Arthur Collins Maclay

A Budget of Letters from Japan

Reminiscences of Work and Travel in Japan. Second Edition

Arthur Collins Maclay

A Budget of Letters from Japan
Reminiscences of Work and Travel in Japan. Second Edition

ISBN/EAN: 9783337170929

Printed in Europe, USA, Canada, Australia, Japan

Cover: Foto ©ninafisch / pixelio.de

More available books at **www.hansebooks.com**

A BUDGET

OF

LETTERS FROM JAPAN

REMINISCENCES OF WORK AND
TRAVEL IN JAPAN

BY

ARTHUR COLLINS MACLAY, A.M., LL.B.

FORMERLY INSTRUCTOR OF ENGLISH IN THE KO-GAKKO-RIO,
TOKIO, JAPAN

SECOND EDITION.

NEW YORK

A. C. ARMSTRONG & SON

714 BROADWAY

1889

I DEDICATE THIS BOOK

TO THE MEMORY

OF

MY MOTHER

PREFACE.

DURING my leisure hours, while a sojourner in " the land of the gods and of the rising sun," I made it a practice—partly as a matter of recreation, and partly from a desire to secure accurate information—to carefully reduce to writing my observations and experiences while dwelling in that beautiful country, in order that I might always have something tangible wherewith to refresh my memory in coming years when those vivid impressions had become dimmed through lapse of time. In the course of years, these " wayside jottings " accumulated in a manner quite surprising to myself. Throwing out all matter that had been dwelt upon to any extent by other writers upon Japan, and retaining only that which seemed to me to be fresh material upon this subject, I reduced the substance of my journals to a book, adopting the form of correspondence as being conversational in its nature and best suited for conveying to other minds the results of my own observations and experiences. Submitting the work to several impartial readers, I was strongly urged by them to have it published as containing matter of general interest presented in a readable manner. Bowing to their judgment in the matter, I now submit this " Budget of Letters " to the individual opinion of each reader, hoping that each may derive as much profit and pleasure from the perusal thereof as I have derived from the composing.

ARTHUR C. MACLAY.

32 PARK PLACE, NEW YORK CITY,
    July 1, 1886.

PREFACE TO THE SECOND EDITION.

THE unexpected kindness and commendation with which my *Budget* was received by the critics of the Press in the United States, Canada, and Japan, very naturally afforded me much pleasure and encouragement. As was predicted by the New York *Herald*, that portion of my book which shows the measureless inferiority of Buddhism when compared with Christianity,—"although the logic is unassailable,"—did not much recommend it to the favor of the Theosophists. In 1883 I attended a missionary meeting in one of the most orthodox churches of one of the most orthodox sects in the city of Brooklyn. I there heard one of the clergymen addressing the meeting commit himself unreservedly to the statement that the fundamental principles of Christianity were substantially the same as those of Buddhism. Of course, the Bishop in whose presence this reckless assertion was made strongly protested against any such doctrine. I noticed, however, that the people seemed to be rather amused than offended at the statement of the speaker. Subsequent inquiry revealed to me the fact that there existed a widespread sentiment in the community that perhaps the assertion was based on fact after all. This incident set me to thinking. The first broad conviction that forced itself upon my mind was that the speaker's statement certainly did not coincide with my conclusions on that subject, as drawn from many years of observation and study in China and Japan. Can it be possible, queried I to myself, that one who has been brought up among Buddhists, and who has imbibed their doctrines from childhood up to mature years, must be informed that Buddhism is not understood by those who practice its precepts? Can it be possible that the time spent with the monks up in the serene altitudes of the Kushan Monastery among the mountains of Fookien in southern China, discussing with them in their own language the mysteries and the ceremonies of their creed, was productive of no insight into their doctrines? Did the scholarly missionaries who discussed the subjects with them, not understand the fundamental principles of Buddhism when they urged the religion of Christ upon them? And, then, when I remembered that all that I had learned about Buddhism in China had been corroborated and verified by four years of study and observation in Japan, I further queried to myself, "What is this thing called Buddhism in the United States?" It surely differs vastly from the original article. Surely, if there had been such doctrines in Buddhism as people here claim, what prevented me from being a Buddhist myself?—for their magnificent ritual created a far deeper impression on my youthful mind than the simple services of the Christian religion. It did not take me very long, however, to discover that Buddhism as understood and practised by the pagans themselves was a very different article from the spurious substance held up by those people in this country who were anxious to elevate some heathen creed up to the level of Christianity in order to deal the latter religion a foul blow, and, if possible, thus to neutralize its claim to being of divine origin. Buddhism as understood by pagans is one thing, and Buddhism as pictured by those who would like to twist it to suit their own views, is quite another thing. Having made these interesting discoveries, I came to the conclusion that when a layman must listen to an orthodox clergyman recklessly asserting that the fundamental principles of that religion which has everywhere dignified and elevated human existence, and has rendered human life worth living, are substantially the same as those of a creed which has stagnated and degraded human existence wherever it prevails, and which pronounces human existence to be but a curse,—that then it was about time for some protest to be heard from the pews. Accordingly I wrote my chapter on Hiyeisan, which shows that the fundamental principles that were incorporated into Buddhism by its founder are totally different from the fundamental principles incorporated into Christianity by its founder. This chapter has run a severe gauntlet and has come forth verified. Not a single statement has been refuted. The *Boston Daily Advertiser* pronounces the remarks to the point, and adds, " We do not remember to have seen the wide difference between the two (religions) better set forth in a few pages than in this volume." In this matter I desire to see fair play, and no foul blows delivered. If the fundamental principles of these two religions be the same, in the name of justice, let that fact be established *fairly.* Until that be shown by such evidence as would hold in a court of reasonable and fair-minded persons, I shall continue to assert the divine origin of Christianity, and to assert the human origin of every other religion the world has ever produced. As the *Alta California* well expresses it, " The author denies that Christianity is a mere development of human wisdom and experience, and gives the unnamed Boston philosopher, whom he so ably refutes, something to ponder over besides the unproven vagaries of Buddhism."

But how about the " Light of Asia "? some one has asked. Doesn't that sweep away the distinction between the two religions? By no means. In the first place, I most cordially admit that the " Light of Asia " is a most beautiful poem. In the second place, it pictures the doctrine of Nirvana in an exquisite and correct manner. In the third place, the gifted author has woven through his verses (unconsciously, I presume.) a vast mass of Christian sentiment that does not belong to Buddhism, and which greatly misleads the reader, who is thus made to believe that the difference between the two religions is merely nominal. I will venture to assert that a Buddhist could never have written the " Light of Asia." That is to say, a mind that was the product of many generations of Buddhistic thought and teachings, and whose sentiments by the laws of heredity were the outgrowth of such doctrines, could never have written such a poem. At all events, Buddhistic intellect has had twenty-five centuries wherein to produce some such poem, and has not done so. I will venture the further assertion that none but a Christian intellect could have written the " Light of Asia." That is to say, none but a mind evolved from a Christian ancestry whose sentiments and inspirations had been transmitted to it by the laws of heredity, could have produced such a poem. At all events, this poem has been produced within one century from the time when intellects that had been developed and operated upon by the principles of Christianity came into familiar contact with the teachings of Buddhism.

In conclusion I fain would propound this query to those Christianized intellects that have so generously rushed to the rescue of this form of paganism : If the fundamental principles of these two religions be the same, why is it that the Empire of Japan to-day trembles on the verge of Christianization ? Why has that haughty and aristocratic nation cast aside a religion founded by a king's son, and, after but thirty years of inspection, become willing to adopt one founded by a Jewish peasant? Verily that was a shrewd summing up of the case by one of my pagan pupils : " You foreigners in Europe and America have shown yourselves to be the leaders of the Nineteenth Century in the arts, the sciences, and in literary culture and political development. You are keen, observing, and profound in of all your investigations. Your intellectual capacity is wonderful. Yet, if we are to believe infidels, you worship a man who was a bastard, a lying impostor, and a criminal justly executed under the laws of his country for his insolent blasphemy in claiming to be the son of the great God that created the universe ! It is incredible that you foreigners, who have shown yourselves to be no fools in other things, should be such colossal idiots in this matter of Christ. Therefore, when such great nations manifest such credulity, it is better not to scoff at them, but to carefully investigate the grounds of their belief. Therefore, I wish to carefully study your Bible, and to probe this mystery for myself, because I deem the subject worthy of my closest attention." Accordingly that young man investigated the subject for two years, and came to the conclusion that Jesus of Nazareth *must have been precisely what he claimed to be, the Son of God.* Any other hypothesis branded the Caucasian race as an aggregation of colossal fools. No sane Jew could honestly have made such a claim. To suppose that some Nazarene could have been hallucinated with such an idea, thus courting torture and crucifixion, involved a supposition entirely too violent for this "hard-headed" young man. Nor could he see any sense in the hypothesis that a madman, or a mild idiot, could have produced a system of moral ethics so matchlessly pure and perfect. In short, he found that all other hypotheses required far greater stretch of credulity to accept than merely to take Christ at his word, and to believe on him as the Son of God, the Redeemer of the human race from that subtle and mysterious innoculation of sin instilled into our blood by our common progenitor, that innate tendency toward degradation and corruption to which every family and nation under heaven have borne abundant testimony. In one of his letters he exclaimed : " I wish to become a disciple of this Christ !" So says the Empire of Japan to-day. What say you to this, infidel ? In the light of your alleged exposures and denunciations, be they fools?

ARTHUR C. MACLAY.

NEW YORK CITY, *September,* 1888.

EXPLANATORY REMARKS.

New York City, *February* 1, 1886.

DEAR PUBLIC:

INASMUCH as introductions are, subjectively and objectively, a bore, permit me to be very brief in introducing to you my friend Theophilus Pratt. He was a school-teacher in Japan for four years. He taught in various parts of the Japanese Empire from the year 1873 to the year 1878. During that time he wrote me quite a number of letters, which to me were very interesting. They are upon a variety of topics, including house-keeping, rebellions, and assassinations. They describe the halcyon days of school-teaching in Japan. They also touch upon events of general interest to Americans and Europeans.

These letters, I repeat, were very interesting to me. Hence I naturally inferred that they might interest others. Therefore I have arranged them in book form, and now present them for your perusal. Hoping that our tastes in this matter will coincide, I remain,

Very respectfully yours,

JULIUS MARCELLUS VAN TAG.

CONTENTS.

LETTER I.

PAGE

THE FAREWELL... 1

LETTER II.

A VOYAGE ACROSS THE PACIFIC............................ 6

LETTER III.

YOKOHAMA.. 21

LETTER IV.

HIROSAKI... 35

LETTER V.

A GLIMPSE OF OLD FEUDAL TIMES IN JAPAN................ 57

LETTER VI.

A FEW IDEAS ABOUT LIFE IN THE INTERIOR 81

LETTER VII.

A TRAGEDY.. 99

LETTER VIII.

A FEW REMINISCENCES....................................... III

LETTER IX.

TOKIO.. 130

LETTER X.

PAGE

SCHOOL-TEACHING IN TOKIO................................... 162

LETTER XI.

A SUMMER VACATION.................................... 173

LETTER XII.

MISSIONARY WORK IN JAPAN............................. 196

LETTER XIII.

A TRIP THROUGH CLASSIC JAPAN......................... 219

LETTER XIV.

KIOTO... 243

LETTER XV.

AN EXCURSION TO NARA................................. 258

LETTER XVI.

FUJIYAMA 272

LETTER XVII.

THE SATSUMA REBELLION 287

LETTER XVIII.

HIYEISAN.. 303

LETTER XIX.

SOCIAL PROBLEMS IN JAPAN............................. 333

LETTER XX.

OUR IMPERIAL COUSINS 365

LETTER XXI.

FAREWELL TO JAPAN............. 385

ILLUSTRATIONS.

	PAGE
THE YOMEI GATEWAY	*Frontispiece*
CASTING UP ACCOUNTS	21
IWA-KI-SAN	35
STREET VENDER	43
GOSSIPING AT THE WELL	51
OLD-STYLE WARRIORS	57
THIRD MOAT OF THE TOKIO CASTLE	68
OUR POSTAL SERVICE	81
MAYÈBARA	99
STREET SCENE IN HIROSAKI	111
AINOS	130
THE UBIQUITOUS JINRIKISHA	145
THE KAGO	162
THE TOMB OF TOKUGAWA IYEYAS	173
GLIMPSE OF CHIUSENJI LAKE	186
VIEW OF THE THIRD TERRACE, NIKKO TEMPLES	196
THE CITADEL OF OWARI CASTLE	219
THE GREAT BELL AT DAI-BUTZ TEMPLE, KIOTO	243
THE DEATH OF BUDDHA	258
IMAGE OF DAI-BUTZ AT KAMAKURA	272
THE CITADEL OF KUMAMOTO CASTLE	287
RUINS OF THE CITADEL OF AIDZU CASTLE	303
A QUIET CORNER IN A BUDDHIST CEMETERY	333
AT HOME	346
THE THREE ESTATES	365

A BUDGET OF LETTERS
FROM JAPAN.

LETTER I.

THE FAREWELL.

San Francisco, California, *October* 10, 1873.

Dear Julius Marcellus:

I am off for Japan. I left New York in such a hurry that I was unable to give you a parting call. I therefore present my apologies and explanations by letter. I expect to be gone for three or four years; and I wish to open a regular correspondence with you during my sojourn abroad. If you agree to this plan, be so kind as to notify me to that effect.

Why did I decide so suddenly to go to Japan? Permit me to explain. You will remember that my studies were interrupted by the failure of my eyesight last year. This inopportune event laid me on the shelf, colloquially speaking. About six weeks ago I received a letter from my friend Adamson, in Yokohama, urging me to go out to

Japan and teach school. He said the work would be agreeable and not too hard for my eyes. He also said that the pecuniary considerations were by no means to be overlooked. He advised me to go right on to Yokohama so as to be ready to make application for the first vacancy that might occur. This was the only way to do, for there was no probability that a Japanese delegation would wait upon me in the United States. He said I might have to wait a year, or I might have to wait only a month, for one of these flitting opportunities.

In almost every transaction in life we are obliged to incur a certain amount of risk. Success is the result of an ever-varying equation. The science of life is to calculate that there is a reasonable prob-ability of a given set of circumstances producing a plus quantity, and then to go ahead. In the pres-ent case, the circumstances and conditions augur well for success.

The journey across the continent was not spe-cially exciting. We came through from New York with the same car-load of passengers with which we started. We had the usual assortment of travelers. There was the bridal couple going to visit the Yosemite. There was the Englishman returning to China *via* America despite the warning of anxious friends who had cautioned him to be-ware of the free fights and the railway disasters of the reckless Americans. There was the elderly lady with spectacles, who had come to write a book on Mormonism, and wanted to silence all assailants with the fact that she had seen the things therein stated with her own eyes and could not be mistaken. There was the man going to get up a lecture on the Chinese immigration question, and wanted to convince his audiences of his impartiality by stating that he had been in California and could testify whereof he knew. And then there was the party of ubiquitous "Globe-Trotters" with their *Cook's Guide.* We were given to understand that they represented several millions of dollars and also a rare assortment of refinement and culture. And, finally, there were Mrs. What's-her-name, from Boston, and her husband,—but he didn't count. She had strong scientific tastes, and made many very wise observations. She thought that the country, through which we passed yesterday, gave strong evidence of glacial erosion. To-day she wishes that she could obtain some of those fossils in the ledge of rocks to our right, for she feels positive that the place gives indications of much geological interest. Her meek husband then expresses profound regret that the sordid aspirations of the lucre-loving railroad company will not allow the scientific passengers to spend an hour or two per day at these carboniferous outcroppings. She then pines for some of those lovely endogenous bulbiferous plants that are growing beside yonder marsh, for she feels sure that they must be some new species, and heaves a regretful sigh as the train passes on. Whereupon her husband turns around and looks wildly down the car, as if seriously contemplating the immediate stopping of the train, or some other desperate maneuver whereby the bulbiferous endogens may be procured. But, on second thought, he settles down and delivers himself of a diatribe against the vile mercenary spirit of railroad corporations in general and of the Union Pacific in particular. Enlisting the florid effusions of some of his choice oratorical efforts, he warmly asserts that corruption in high places should be closely scrutinized; that bribery and trickery among our public officials should be ferreted out, and an indignant public should excoriate the same with withering scorn; and that the surest way of staying this frightful torrent of chicanery, and of heralding in pure politics, was to grant universal and unrestricted suffrage to the much-abused and downtrodden female sex. To all of which an approving amen was smiled by the budding scientist whose genius was thus being rudely blighted by the grasping avarice of the Union Pacific.

It took us about seven days to cover the distance between the oceans. The journey was a most enjoyable one. The greater part of our company will take the same steamer for Yokohama. This will make it quite home-like. I have not cumbered myself with very much luggage. A trunk and a box of books tell the tale. They say that Yokohama furnishes all articles needed by Europeans and Americans. I hope you will excuse the brevity of this letter. Also, its abrupt termination, for I must go down to Santa Clara this afternoon to visit some cousins living there. Keep me posted on all home news, and I will post you on all news relating to Japan.

Truly yours,

THEOPHILUS PRATT.

LETTER II.

YOKOHAMA, JAPAN, *December* 18, 1873.

DEAR JULIUS MARCELLUS:

I HAVE been here about a month. I have not yet secured a position; but my friend Adamson says that patience is a great virtue, particularly in Japan. He says that more than half the battle is won by being here on the ground. I hope to report progress in my next letter. My mornings I spend in walking over the delightful hills surrounding Yokohama. For two hours after tiffin I am engaged in teaching a couple of Japanese gentlemen. After that, I have some time for reading. And then before dinner I take another walk through the city or along the Bluffs. I have already been over almost every path within a radius of five miles of this place. Everything is so novel that it seems as if I were in a new world. Private teaching here is not very remunerative. Japanese do not feel able to pay more than five dollars per month for tuition; and the majority feel heavily taxed when they have to pay two dollars per month. Unless a person can secure a contract under the government, he will find school-teaching a poor business. But all this is not answering your questions about my voyage across the Pacific.

Let us imagine ourselves on the wharves at San Francisco. We pass up the gangway of the huge paddle-wheel steamer chained to the pier. Its accommodations are superb. Upon the upper deck is a social hall where we can have music and dancing. Upon the same deck is a fine broad promenade. Here, the children, the terror of sea-going folks, spend most of their time. These steamers take about twenty-six days to reach Yokohama in moderately fair weather. The propellers take about eighteen days. They are not, however, so comfortable, and many of the ladies prefer the extra time, with comfort.

Having arranged our stateroom, we lean over the taffrail beside the main gangway, and watch the passengers coming up from the pier. Here comes the English party. They recognize us and exchange nods, for in journeying we dispense with formal introductions. Behind this party come three or four Japanese gentlemen dressed in European style and armed with patent leather valises. Then follows a Chinese Commissioner leading his two boys. They are all dressed in their native costume. And their well-greased pig-tails flaunt gently in the breeze. They come stalking up the gangway as consequentially as if they owned the ship. The contrast between them and the Japanese is characteristic of the two nations.

The tide of passengers and leave-taking friends is now surging up and down the plank in a continuous stream. It is within a few minutes of high noon, and we are preparing to start. Ah! here comes the admirer of bulbiferous endogens. And beside her is the denouncer of corrupt railroad corporations, our friend Mustaches. That feeble old gentleman meekly following them is the father of the gushing scientist. We came near being deprived of their society across the Pacific. Time's up! The gang-plank is drawn away. The hawsers are cast loose, and the vessel swings from the wharf. Round go the wheels, and the spray sprinkles the crowd on the pier. The extending wake of boiling waters now marks our course down the bay.

Have you ever seen your native cliffs sinking beneath the waves? And have you ever felt as you gazed mournfully astern through the misty air that your farewell might be final, and that you might never see those blue mountains rising from the sea? Then you can appreciate our feelings.

The passengers crowd the hurricane deck and wave their handkerchiefs to the crowded shore. Many eyes moisten as the gap widens and the responsive flutterings become obscured by the distance. Even the officers wear a resigned expression. But the saddest group of all is the little party of missionaries just abaft the paddle-box. They necessarily feel the situation far more keenly than people who are going abroad for self-interest, expecting to return in a few months, or two or three years at most. Their outlook is gloomy. For they are to be gone for ten years at least, unless death or disease steps in to shorten their exile. Now, in the Sunday schools we used to get the impression that missionaries were a species of beings so divinely constituted that they were not apt to be affected by ordinary human woes; but here we see simply a sad little company of devoted people who are greviously afflicted, like ordinary mortals, with homesickness. And as they hurry down into the cabin we grimly wonder how many of the church members at home, who believe in missionaries never leaving the foreign field, and in their going to heaven by way of India and China, and who are so loud in dictating about the economical disposal of missionaries, as if they were pieces of church furniture, would thus ostracize themselves from home, friends, and civilized society.

But our voyage is begun. The peculiarity of a sea-voyage across the Pacific is that you get almost all nationalities represented. English, French, Germans, Jews, Chinese, Japanese, and Americans are apt to be well represented. All grades of society, all creeds, and all professions are also apt to be represented. The cosmopolitan character of the passengers usually promotes good nature and sociability. You, of course, know what a sea-voyage is. There is much sameness in the general run of events. Eating is our prime occupation. Coffee and toast at seven; breakfast at eight; tiffin at twelve ; a regular dinner at five ; and tea at nine ; there you have it.

Our interludes we fill in with reading and gossip. Sometimes the Japanese passengers are criticised. You are duly informed how many cigars they smoke per day; how many bottles of wine they drink at dinner ; how often they pace up and down the spar-deck indorsing the civilized method of exercise; how little *Tanaka*, while pacing the deck with the dignity of a tycoon, had his high hat blown over the quarter-rail and came very near going over himself while frantically hopping after it ; and how sociable, genial, and chatty they are.

Then you will hear a long yarn about the missionaries. How the stewardess says the ship always meets a storm when they come aboard ; and how foolish it is for people to spend thousands of dollars in sending them abroad when there are so many heathens at home.

Then you will hear about the English. How they bet on every imaginable thing,—on the weather, on the number of miles run per day, on the prospects of rain, on the continuance of the wind, and on the length of the voyage.

Then the Americans catch it. And our English cousins furnish us with a series of dissolving views upon society, politics, and morality in all that portion of dangerous territory called by civilized nations America, but which we designate the United States.

They always advance the same arguments, and

tenaciously cling to the same line of assertion. They get most of their ideas from English newspapers and journals, and never think for themselves as to whether their ideas are accurate. I have had several tilts with them and have now become so familiar with their mode of attack that I begin to wish they would start a new journal in England so that we can have a little variety in our discourses. After a short conversation you can tell by what London newspaper an Englishman swears.

We have had several animated after-dinner discussions. As a matter of recreation, I have dramatized these belligerent talks. I here insert a copy of my humble efforts. It will serve as a sample.

ACT I.

SCENE I.

(CAPTAIN'S TABLE. *Dramatis Personæ.*—Captain, two Germans, three Englishmen, and two Americans. All busily engaged in eating nuts and raisins.)

Dr. Smith of London.—I say, would you mind just passing that dish of almonds?

Mr. Brown of New York.—With pleasure.

Dr. S.—An uncommonly auspicious beginning for our passage, you know.

Mr. B.—It is, indeed. But I fear we shall have some cases of seasickness before we reach Japan.

Dr. S.—I am rather inclined to think so myself, you know.

Mr. B.—This Pacific has a false reputation, I think. The captain thinks we will have some rough weather before we're through.

Dr. S.—So the "*fright clark*" told me.

Mr. B.—Excuse me, but I didn't catch the gentleman's name.

Dr. S.—That gentleman near the purser.

Mr. B.—Oh ! *Freight clerk*, you mean—that individual with a red moustache.

Dr. S.—Ah ! That's another one of the peculiarities of the American language. You know, I am often floored by some of your odd provincialisms. You never know when you are going to turn the corner sharp upon one of them. It's confoundedly awkward, you know.

Mr. B.—I don't think much difference exists in the cultivated language of the two countries. The colloquial does vary somewhat, I believe.

Dr. S.—But you Americans are changing the English language, you know.

Mr. B.—All languages, sir, that live must grow, you know. Even in England the language has changed within a century.

Dr. S.—But your American phrases and *patois*, so to speak, are sometimes quite unintelligible.

Captain.—To hear you talk, doctor, one would think that the English language was spoken in full perfection in England. But I have been to places within two hours' ride of London where you positively can't understand the people and they can't understand you. Just go over the Sussex Downs some time. And as for *patois*, you have a number of them even in so small a space as England ; to say nothing of the barbaric lingo you find in Wales, Ireland, and Scotland.

Mr. Jones of Liverpool.—And don't you find the same thing in America ?

Captain.—No. You can go from Maine to California and be perfectly understood, except among the Indians.

Dr. S.—Quite true. Yes, quite true. But I'm afraid you don't fully grasp my meaning, you know. I refer more particularly to the newspaper literature of America. I think you'll own that American editors are guilty of the most un-justifiable liberties in distorting the English language. Look at the *Police Gazette*, the *Buckeye Democrat*, and the infernal orthography of Artemus Ward and Naseby.

Mr. B.—Be fair, doctor. You are not selecting standard papers. And then you must remember that no American pretends to recommend the spelling of Ward and Naseby. These writers are popular both in England and America because they are humorous and witty.

Mr. Griggs of New York.—Guess you'd better try again, doctor. Why don't you quote the *Harpers'*, the *Atlantic Monthly*, and the *North American Review?*

Dr. S.—Well, take the *Harper's Weekly* then. See how it copies pictures from English papers. You will often find the same picture in both papers.

Mr. B.—Well, supposing we do. Don't you copy American jokes into your English papers? We copy your choice illustrations, and you copy our witticisms. Doesn't that leave the sides equally balanced?

Mr. Jones.—But your American papers are so addicted to exaggeration that a stranger finds himself sorely puzzled what to believe. I have met a great many Americans who, when I say that a certain thing is stated so and so in the newspaper, immediately burst out laughing and say that is just why they don't believe it. A man can't tell what to believe, you know. It's intensely awkward, indeed it is.

Mr. Griggs.—I regret to say that your remarks are quite just respecting what we designate as our newspaper "trash." Some of these papers are very vile, I admit. But our first-class newspapers are not generally unreliable. You must remember that your English papers frequently make blunders. And they sometimes get decidedly personal.

Mr. Pinker of London.—Then you Americans are so superficial. You don't do things thoroughly. Why, I met an American in Paris who had been there just a week and was talking of returning home. He thought he had " done "

Europe! You Americans think you can do Europe in three months!

Captain.—Pray how long have you been in the United States?

Mr. Pinker.—Just long enough to come across and take Niagara in.

Captain.—I thought so. That's just the way nine out of every ten Englishmen do up the States. I've met lots of them on this route. You fellows jump on the train at New York. Then you make a rush because you have heard that railway traveling is dangerous in America, and you never know when a band of Sioux will board the train. At Niagara you scamper on to the Canadian side, and then thank your stars that you are safe. Then you make a bee-line for San Francisco and board the first steamer for Japan. And after that you consider yourselves fit to discuss America, socially, politically, and otherwise. You fellows lack consistency.

Mr. Pinker.—Well, I saw enough to see that Americans all live in hotels. Your daughters trail their dresses through public drawing-rooms everywhere.

Mr. Dobbs.—After what you have said, it can hardly be expected that you should possess an exhaustive and critical comprehension of our institutions. I have lived in America thirty years, and I feel confident in asserting that as regards America outside of the large cities, your statement is essentially incorrect.

Mr. Pinker.—I've been told so by many travelers. Then there's an awful amount of rascality in America. The venality is something frightful. The papers are full of it. Even the railroad corporations are corrupt. In coming over on the train, it was a subject of remark how the Union Pacific Company ignored the interests of the passengers. And besides, the cars in America never go over twenty-five miles an hour. Now between London and Liverpool we have trains that go over fifty miles per hour.

Mr. Griggs.—Have you ever heard of the Erie road ?

Mr. Pinker.—No.

Mr. Griggs.—Well, what are you blowing for then? We have got trains there that go as fast as any in England.

Mr. Pinker.—I don't believe it.

Mr. Griggs.—Look here, my friend. I see what you English want. You want us to make a clean, unadulterated, up-and-down, out-and-out confession that republicanism is a failure ; that the American social system is mawkishly tame ; that our political institutions are corrupt to the core ; that our people are rapidly degenerating into effeminacy and imbecility ; that education of the masses is bosh ; that the abolishing of our Constitution and the adoption of British institutions is merely a question of time ; and that our benighted citizens are gradually becoming aware of these facts, and are beginning to see the error they committed a hundred years ago in separating from the essence of political freedom. When we have humiliated ourselves to that extent and sufficiently groveled in the dust, you may possibly be induced to smile upon us ; and may condescend to appoint governors to fatten off us; and may modestly send over tax-collectors to fill the depleted treasuries of your bankrupt government, and to squeeze out of us wherewith to help support your useless, scrofulous breed of nobles that now greedily looks upon our prosperity.

All.—I say, hold on ! Are you wound up for any special length of time ?

Mr. Jones.—Let the steward clear the table, and we'll adjourn to the smoking-room, where brother Griggs may continue his speech.

(*Exeunt.*)

That's about the way it goes. I always thought that Americans were given to bragging. But I must confess that the English are just as bad. I

find that the elements of human nature are the
same all over the world.   And it takes a sea voyage
to bring out all its phases.   Take the Bulbiferous
Endogen, for example, and her partner.   There
you have an aggressive female linked to an insipid
man.   She represents a type of womanhood which,
thank heavens, will never be very popular.   It certainly is not a fair specimen of our American ladies.
She has energy and positiveness enough for a school-
boy, but she lacks the true instincts of a lady.   She
is well read and has considerable intelligence, but
she parades her knowledge so incessantly that you
become disgusted.   She takes endless pains to let
you know that she is intellectual and scholarly ; yet
she is oblivious of the fact that true scholarship is
always modest, and that only pedants love to display.   Once in a while she gets off a clever remark,
but the superficiality that invariably accompanies
these hits quite destroys their effect ; and the air
of conscious superiority that she assumes fairly
makes you pity her.   After conversing with her
about ten minutes you are usually refreshed with
the information that she graduated at the head of
her class in some college ; that there were some
men in the same class. but that they, of course, were
entirely inferior to the *ladies* in scholarship ; that
she has studied Latin, Greek, higher mathematics,
logic, rhetoric, chemistry, and lots of other things ;
that she is proficient in French and German ; that
she considers herself equal to any Harvard or Yale
graduate ; that it is all bosh to say any intellectual

difference exists between men and women,—that if any does exist it is in favor of women ; and finally, that female suffrage is only a question of time. For emphasis, she gravely looks over her glasses and slowly taps the arm of her chair with her fan so as to direct with greater force the arrow of conviction, and looks around ready to an- nihilate any one should they chance to question her views. And Mustaches sits by tamely breath- ing forth an occasional "That's so! By Jingo!" and fills in the pauses by telling how he prepared for Yale College but did not enter (for reasons quite obvious), and that he hopes to see the day when co-education and woman suffrage shall prevail all over the United States. Bah! Let us drop this compound of nauseating egotism and pedantic prig- gishness.

On the twenty-sixth day we sighted the Japan coast. I went on deck to get a view, but could see nothing that looked like land. Finally, just over the bows, I was able to see the dim outlines of snowy Fujisan some eighty miles away, rising and falling with the ship.

At mid-day, we passed several fishing boats. By three o'clock in the afternoon we rounded Cape King and entered Yeddo Bay. From this point up to Yokohama is a sail that the visitor will never forget. Fishing boats are swarming in all the inlets that branch from the bay. The nude condition of the boatmen much mortified our Jap- anese passengers, who were highly disgusted at this

2

prominent display of nature unadorned on the part of their countrymen.

We steam rapidly up the bay, and leave behind us a lengthened vista of hills, groves, temples, and fishing hamlets. And we drop anchor in Yokohama harbor just as the evening mists begin to float from the distant valleys and repose against the sides of the lordly cone that we sighted this morning.

We let down the gangway and are immediately beset by a fleet of boats scuffling for the first place beside it. While waiting the arrival of Fred, I lean over the railing and watch the surging crowd of half-naked savages scrambling, yelling, and gesticulating in the most demoralized manner beneath. It amuses us immensely. And so this is Japan, the civilized Japan, about which I have heard so much. Incredible! There must be some mistake! These wretches must be imported. I turn to see who is grasping my arm.—"Why, bless me! Fred, my boy, how are you! I didn't know you were anywhere within a league.

Fred.—"I have been on the Bluffs the past hour watching you coming up the bay. I was just going out for my afternoon walk around Mississippi Bay when the gun went off. Come, get your baggage, and let's be going. My boat is waiting. I want you to stay with me in Yokohama until you have negotiated a contract."

In ten minutes we are sculling for the shore at a furious rate.

"I say, Fred, you don't mean to say that these howling cannibals are Japanese, do you?"

Fred.—"They are, my dear fellow."

"Shades of Pompey! Well, how are the people in the interior? Do they sport any more fine-twined linen vesture than these yelling hoodlums?"

"My dear sir, these boatmen are high-toned, civilized gentlemen compared with some of the specimens that you find in the interior. Why, we old residents don't notice these things. In the interior the summer costume is nothing for the children, a waist-cloth for the men, and nothing above the waist for the women. The *Samurai* class, however, are not so economical in their vesture. They usually appear in public fully dressed. But they only constitute about three millions out of thirty millions. The merchants are also a little more careful in their dress. But the masses dispense with as much as possible. But around the Treaty Ports, the government has commenced civilization, and are trying to cure these people of some of their startling tricks. They have issued an edict commanding all coming within five miles of Yokohama to don a short cotton tunic. I want you to understand that some of our Yokohama coolies are really stylish. For, in addition to their regulation shirts, some of those in the more advanced stages of civilization will put on a pair of knee-breeches. But the moment they are beyond the charmed circle, off comes the eccentric western paraphernalia, to be slipped on again when a

" bobby " heaves in sight. But here we are at the French *Hatoba*. Just walk up the steps. As soon as this custom-house officer has satisfied himself that you are not trying to smuggle Krupp guns in your trunk, we will ride up to my house."

Now, Julius Marcellus, you must not be shocked at these closing scenes. I have given you a faithful picture of my first impressions of Japan. We must describe people as we find them, not as we expect to find them. In ten years such scenes will be rare. Old residents here say that Yokohama has greatly improved during the past five years. The people have really made great progress. But we strangers coming here, with our minds filled with the vivid descriptions of book-makers, are apt to expect too much. My impressions are, on the whole, favorable.

I will keep you posted on my progress in my next.

Truly yours,

THEOPHILUS PRATT.

CASTING UP ACCOUNTS.

LETTER III.

YOKOHAMA, *February* 2, 1874.

DEAR JULIUS MARCELLUS:

I SAT down with the intention of telling you something about Yokohama. But when I come to consider how much has been written about the place, I almost despair of telling you anything new. My letter will, therefore, be very rambling, as I wish to avoid broken ground.

In the first place, Yokohama is not Japan. It is one of the most cosmopolitan places I can imagine. Almost all nationalities are here represented. So that you will hear very little about the Japanese this time.

The city is built upon a broad tongue of land jutting into Yeddo Bay. On one side is Yokohama harbor; on the other is Mississippi Bay. Through the center of this tongue passes a line of low hills, known as the Bluffs. On the harbor side are re-claimed rice fields, built up with "godowns" and houses. This is known as the "Settlement." Ad-joining this you have the native town. On the Mississippi side of the Bluff you have the race-course, the rifle range, and a continued series of

hills covered with picturesque woods and wheat
fields. Between the hills are spongy rice flats. The
Bluff itself is covered along its entire length with
villas, which are separated from the long, straggling
road by shrubbery. On New Year's Day this road
presents a gay appearance with its gates decorated
with arches of pine and bamboo trees covered with
Mandarin oranges.

The stranger in Yokohama usually spends his
first morning in Curio Street, just outside the "Settlement." Here he will find the best and most
extensive assortment of bronzes, lacquer-ware, and
silks to be found in the empire (1874). On entering a shop, the salesman tries to find out whether
you are a resident or a visitor from off the ships.
If you are a visitor, the countenances of the shop-
keeper and his interesting family brighten. And
he forthwith proceeds to tuck on the prices with a
cheerful face and a clear conscience. Should you
chance, however, to be an old resident, he loses all
inspiration. And the sale goes on in a listless,
hangdog sort of way, as if he were feeling discouraged at the financial condition of the country. The
old residents are at a decided discount, while
strangers are always welcome visitors, to be politely
enticed into the store and relieved of as much
cash for the least compensation as possible.

In the afternoon you leave the Settlement, climb
the Bluffs, and walk along the beautiful garden-
like road that leads out by Mississippi Bay and the
race-course. This course is not a very good one.

But the apparently indispensable nature of the institution has inspired the soul of the indomitable Saxon to such an extent that the hilly nature of the country has been tolerably pruned into the required classic shape. Twice a year Yokohama suspends its business and pours forth its people to resort hither to recall inspiring visions of Derby and Doncaster, to watch the striped jockeys bobbing round the track, to bet upon some ill-starred brute that comes limping down in the rear, to testify their keen appreciation of trained horseflesh by judicious applause, and to show the assembled heathen multitudes how this thing is done in civilized countries.

Passing the race-course we take the pretty road down by Mississippi Bay. Going through three or four miles of rice-fields, it sweeps around toward the other end of the Bluff. This is the popular drive for foreigners. We now come to the rifle range. This is where the French and English soldiers practice with their *Chassepôts* and Snyders. Here, also, are the grounds of the athletic association. In the spring and autumn the community resorts hither to enjoy the " spawts." Running, jumping, fencing, flinging the cricket-ball, throwing the hammer, and a variety of other physical contortions supposed to be indicative of strength and agility, furnish abundant amusement to immense crowds of natives, who view the proceedings with much the same appreciation manifested by the Corean Ambassadors when witnessing the agile climbing of the naval cadets. With languid sympathy, they remarked that there were monkeys in Corea that could do such things much better!

We now climb what is known as the English Bluff. We here have a peerless view down the bay. We will omit the accustomed ode to Fujisan, which can be seen to best advantage at this point. Next in order comes the English camp, the U. S. Naval Hospital, and the American Bluffs. This dash of the pen will give you a fair general idea of Yokohama.

As to the social features, the Japanese regard it as the wickedest place in the empire. Not but what many good people live here, but it possesses a vast capacity for working iniquity. In this respect it is like all Oriental settlements where the lower forms of our civilization come in contact with a degraded Eastern society. The most iniquitous people are generally to be found in the immediate vicinity of the civilization of the nineteenth century. The polite countryman, who expects to find in the foreigner a model of propriety and intelligence, seeks in vain for his ideal among the average community. And after six months' experience in the Settlement, becomes transformed into a brazen-faced *jinriksha* man, or a saucy boy, laying aside his manners and honesty as articles not appreciated by the coarse Saxons, who rarely lose an opportunity to drive merciless bargains, and who frequently adopt questionable methods of securing the main chance.

To understand life in Yokohama, you must come here and live. The moral tone of the European community is very low. In the majority of cases, a young man settles down to a life of license and shame. The prevalence of this custom would seem incredible to you folks at home. The tone of the community is, however, better than it was several years ago. The presence of large numbers of missionaries has done much to elevate public sentiment on this point. Consequently they are bitterly hated by the corrupt portion of the foreign settlement.

Outside of business hours, the main occupation of the community is to kill time in the easiest and most fashionable manner possible. Various are the expedients for the consummation of this complicated object. Till four o'clock in the afternoon, the Bluff roads present quite a deserted appearance, while the Settlement is all alive. Then the tide changes, and all the Bluff becomes alive with pedestrians, horsemen, and carriages, presenting a gay and lively appearance. Horseback riding is much favored. Your thorough-bred cockney, preceded by about half-a-dozen hounds, mounts his pony, and, accompanied by a yelling groom who goes scampering alongside, comes thundering down the road, scattering the natives to right and left, bows graciously to his lady acquaintances, and allows no mortal object to check his career until he chances to spy Sir Harry coming down the Bluff, when it is considered the proper thing to rein up and salute this servant of the British public.

The paper chase is a popular item of recreation that comes off about half-a-dozen times during the winter—these delightful winters that never trouble you with sleet and slush. These hunts are sometimes on foot, and sometimes on horseback. Torn-up paper is scattered along the hedges, across the neat, garden-like fields, through the thickets, and over the hills. Excellent opportunity is then afforded for ambitious athletes to bark their shins, wade knee-deep through mud, annihilate their habiliments generally, and then come rushing home to receive a silver cup from the hands of some fair damsel. And the gaping peasants wonder how much per hour the *danna-san* charges for that species of self-immolation. It at first seemed to me that this chasing over the fields was an arrogant infringement of the right of property; and that thirty or forty brogans tramping over the fields would be ruinous to the crops. But after several conversations with our enlightened cousins, and after thoroughly imbibing the spirit of the matchless press of this community, I clearly perceive that my base-born republican views were to blame. I am now fully convinced that my plebeian ideas of the rights of the vulgar peasantry were utterly incompatible with the liberal sentiments of this enlightened Settlement. Truly it would be a shame to interrupt a party of gentlemen in pursuit of manly "spawts." On such occasions, persons attempting any interference must not be surprised at a cuff over the ears, or a cut from a riding-whip. And I shudder as I consider the benighted pugnacity that would be displayed by some of our democratic farmers as, slinging shot-guns over their shoulders, they would lead on a couple of bull-dogs to join in the chase.

Another popular source of amusement is football. During the beautiful winters matches are of frequent occurrence. Sometimes it is England against the world. Sometimes it is old residents against new residents. And sometimes it is the fleet against the Settlement. On these occasions, the brass band from the flagship will kindly lend its services.

Then we have the Dramatic Association, which furnishes its quota of entertainment during the cold season. The theater on these occasions is well patronized by the community. During the warm season this association will give an open-air entertainment in the Public Gardens on the Bluff. This is a rare treat,—at least for the spectators. But the rarity of such performances would rather indicate that the parties directly concerned considered it no joke to sweat through quarter of an inch of powdering on time.

We may also mention boating in our list. For about five weeks in the spring your Yokohama athlete drops his pipe and beer long enough to bring his body into trim. The races are generally between Scotch and English crews. The Americans rarely participate, and consequently sink below zero in the estimation of the sporting public. The newspapers frequently suggest that races be arranged between Yokohama, Kobè, Nagasaki, and Shanghai. An occasional regatta is the result. But the distance between places, and the fact that the participants cannot often leave their business, will always more or less interfere with these amusements.

But I may safely say that hunting and loafing constitute the ideal recreations of Yokohama. To don a loose suit of clothing, to stretch back in a long chair, to languidly suck your pipe and sleepily read the latest novel in the deep shade of your cool veranda, form delicious relaxations preferable to all others. And when your bosom friend, Slukes, lounges in, you can order the boy to bring the iced drinks, and then dreamily slip into an exquisite dissertation on Japanese inefficiency and the latest missionary scandal concocted by the outside committee of Yokohama, which, by the way, appears to hold perpetual session on the private affairs of the community at large.

But should all these afore-mentioned diversions fail to satisfy the public appetite, it then devolves upon the three and a half local papers to enliven the *ennui.* It is sometimes quite difficult for the ingenious members of the combined editorial staffs to furnish the required amount and variety of material to suit the fastidious taste of our highly discriminating community. An acute diatribe, however, severely handling the legislative performances of the government is always in order. Selections of choice jokes and witticisms culled from American papers are peculiarly acceptable. And a bitter controversy between the chaplain and the community, upon some trifling church affair, is an invigorating species of diversion that appears to have peculiar charms, and is devoutly encouraged on all possible occasions. And should some evangelist chance to come to town, his appearance in the pulpit will not only secure a full house but columns replete with attempted wit, theological lore, and sublime nonsense upon the folly of filling the minds of the simple-minded natives with a lot of religious bosh. For you must remember that our Oriental *connoisseur* dearly loves an opportunity to criticise "religious buffoonery." And some unfortunate expression or objectionable view uttered by the reverend gentleman, will furnish the magnanimous and casual anonymous correspondents with teeming sheets long after the victim has fled the unkindly shores.

Moreover, the missionary furnishes an apparently unfailing source of recreation. He is served up with peculiar relish. The Oriental settlements seem to take unbounded interest in the private affairs of this harmless portion of the community. It does not appear to be considered impertinent to publicly investigate their respective salaries, the houses they live in, the number of their servants, what kind of clothes they wear, what society they keep, the petty misunderstandings that may chance to arise

among them, and whether or not they are actuated
by mercenary motives. These gentlemen of the
imperial race run amuck with the whole clerical
brotherhood, and mercilessly appropriate, as legitimate subjects for literary cuteness and witticism,
the most trivial circumstances.

But should all these themes become exhausted,
it is then the solemn duty of the fractional editorial
trinity to launch invectives against the vile corruptions and mercenary venality of the republican institutions of America. They execrate in withering
terms the naughty doings of " that clever but wicked
people." And should some dyspeptic article against
the government be found in some democratic sheet
that longs for the days of Buchanan, it must be
copied verbatim as incontestible proof of the speedy
dissolution of the " great Yankee farce." I never
knew so much about America until I came to the
east. And I must confess with humiliation and regret my utter ignorance of the genius of our people
until I was enlightened by these comprehensive
philosophers. I now see clearly that our Constitution is based upon false principles; that we will be
compelled soon by the force of natural political
evolution and social differentiation to have a mon-
arch and a nobility; that Washington, Adams,
Jackson, and Jefferson were fanatical monomaniacs;
that but for the immigration from Europe our effete breed would soon become extinct; that we are
thorough in nothing, our best work of every description being done by imported foreigners; and

that we were blind to our interests when we left the protecting wing of Britannia.

Am I getting excited? Not at all. But this is the only way an American can express himself. The press is entirely English. And, having no opposing paper, they rather drift into a characteristic disposition to bully our portion of the community. An occasional letter in one of our home papers checks them for a while; but they soon forget themselves and drift into their unfair and cynical style of criticism. So you must not be startled at this mild ebullition.

To change the subject, it is interesting to conjecture what the future of Yokohama will be. Some think that the foreign population will increase until we have a city like Hong-Kong or Shanghai. Others think that it will remain the same. While others, whose views I am rather inclined to endorse, hold that the foreign element will gradually dwindle down to a few scores of professional residents, while the mercantile business will be in native hands. This ground is certainly plausible. There was a time when the foreign merchants here made money rapidly. But those times have passed. Money now comes slowly. There are too many merchants for the place. And, besides, the natives are beginning to take much of the trade into their own hands. They have monopolized all of the cheaper custom. They are particularly apt in photography and outfitting. And as each successive year rolls away they become more competent to push themselves into the higher departments of business. Being able to live upon about one-tenth of what it costs a foreigner to live, having no expensive establishment to keep up, and being contented with a lifetime of small gains, they can defy the competition of the European, who must make his fortune within ten or fifteen years at the most.

It is amusing to listen to the common run of trades gossip here. You gather the impression that five years is the proper time wherein to make a fortune. And if cash is not fairly coined within the allotted time, you hear no end of talk about hard times and the rascally nature of the Japanese in general. Importers of dry goods and European clothing, in particular, have lost heavily. When the fact that Japan had become civilized had fully dawned upon Europe, the keen tradesmen of that part of the globe, with a sharp eye to business, at once clearly perceived that these unclothed millions must have a general outfit of civilized vesture. Forthwith, the incoming steamers brought cargoes of nondescript dry goods. Felt caps, superannuated "plug" hats, antiquated neckties, thousands of shirts and singlets, combs, buttons of every variety, innumerable pieces of woolens, hosiery of endless assortments, brogans of all known sizes,—in truth, beloved Julius Marcellus, you might easily have imagined that the combined efforts of all the old-clothes dealers in Europe had been employed to ransack the four corners of that continent for all species of Noachian apparel.

But there was a miscalculation somewhere. The market was overstocked, and the goods had to be sold at auction with immense loss. Your average native, after having invested in a hat, shirt, and a pair of colored spectacles, appeared to have reached the height of his ambition. He would cut no end of a swell meandering down the streets of his native village, reposing in the sublime consciousness of having fully solved the intricate problem of civilization. This primitive simplicity of taste, however, does not appear to have suited the importer, thus reduced to the disagreeable alternative of having his wares mildew in the *godowns* or thrown away at auction. Some of the heavy losers then lost faith in humanity in general, and in the Japanese in particular. They accused the unwitting offenders of downright meanness. Some wanted the country to be reduced to a condition resembling that of Hindustan. Some wanted all the missionaries packed out of the country as being in some way connected with mercantile reverses. And some of the most radical threatened to turn apostles themselves, laboring under the delusion that the laborers in the vineyard were in receipt of some three thousand dollars per year.

But the reasons for the commercial collapse are easily found. The vast mass of the natives are too miserably poor to invest in anything beyond headgear. Imagine a man, whose yearly income is barely forty dollars, investing in our expensive clothing! When such a party has been improvident enough to become the possessor of a pair of trowsers, his prodigality has reached a height of extravagance at which he fairly trembles. And the vast mass of the people live on less than six dollars a month. Five dollars a month is considered good pay. Seven dollars is very good pay,—sufficient to keep a wife in considerable style. While ten dollars per month would fairly stagger the soaring ambition of the countryman, being enough to furnish a new suit for his father, a brand new girdle for his wife, and no end of kites for the children. A man in receipt of such a sum would feel called upon to allow his intimate, less-favored friends to sponge numberless meals off him, intending, of course, to return the compliment when the fickle goddess should cease to smile.

The truth is, the Japanese are liberal beyond their means. That their means are limited, from our stand-point, is a melancholy circumstance for which they can hardly be held accountable. Should I return to Yokohama in twenty-five years, I don't think I would recognize it. By that time I imagine the European population will have dwindled from twelve hundred to three hundred. And the natives will probably be dressed in full foreign costume. But it will always retain a larger foreign population than any of the treaty ports, because of its central locality.

My next letter will probably be dated from some point in the interior. Write soon and often.

Truly yours,

THEOPHILUS PRATT.

IWA-KI-SAN (STONE-AND-TREE MOUNTAIN) AS SEEN FROM THE RAMPARTS OF HIROSAKI CASTLE.

(*From a Native Photograph.*)

LETTER IV.

HIROSAKI.

DEAR JULIUS MARCELLUS:

SINCE writing to you from Yokohama, my fortunes have changed considerably. I am now in the northern part of Japan. I have just entered upon my first contract with the government as teacher of English. So here I am in the extreme northern end of Nippon, about nineteen miles from the Japan Sea, on the west, and thirty miles from Awomori Bay and the Tsugaru Straits on the north.

As I am the only white man in the province and consequently expect to have abundant spare time, I shall open an extensive correspondence with you during my stay here. Hirosaki was formerly the capital of this province. It is a city of about thirty thousand inhabitants. It is picturesquely located near some low mountains that skirt the base of an extinct volcanic cone which swells up from the shores of the Japan Sea to the height of about six thousand feet. This cone is much venerated by all the people, who call it *Iwaki-san*, rock and tree mountain. Standing guard beside a gap at the

lower end of the valley, it overlooks the lesser
heights that sweep around its base through the adjoining provinces.   From its summit you can gaze
beyond the Straits as far as the dim outlines of
Yesso.

Hirosaki is like all Japanese Daimiate cities.
You find the usual above-ground drainage in gutters; the same style of long, shambling streets; the
usual pretty suburbs filled with monasteries and
sacred groves ; and, finally, the more cleanly aristocratic portion encircling the Castle, where, in old
times, the relatives and friends of the *Daimios* were
accustomed to live.

And now before telling you anything more about
Hirosaki, I will tell you how I secured my contract and how I came here.

As you know, I did not come to Japan with any
specific opening in view.   My friend, Adamson,
wrote to me to come on, for if I could be on the
ground the chances were very favorable for a contract.   And he was right.   When I had been several weeks in Yokohama the Directors of the
Toögu-Gakko (School) in Hirosaki came to him
and requested his aid in securing a teacher for
them.   Their terms were very favorable.   But I
did not want to make a contract for a longer term
than eight months,—that is, so as to cover the
months between February and November, for the
northern weather is very severe.   The loneliness
was also another objection.   Our negotiations were
protracted nearly a month, and finally resulted in a

contract upon my terms. Our contract was reduced to writing and sealed. This is the usual way of making such agreements. The Japanese always strictly carry out these contracts. When a native has once put his signature or seal to a document he invariably fulfills the terms. Until he has done so, he is as unreliable as the winds.

I agreed to teach English six hours per day (Saturdays and Sundays excepted), and to furnish all advice that I thought requisite in the management of the school. They agreed to pay all my traveling expenses ; to allow me the month of August for a vacation ; to duly respect my rights as a citizen of the United States, and, in case of grave misdemeanors, to hand me over to the nearest American Consul ; to pay me on the twenty-fifth of every month ; to provide a first-class native house, comfortably furnished ; to give due notice should a renewal of the contract not be desired ; and, in fullness of time, to return me safely to Yokohama.

Having thus balanced our minds, we began discussing the route that we should select. To reach Hirosaki, you may choose two courses. Either go entirely by land, passing up through the extended provinces of Sendai and Nambu, or go to Hakodatè and Awomori by steamer, and then go some thirty miles by land.

I chose the latter course. The directors were to accompany me. These gentlemen had been retainers of the former *Daimio* of Hirosaki. They

dressed in native costume. They understood very
little English, but with the assistance of Hep-
burn's *Dictionary*, we got along first rate. They
were exceedingly obliging and attentive, and never
allowed even seasickness to interfere with their
many little acts of kindness. When we went
aboard the steamer they thoughtfully placed some
oranges in my stateroom to relieve my seasickness,
as they said. Weighing anchor, we set sail. The
distance up to Hakodatè is about five hundred and
fifty miles. We had a rough passage up the coast,
and were out facing the head-winds nearly three
days. Hakodatè is built on the landward side of a
bold promontory that is almost insulated, being
connected with Yesso by a narrow isthmus but a
few feet above high tide. The native population
is about forty thousand. The houses are built
along the steep and curving mountain side, presenting a pretty view to the incoming ship. Great
numbers of fishermen reside here. They find the
surrounding waters teeming with vast varieties of
marine life. The Japanese do not like the severe
climate of this place and shun it as much as possible during the cold weather. This makes the
community very floating. During the warm weather
the tide turns, and merchants, laborers, and travelers, stream up from the south. Although the
climate is about like that of New York State, yet
the natives, having none of our heating appliances,
find it very trying. Fish and sea-weed form the
chief exports of the place. Very few vessels float

in the harbor during the year. The *patois* is said
to be the coarsest in Japan. The customs and
manners are regarded as very rude and uncultured.
The refined Tokio gentlemen regard the social institutions of Hakodatè with much the same feelings
manifested by the Romans for the truculent Hel-
vetii. If you chance to breathe the word Yesso to
a warm-blooded southerner, a chill instantly passes
down his back, and with a shiver he will inform
you that it is cold up there, and that the people are
barbarous.

The foreign population in Hakodatè does not exceed thirty. With about half-a-dozen exceptions,
the white delegation is decidedly discreditable to
civilization. Licentiousness and depravity are here
given full swing. The forms of degraded vileness
that you come across here fairly make you blush
for your race.

Hakodatè is desolate enough for the natives, but
it is more so for the foreigners. There are no en-
tertainments at all. Hunting is the chief sport.
Excitement of any kind rarely occurs. Six years
ago, however, the place at last became registered
in Japanese history. Here the rebellious forces of
the Shogun made their final stand. For several
days the harbor and Head presented a lively appearance. Several gunboats were destroyed. And
early one morning, before the mist had lifted, the
Imperial forces made a masterly maneuver around
the Head and struck the rebels in the rear. A
hot scuffle ensued. The rebels were demolished,

and the place then settled down to its ancient repose.

We remained in Hakodatè several days. We then took steamer for Awomori. The distance is fifty-six miles. At this season the passage is intensely rough. If this route were in the direct line of travel, it would speedily acquire a most unenviable reputation. The fierce gales rushing down the Tsugaru Straits, together with the swift current, make a wild, chopped sea, very disagreeable to encounter. During these trips the native passengers strew the decks, being fearfully seasick. The women, in particular, are great sufferers. At dusk our little steamer dropped anchor near Awomori beach. The bay is a large one, and is enclosed by headlands stretching northward. Behind the groves and villages rise the snow-clad mountains. Before going ashore, my attendants brought me some bread that they had purchased in Hakodatè. For you must bear in mind that, although this place is but a few hours steaming from that place, yet it is almost impossible to obtain foreign provisions here. In going into the interior, even for a few miles, you have to carry your "chow," as it is called. I was much impressed with their kind thoughtfulness in the matter.

On the beach we were met by two of my future scholars, who had come up to anticipate our arrival. They spoke English fairly well. Considering that they had only studied it for one year, off in the interior, where they could never hear it spoken, the wonder is that they were intelligible at all. They committed the common error of putting English words to Japanese idioms. As they had simply studied text-books, their supply of conversational English was very limited. To illustrate:

" We welcome you, dear master."

" How is your health?"

" If you desire anything, command us to do it. How do you call your name?"

I was so much pleased to meet them, however, that I took no notice of their rather obscure address, and guessed at their meaning and answered all questions.

" Follow me and I will guide you," said the spokesman, taking a lantern and leading the way through the long lines of boats and nets upon the beach.

We soon reached the streets. Everything was silent and dark. No street lamps anywhere. Here indeed was real Japan. There was nothing to remind one of civilization save a slight sprinkling of ancient hats and neckties. The sidewalks were about four feet wide. They were of hard ground and were covered with a shed, so that locomotion need not be obstructed during the severe winters, when the snow is heaped up nearly to the eaves of the houses. We must have made a weird appearance as we marched along in single file up the sheds dimly lighted by the swaying lanterns of the company, whose clattering clogs filled the streets with a prolonged din, and whose petticoat-

like *hakamas* grotesquely flaunted from side to side
as we lengthened our strides. After some ten
minutes' brisk walking, our leader suddenly stopped beside a wicket-like door and called out to
somebody inside. The door was slid back, and a
top-knot popped out to view the situation. He
told us to come in. We stooped and entered the
hotel, for such it was.

The landlord welcomed us by bowing his head
three times down to the *tatamis* * (mats). My
future "boy" was then brought forward. He
fetched a tub of warm water and a towel and began washing the mud off my shoes. He was ex-
cessively timid and cowering. We then went upstairs in our stocking feet. The entire upper story
had been set apart for our accommodation. In
honor of the occasion the landlord had borrowed
a chair from a friend who had been enterprising
enough to import it from Hakodatè. It was not
remarkably strong. I sat upon it and warmed my-

---

* The word *tatami* has almost become anglicized in Japan, there
being no English word that adequately represents it ; and it is a
word that from necessity will be much used in these letters. *Tatamis* are heavy padded mats about seven feet long, three feet wide,
and about two inches thick. They are the only covering that the
Japanese ever use for their floors. They constitute the principal
feature in a native house, for, from their soft nature, they serve as
beds, chairs, and tables. Being all of the same size, they form the
unit of measure in estimating the dimensions of native structures,
which are usually cited as containing such and such a number of
tatamis, the temple of *Chioin* in Kioto, for instance, being quoted
as having five hundred. They are manufactured of soft rushes, and
are bordered with silken edges.

STREET VENDER.

self over a *hebachi* (brazier filled with charcoal),
while my attendants sat around on the floor in a
circle warming their finger-tips, for this seems to
be the only part of the Japanese body suscepti-
ble of cold. I suffered much from the cold. The
change from Yokohama, with its green grass and
budding flowers, to these chilling March storms
blowing right off from Siberia, was too sudden
to be comfortable. While my boy was preparing supper, they compared notes and tapped their
pipes perpetually on the rim of the *hebachi;*
and I examined the pretty designs on the sliding doors. Finally my supper was ready, but
there was no table, and how was it to be served?
Here was a complication that taxed the ingenuity of the whole group. They unanimously voted
that it would never do to serve it on the floor.
After much discussion and smoking, decision was
finally rendered in favor of placing two orange
boxes on top of each other and spreading a red
blanket over them. The company then filed out
of the room, and I took my seat and awaited the
opening of the programme. Fish, rice, pears, and
omelets were brought in on little dishes. After
the boy had placed them, he knelt down to await
orders. Calling in my interpreter, I intimated that
it would be more agreeable to me to have him
standing. Thereafter he stood up, but always
wore a troubled expression, as if wondering at his
own audacity. After supper I had quite a conversation with my interpreter. I found him to be

a person of excellent parts. He was extremely anxious to travel abroad. I was much amused at the ponderous words he used in apologizing for the necessity of my sleeping on the floor, as there was no bedstead in the hotel.

Our plan was to start for Hirosaki at five o'clock the following morning. But the negotiation for horses delayed us until eight. It took quite a while to load the beasts, for they were restless until they were satisfied with kicking and biting each other. At last we got off amid a drizzle of sleet. I had expected to go cantering over the road in jolly style. But as none of the party could keep up so as to show me the way, I had to drag along with the crowd. This horseback riding was a new feature in my experience. It was positively the most entertaining—nay, more, I confess it was the most absurd piece of atrocity ever inflicted upon your humble servant. A full-grown, able bodied man leads each horse with a straw rope. Just fancy four men riding in this imbecile manner over a plain road! And you can't hurry them up. Whenever one of the nags endeavors to shake up the funeral a trifle, his man harshly admonishes him.

We met long strings of horses and men coming down the mountains. They were all pacing along at a miserable hang-dog gait that nearly drove me wild. Merciful Zeus! What next?

These nags are an unreliable set. The zest with which they improve all opportunities to kick each other is marvelous. A couple of model specimens of horse flesh will be meandering along as if profoundly considering the true inwardness of nags in general, until they come side by side, when, with inspired rapidity, they begin slamming their hoofs into each other's sides, utterly regardless how far their riders are flung over their heads into the deep mud of the rice fields. As their shoes are made of straw, they never damage each other very much by these displays of temper.

By mid-day we had passed over the mountains. There was much rugged scenery. My boy had gone on to prepare dinner at the mid-way village. Our road was now level. All the country is under a high state of cultivation. Rice is produced in every available spot. The long valleys, that go winding up into the mountains, are all terraced and flooded for this purpose. In the valley, to our right and left, extensive rice fields stretch off to the hazy mountains. Innumerable villages, picturesquely shaded by clumps of trees, are scattered along the winding road where endless squads of pack-horses are passing and repassing. All the houses up here are covered with tissue shingle weighted down by stones. Those who can not afford this, thatch theirs with rice straw. All the yards are surrounded with pretty hedges. Across the north-west face of every house you will see a high screen made of rush mats to protect the tenants from the deep drifting snows which are hurled down the valley during the bitter winter months.

Life in these villages must be dreary in the extreme during cold weather.

About four miles from Hirosaki I met the whole school. They had waded through a quantity of slush that I would not have gone through even to see the Nana Sahib. They were drawn up along each side of the main street of a large village. As we appeared they welcomed us with profuse bowings. The entire village, numbering some two thousand pieces of humanity, had also turned out. It is impossible to describe the sensation of a person lionized for the first time. When you are hard at work on a match game of base-ball and have the entire field to yourself, you don't mind three or four thousand pairs of eyes watching you. But to ride through a crowd that is drinking in all your gestures, with mingled feelings of curiosity and admiration, makes one feel like evaporating.

Arriving in front of the crowded hotel, his Highness (!) was assisted from his fiery nag and duly escorted into a suite of rooms where the entire school, numbering some ninety scholars, were sitting in semicircular rows upon the *tatamis*. Around an extemporized table beside the window was grouped a party of school officials. Through the medium of the interpreters, a mutual introduction followed. Then came some of the steepest bowing on record in the annals of this obscure village. First the interpreters bowed to the officials. Then the officials bowed to the interpreters. In bowing, they got down on all fours and mutually bent their foreheads down to the *tatamis* three times in succession, at the same time sucking their breath between their teeth, expressive of their intense pleasure at the honor of the salutation. Then the scholars saluted the officials, the directors, the interpreters, and his Highness, with repeated waves of obeisances. His Highness returned the salute by unloosing the vertebræ of his neck sufficiently to allow his head to duck forward a few degrees. Then followed a tempest of mutual *kowtowing* that beggared description. The entire crowd dissolved into incoherent atoms of bobbing heads. There were special salutations between special friends. And the special friends, to make things doubly sure, repeated their special salutations. And to help on the good work, the landlord and his lady came in and showered indiscriminate greetings upon the special friends, the directors, the officials, the interpreters, and his Highness combined. I must confess that his Highness was bewildered with the scene. Bowing with the Japanese is a real means of social grace. They revel in it; they really seem to love it. In their efforts to outdo each other, the assembly seemed to him to be almost frantic. He became exhilarated, inspired,—nay, almost infatuated with the desire to bounce down and root over the *tatamis* like a wild rhinoceros. But, like a rock upon a surf-swept shore, he calmly surveyed the wild " confusion thrice confounded," and helped himself to some tea and cakes !

After things had somewhat subsided, the spokesman of the senior class made a little address in fair
English, wherein were contained sundry glowing
congratulations upon the safe arrival of his Highness, boundless pleasure that the weather and the
ocean had been propitious, sincere desires that the
fatigues of the journey would soon vanish, and
ardent hopes that the future would be quite as
favorable in all respects.

Now his Highness was not expert at impromptu
addresses, so he was cornered. He, therefore, re-
sponded with an approving bow and a few words
of thanks, supplemented with some rather indefinite sentiments about the cordial relations that
ought to exist between instructor and pupil, and
coupled with a rather hazy observation about
general good understanding between all parties
present.

The assembly now dissolved ; his Highness to resume his journey in the dusk, the scholars to plod
back through the slush on the morrow.

It was late in the night before our weary party
entered the deserted streets of Hirosaki. It was
raining heavily, and the sleepy horsemen were
obliged to carefully pick their way through the dark-
ness. Yonder, to our right, the trees around the
castle loomed up grandly in the night. Our road
led along the borders of the ditch and then turned
sharply to the left,—" Look out, man ! You'll have
me in the moat ! Where are you going, you loon ? "
The drowsy fellow had well-nigh walked the horse

into the stagnant waters. He rouses himself; and in a few moments leads me, half-frozen, into the gateway of my future home.

My house was a good native dwelling, having eight rooms. My boy had already arrived, and, with the partner of his mundane vicissitudes, was the first to welcome the new master of the house. I found the interior decidedly homelike. There were a couple of genuine tables, a first-rate writing-desk, five or six folding-chairs, two large rugs, two bureaus, a stove, and glass windows. The fire was lighted and I began rapidly to thaw out. Feeling very ravenous, I made short work of a roast chicken some fried potatoes, and some griddle cakes. I then slept the sleep that none but the weary know.

The next morning, the directors and scholars called upon me. They were all dressed in native costume. Many of them wore Manchester singlets and woolen shirts. A few of those who desired to be stylish, and set the fashion for my future levees, wore collars and neckties. We shook hands all around instead of bowing. They all had their hair cut in foreign style. But a glance at the method of tonsure made me form a mighty resolve to cut my own hair while a sojourner here.

Then followed the indispensable exchange of compliments. It was hoped that the teacher would find this poor house fit to live in; that there was no better accommodation in the city, but, inferior as it was, they hoped the teacher who had left so many civilized luxuries would find it comfortable;

4

and that they were delighted with my prosperous journey and safe arrival.

To which, reply was made that the house and furniture were much beyond expectation; that they would furnish much comfort and pleasure; and that very many thanks were returned for the kind attentions shown.

Formalities being finished, they proposed to assist me in unpacking my baggage. Although there could be no use for ninety pairs of hands, yet I accepted the well-meant offer, intending, however, to perform all the work myself. Taking my hammer, I began on my box of books. But that would never do! It was abhorrent to their ideas of etiquette that I should work while so many stood around idle. In deference to their importunity, I submitted, and handed the hammer to one of the senior scholars, who immediately flung back his loose dress over his shoulders and began energetically pounding away without having any definite idea how the thing was done; for the Japanese never use nails in their frail, shell-like boxes, so that one of our ponderous dry-goods boxes assumes formidable proportions to them.

Five minutes' thumping fetched out profuse perspiration, half a dozen chips, and about a square inch of skin from the knuckles. This mishap caused intense merriment among the bystanders. While number one was sucking the back of his hand, number two vigorously grasped the instrument and speedily succeeded in giving himself a black and

GOSSIPING AT THE WELL.

blue nail amid peals of laughter. He dropped the hammer like a hot coal. Number three then picked it up with a gusto that foreboded the immediate lifting of the obstinate lid. He stood up to his work right manfully until a tremendous whack glanced from the edge of the box upon his shin, while the small boys of the third class nearly died laughing. Number four, five, and six then retired from the field more or less grievously wounded. The senior class was nearly decimated ; and there was a fair prospect of the entire school being numbered among the victims before the boxes were opened. The directors stood scratching their heads and were muttering that it was decidedly *mudzu-kashi* (difficult). In this perplexing dilemma, we were observed to carelessly pick up the luckless hammer and knock off the wood from around a crevice. Then inserting the other end of the instrument, we pried up the lid with the greatest imaginable ease amid a subdued murmuring of " *Nara-hodo ! So-dis-ne ?*" which may be liberally translated, " 'Pon my honor! That's the way, isn't it ?"

The box was now fairly opened. The books were then unpacked and passed down a long line of hands to the shelves in the next room. Considerable surprise was expressed over such an array of printed matter.

The next box contained the provisions. They were quite willing that I should remove the lid. They were then passed down into the store-room, where a special committee deposited them in the

closets. Each article excited considerable comment. The tin-can, and bottled fruits were riddled
with criticisms. But the base-ball and the dumb-
bells created the most interest. They failed to see
any fun in catching so hard a ball.

And so the morning was passed. Everything
was duly arranged. At dinner time the kind-
hearted assistants retired with sufficient material
for six weeks' conversation. For you must understand that these natives are essential gossips.
Their language is eminently fitted for this species
of recreation. Off in the interior, where social
stagnation prevails, an unusual event is something
to be treasured up and handed down, and the
coming of a foreigner forms an epoch in the history
of a place. It will long be remembered how pompously he came into town ; how his fierce dogs drove
the native curs beyond the village; how it took
three pack-horses to carry his provisions and baggage; how he had to stoop in entering the hotel ;
how shaggy his beard was : how he drank immense
quantities of beer ; how he used a murderous word
that his boy and groom had also learned to speak ;
and how strange it was that so majestic an individual should condescend to fool with the insignificant waiter girls at the hotels. While the natives
are by no means saints, it is a great pity that they
should be spoiled by the coarse specimens of foreigners that go swaggering through the country
creating the impression that all of them are a set
of licentious beasts.

And now, before closing this rambling letter, I must tell you a little about Hirosaki.

As I said in the beginning of my letter, the great feature of this valley is the lovely cone of Iwaki-san. Whether seen in the rosy dawn, or at mid-day, or in the twilight, or when swathed in clouds, it is always lovely. The people love to watch the sunset bathing its stately form, resting against the deep hues of the evening sky, as they sip their tea in their gardens after the labors of the day. It is the lord of the valley. From its summit you can gaze beyond the straits as far as the dim outlines of Yesso.

Concerning the origin of the mountain, the legends say that ages ago an old woman saw it rising up in the night, and in great trepidation reported the affair to her astonished neighbors. This same story is told about Fujisan and several other noted peaks. In fact, an old lady meandering around promiscuously at unseasonable hours, seems to have been considered a necessary witness to the production of one of these volcanic cones. A goddess is enshrined beside the crater. From all accounts, she appears to possess considerable characteristic capriciousness; for she expects annual visits from all the men in the surrounding country, but forbids delegations of her own sex to appear at the chilly crests, under penalty of being whisked off into the limitless realms of air should they dare to disobey her exacting mandates. Whether the ancient priests invented this myth as an excuse to save the ladies a fatiguing climb up the misty heights, or whether her divine ladyship bears a sweeping grudge against the old crone that witnessed her *début*, will forever be fertile subjects of conjecture to knights of the quill who delight in speculation and classical description. Many thousand votaries worship at this shrine every year. They come from villages a hundred miles away. The vast majority are farmers, who organize themselves into companies while the crops are ripening, and, arming themselves with gongs and drums, flock toward the cone from all directions. During the cool hours of the autumnal nights you will be kept awake by the crash of the drums and the din of the chanting as the immense crowds of pilgrims stream through the city.

The great architectural feature of Hirosaki is the castle which environs the bluffs in the center of the city. Its foundation was laid some three centuries ago, when the present style of building came into vogue. The Daimio was the most powerful in northern Nippon. His eastern neighbor was Nambu, with whom he was upon very good terms. His southern neighbor was Akitah, with which lord a bitter feud existed, leading to many a wild foray across the rugged borders. The entire surface of Awomori Province, as well as that of all the provinces that stretch northward from Kinka-san (a bold promontory half-way up the coast) is grandly mountainous. And, like all the provinces that face the Japan Sea, it has an immense snowfall during the winter.

Judging from the appearance of the people of these northern provinces, you would not infer that a double tide of immigration had swept over the country. First, at least twenty-five centuries ago, came the aboriginal Ainos from Siberia, Saghalien, and Yesso. They spread southward over the Japan Islands and were met by an opposing tide of Malays (*vide* Asiatic Reports) that had drifted up on the Kuro-siwo from the archipelago beneath the tropics. The Ainos were no match for their hot-blooded competitors. And, after centuries of strife, they were pressed northward by the overcrowding population of the south ; and were finally expelled from Nippon and banished to the cheerless wilds of Yesso, whither their unrelenting enemies desired not to follow.

The early history of Hirosaki and these northern provinces is composed mostly of feudatory skirmishing which can hardly be designated war. The country was broken up into a series of petty chieftainships. Instead of a Daimio for a large province, we find innumerable petty leaders of a few villagers who lived in little moated enclosures. This epoch was one of perpetual frays.

About the fifteenth century, however, some ambitious master-spirit arose. Subduing the petty lords and compelling them to be his vassals, he selected the present site of Hirosaki for his headquarters, and founded an enduring castle, leaving the primitive strongholds to become obscured by tillage until their original lines of demarcation had become obliterated by herbage. Houses sprang up all around the castle, and we have the present city. Excepting the castle, it presents but few points of interest to the foreigner.

As I intend giving a full account of Japanese castles in a future letter, I will put my period here.

Truly yours,

THEOPHILUS PRATT.

OLD-STYLE WARRIORS.

LETTER V.

HIROSAKI, *July* 10, 1874.

DEAR JULIUS MARCELLUS:

ABOUT the only thing here that reminds me of civilization is the castle. There is something very inspiring in the lively notes of the bugle that make the entire place vocal in the morning, at noon, and at sundown. It contains a garrison of about a thousand men. They are dressed in blue uniform trimmed with yellow, and are armed with Snyder and Sharpe rifles. These soldiers come from all the provinces; for the government will not allow the regiments to be composed of men coming from one clan lest it tend to promote sedition. They are small men, but are very plucky and hardy. They are kept under excellent discipline, giving implicit obedience to their officers, and are very quiet and orderly. It is a rare thing to find one of them drunk. When they do get drunk, however, they become childish rather than pugnacious.

About once a week the garrison will turn out in force for a march into the country. They file through the streets with great regularity and are

treated with great respect by the townsfolk, although many of them are from hostile clans. The
government keeps a standing army of about thirty-
five thousand men. The mass of these are in can-
tonments at Tokio. But the others are occupying
the many castles throughout the empire.

I was quite desirous of seeing the inside of the
Hirosaki Castle, as it was in an excellent state of
preservation. I therefore made a formal request
through the school authorities. They were, for a
while, in quite a dilemma, for no white person had
ever been beyond the second moat, and they much
dreaded a refusal. But it happened that one of the
scholars had a brother who was an officer in the
regiment, and through his kindness, permission was
granted to visit it one Sunday afternoon, as on that
day all the officers were at leisure. So, on the appointed day, the whole school put on their best
clothes and escorted me through the spacious
grounds. The afternoon was very genial, the officers were exceedingly courteous, no restrictions
were placed upon our inspection, and we had a most
delightful time indeed.

Japanese castles are singular structures. They
are all built upon the same general plan. Throughout the empire there are about one hundred and
fifty of them, varying in size and antiquity. The
origin of this style of building feudal strongholds
has been ascribed to Yamamoto, a Daimio of the
thirteenth century. Other authorities date their
rise some four centuries before this, holding that

the first one was built in Shikoku, the large island just south of Nippon.

The term "castle" is misleading. For, unlike the flinty masses of masonry of Europe that delight to perch themselves upon lofty cliffs, these strongholds rarely present high walls to the sight, and are generally built upon undulating or level ground. The ideal plan is to arrange the moats and embankments so that a moderately rugged hill shall be near the center, thus serving to increase the strength of the Tenshiu, or citadel. As a rule, you will find a triple system of circumvallation, one inside the other; the outermost one being from two to four miles in circumference, while the inmost one is reduced to a massive enclosure of a few hundred yards. The largest castle in Japan is at Tokio. The perimeter of its outlying line of circumvallation exceeds ten miles,—in fact, a part of the metropolis is built between the first and second systems. The next one in size is said to be at Shidzuoka, about one hundred miles south-west of Tokio, but it is not half so large as the one in the metropolis.

Scattered through the different islands of the empire, these mediæval relics, more durable than the institutions they represented, still greet the eye of the inquisitive traveler as he journeys through the provinces.

Imagine yourself standing beside the one in Hirosaki. This first system, here before us, is surrounded by a wide moat that is walled in with

roughly hewn blocks of granite.   On the opposite
side, at a slight angle from the water, rises a thick
swarded embankment to the height of about twelve
feet.   The top of this is defended by a strong picket
fence and plastered wall, and a row of pine trees
just behind not only beautifies the place, but furnishes additional protection to the defenders of the
rampart.   This moat and rampart sweep around
about two miles, passing over an occasional bluff.
In the castle at Tokio, the moat of the outer system
has been carried through the foundations of several
hills, necessitating several enormous cuttings at an
immense outlay of labor.

We now cross the moat by means of this fragile
bridge, which has been purposely so constructed in
order that it may be quickly demolished upon
emergencies.   For you must bear in mind that
the famous drawbridges which spanned the chilly
chasms of the Norman fortresses are not to be
found in Japan.

At the other end stands a double-storied tower
with heavy wooden gates covered with iron plates.
The strongly barred windows of the upper story are
well arranged for a free play of arrows upon assaulting ranks beneath.   From the gable ends of the heavily tiled roof bronze fishes are gayly curveting in the
air ; while from the corners, weird dragons appear
to be ready for a spring upon the advancing foe.
The brilliant white plastering with which the tower
has been finished off presents a pleasing contrast to
the dull gray stones of the rampart and the waters

of the moat. Seen at a distance peeping through the cordon of watchful pines, its appearance is grotesque in the extreme.

We now enter the first inclosure. It covers many acres of ground. A long avenue of pine trees leads down to the second moat. The entire place is neatly swarded. It contains lines of barracks for the retainers of the prince. In the old days you would have found them here practicing fencing and other warlike diversions. This inclosure was used as a kind of promenade for the inmates of the castle. Here we also find the parade ground, the orchards, the wells, and the shady vistas twisting through the camelia and box-wood shrubbery.

The second moat is deeper and broader than the first one. The towers are more massive, and are placed at shorter intervals along the rampart. Passing over another bridge, we enter the second system. The grounds are about one-tenth as extensive as those just viewed. But they are far more rugged. It is a kind of fortified park. The general appearance of the place is that of a pretty garden filled with neat paths winding around through the bamboo groves. Near the gateway are some tea booths, wherein visitors paying their respects to my lord, the Daimio, would tarry awhile chatting with the retainers until his Grace should be pleased to receive them.

Following this path down the hill, we come to a long fire-proof " go-down " serving as an arsenal for the storing of semi-barbaric implements of warfare.

Off to the right, through that vista of fragrant olea, you will find the shooting range. At the foot of the hill, we find a fish pond. In the autumn, the wild ducks from Yesso delight to sport here for a brief period amid the lotus plants and water lilies that line the margin.

This second inclosure was the private promenade of the prince and a few select retainers.

We now come to the third and last system of circumvallation. Here we find the citadel. The towers and ramparts are exceedingly massive. The hilly nature of the ground has been skillfully made to contribute to the strength of the place. The precipitous sides of the ravine seem to be but a continuation of the stony battlements above. But one gateway leads within this last system.

Entering, we see the palace. The garden surrounding it has been laid out with the best native skill. Ponds for gold-fishes, shaded walks, and artificial mounds representing Fujisan, are scattered around in pleasing variety. The palace itself is apt to disappoint you after having been led through all the external display. It is simply a very large and extensive Japanese house, having an immensely heavy roof covered with sheets of bronze. A superb veranda completely environs it. Everything is built of wood. The interior, however, is more interesting. There is but one story. All the rooms are extremely high and airy. They are separated from each other by exquisitely ornamented *shojees* *

---

* The word *shojee*, like the word *tatami*, cannot be rendered prop-

(sliding doors made of paper) set in elegantly lacquered frames. Upon the panels you see beautifully executed designs from nature,—mountain,
field, and flood being presented by the best native
skill. The floors are covered with the finest *tatamis.*
A few lovely screens and some superb pieces of
bronze and lacquerware will complete the furnishing of the apartments, for you must bear in mind
that the Japanese are utterly deficient as regards
upholstery. The ceilings of the rooms are usually
finished off with square panels representing dragons
and fairies upon gilded backgrounds. In the chambers of Nobunaga's palace in Owari the panels are
said to have been originally inlaid with plates of
pure gold.

As was before hinted these palaces cover a vast
amount of ground. The visitor is led through suite
after suite until he becomes bewildered at the apparently never ending maze of elaborate apartments.

As a rule, the finest room is the audience cham-
ber. Here the combined skill of many artists con-
spire to overwhelm the mind of the stranger with
the wealth, the power, and the generosity of his
Highness. Royal tigers are crouching upon the
gilded panels. Here we see two of the ferocious

---

erly into English. It will therefore be frequently used in the following pages. It is a kind of sliding door set in grooves. They
form the walls and partitions of Japanese domiciles. Upon a fragile
sashing of wood, delicate tissue paper is pasted ; this is then set in
a light frame, frequently lacquered, adapted to grooves in the floor.

beasts engaged in fierce combat. There we have the phœnix and the peacock perching upon gorgeous sprays of a species of plant that never existed outside of the artist's brain. While down at the far end of the room is a scene from Chinese history that occupies the entire side of the apartment.

Great ingenuity has been displayed in the endless variety of the designs. No two are precisely similar. Here we have the lotus plant growing in an elaborate jar. There we see it blossoming beside the sedges in the moat. There it unfolds its gorgeous petals beside the mountain streams that flow through the shaded grounds of that monastery. And yet again we catch its impassioned gleam beside the lilies in the Imperial ponds. Very few of the historic scenes relate to Japan. China is the classic source of inspiration.

For elegance and beauty, the palaces of Kioto, Owari, and Yeddo ranked among the highest. As there is a similarity between the castles in Japan, so the palaces furnish but little in the line of startling variety.

Since the Imperial Revolution of 1868–1870, all these provincial strongholds have been turned over to the central government. All the former proprietors have been sent to Tokio to be kept under Imperial surveillance. Many of the castles have been allowed to fall into decay. Some of the choicest, however, are kept in a fair state of repair, and are open to the inspection of tourists from abroad. But the majority have been turned into quarters for garrisons, and all the ancient paraphernalia and ornamentation have about disappeared. Many of the bronzes, and most of the elegant lacquering, now adorn the homes of the wealthy in Europe and America.

You will find long rows of roughly-made bedsteads arranged up and down the spacious chambers. Muskets are stacked in the audience hall. Knapsacks and heavy riding boots are strewn around promiscuously to be kicked under an adjoining bed by some passing foot. The *shojees* and *tatamis* have been removed, and but little remains to remind one of the former condition of things, save the few rooms appropriated by the officers.

And now I hear you inquiring about the parties that lived within these walls. How did they spend their time? What was the social life of the inmates? How was administrative power wielded? In short, give a glimpse of old feudal times in Japan.

Let us begin, then, with my lord, the Daimio, inasmuch as he was the theoretical sovereign unit. In him were centered the executive, the legislative, and the judicial power. These functions were then delegated to favored retainers, who relieved their lord of the drudgery usually connected with those departments.

In discussing the Daimio, we will suppose him to be a person of fair ability and energy. He has under him some ten or twenty thousand *samurai* (feudal retainers) scattered through the Daimiate.

5

Of these some five thousand live in the immediate vicinity of the castle, taking turns in doing garrison duty and in guarding their liege lord.

From these again are selected the most promising as personal attendants. Under the old *régime* it was the ambition of every *samurai* to be so chosen. For if an obscure retainer could win the notice and favor of his master by pleasing manners and bearing, he could flatter himself with the prospect of holding the most honored positions so long as the favor lasted. In some cases, powerful families would hold the princely favor for generations to the exclusion of others, thus causing bitter jealousies, and, too frequently, cruel assassinations. This favor was usually secured and retained by an amount of obsequiousness quite repulsive to our natures.

Now let us follow his lordship through a day's work. After breakfast (composed of rice accompanied with delicate morsels of fish, rice-beer, and choice bits of vegetables, served up and eaten on the *tatamis*), a delegation of *samurai* will wait upon his Grace with a few items of provincial business which are presented for approval or discussion. Perhaps it is a memorial from some farmers petitioning for lower taxes as the rice crops have been a failure. Or perhaps it is a minute description of some foreign articles in an adjoining province. Or, possibly, it may be an account of another intrusion of one of those restless barbarian ships upon the coast. Or, it may be the disorderly conduct of some *samurai*, coupled with the suggestion that he be confined to his house for a few days as punishment.

After this, a well-informed gentleman comes in to instruct his Lordship by edifying conversation upon a variety of topics. The manners, literature, and history of the Chinese will usually form the main topic of conversation. The duration of this private tutoring will entirely depend upon the temperament and mental caliber of the prince.

In the afternoon, a stroll down to the shooting range will be in order. When the long-bows and match-locks have been sufficiently tested, some time will be devoted to fencing with bamboo foils. After which, a half hour or so of horseback riding up and down the avenues will be in order.

About two or three times per month he goes forth from the castle to hunt with his falcons in the country. Occasionally he tackles larger game and brings down a boar or a stag with arrow or spear. Some of these excursions form famous themes for artists. In some of the drawings, my lord is represented leaping his horse over a chasm and chasing a monstrous boar that rivals his steed in dimensions, while his speechless retainers stand gaping in hopeless bewilderment on the further edge, quite unable to follow the mad career of their valorous master.

During the hot summer months when the exhalations from the moat render the immediate vicinity of the *tenshiu* unhealthy, he will journey off to his mountain villa, where he can spend a month or two in composing Chinese poetry in honor of the moon or his favorite concubine. For you must bear in mind that poetizing in this country is not a monopoly, but a mere mechanical process that can be learned by almost any one who desires to become expert in grinding out the requisite metered verses. Some of this princely rhythmic agony, by the way, enjoys considerable reputation. The sentiment, however, is never remarkably overwhelming in its effects. If our prince be public spirited, he will make an occasional journey through his Daimiate to see that all is going well. But the great event of the year will be his visit to Yeddo. The discussion of ways and means will occupy several weeks, and, as many months will elapse before his return, arrangements must be made for guarding the castle and keeping things in order.

Theoretically, the Daimios were supposed to exchange provinces annually in accordance with the laws of *Iyeyas*, the feudal law-giver of Japan. And in the early days of the *Shogunate*, this regulation was undoubtedly enforced. But the rule became practically a dead letter as regards the northern and south-western provinces; although the right to carry out the statute was never relinquished by the house of Tokugawa.

So long as a province sent in its regular tribute of rice, and disturbed not the peace of the general government by hatching conspiracies, it might retain its prince for many generations,—provided

THIRD MOAT OF THE TOKIO CASTLE.
(*Native Photograph.*)

he paid his regular visit to Yeddo to do homage to the Great Lord of Nippon.

But I have been depicting to you an ideal Daimio. Your average lord, it grieves me to say, differed very much from this model. Instead of harkening daily to the edifying conversation of some learned *samurai*, he wasted his hours in frivolous sports and childish chit-chat with his concubines. He loved wine to excess, and was frequently as "boozy" as typical members of nobility are wont to be. So far from practicing his body with daily manly exercise, he resorts to the ingenious expedient of having two or three horse-boys wind his nags, and two or three coolies might strain their backs over the bows and arrows while he complacently watches their gyrations. As to practicing fencing, he merely desires half a dozen retainers to bang each other's heads with the heavy foils until he has thoroughly imbibed the intricacies of this highly scientific art. As to listening to the long-winded disquisitions of aldermanic Yakunins and official *samurai* upon the administration of provincial affairs, they might smoke their pipes over the *hebachis*, *ad libitum*, and adopt any measure they might see fit, so long as they did not compromise his pleasures and revenues, and falconry and hunting might go to the winds. And as to jumping chasms after wild boars,—the—the—well, the horse-boys can do that also.

About three or four times a season he will exert himself sufficiently to visit some hot mineral springs in the mountains to soak out the licentious impurities of a past winter. Occasionally he will rouse his languid curiosity enough to examine some superb pieces of lacquer-ware or bronze, upon which he has squandered half the revenues of his province, perhaps. Should he wish to see some famous court-dancers, wrestlers, or any other performances of a curious nature, several days will be spent before the preliminaries, the preparation of the grounds, and the exhibition can be consummated. For it would be the height of vulgarity for his Grace to visit a house of public resort. He must inspect anything odd and novel through endless formalities. In short, he was a perfect slave to etiquette. And, unless he was a person of more than average resolution, he would inevitably sink into a state of utter and hopeless imbecility,—a condition, in fact, that was rather encouraged by the ambitious head men of the clan who desired to administer affairs to suit themselves without any interference from the prime power. It was a kind of oligarchy. The Daimio was a kind of social figure-head. He was to be petted and humored. He was never to have the placidity of his temper ruffled by any crossing; he was to be treated with the most deferential obsequiousness; to symbolize limitless power, though possessing little of the essence. In short, he was to be kept in a state of perfect animal good nature, and to have his ambition and energy dissipated by abundance of license, so that his consent to all legal proceedings might the more easily be obtained.

The truth is, that about Perry's time, political affairs in Japan had become thoroughly run down. The *samurai* were rapidly degenerating into a herd of voluptuous imbeciles. Feudal customs had become completely worn out. The country was well prepared for a change. I have frequently been informed by Japanese that the patriotic portion of Japan had already become disgusted at the frightful corruption of their country, and were solicitous for speedy reformation. And it was this undercurrent of liberalism that forced the conservative element to open the country to foreign intercourse. This accounts for the marvelous reaction against all ancient *political* institutions that has so astonished us Western people. For you must remember that the Japanese still cling to most of their *social* institutions; and they will continue to do so for generations.

Now as to your next question, concerning administrative regulations in old times, it will be rather difficult to convey a very definite idea. The first course served up in a French revolution is a new constitution. But this country has never been blessed with this modern invention, as it has been characterized. The legacy of Iyeyas, which in many respects was a dead letter, consisted mostly of directions for regulating the succession of the Tokugawa house, and of a few general admonitions for the management of public affairs. Theoretically, the Shogun (Tycoon, we call him), was the prime minister of the invisible emperor (Mikado,

we call him), at Kioto, to whom he did homage for
perpetual lease of unlimited royal power. And he,
in turn, exacted homage from the Daimios for annual lease of provincial power revocable at pleasure.
He stood as a sort of go-between betwixt the
phenix car and the Daimios. The emperor must
not be contaminated by vulgar bickerings with the
masses. That piece of drudgery must be performed
by his head servant, the Shogun. It was his duty
to keep peace within the realm in the name of his
master. He must govern the people. He must
furnish his Imperial Majesty with proper guards,
and appoint proper officers to see that the revenues
of the Province of Yamashiro were duly devoted to
keeping up the simplicity of the imperial court.

While the Shogun was thus supposed to be busy-
ing himself with the secular affairs of the realm at
Yeddo, the inmates of the Gosho in Kioto were
supposed to be wrapped in the sublimest indifference to administrative affairs, being in a kind of
imperial Nirvana, if you please. They would, however, occasionally notice the petitions of their head
servant for some title or rank to be conferred on
some worthy subject. Such was the theory.

Practically, however, the emperor was kept under
a polite but most unrelenting surveillance. A bare
pittance wherewith to keep up a skeleton court
within a few acres of enclosed ground was doled
forth to him at tardy intervals by the officers. He
was respectfully but strictly guarded by Aidzu, the
most zealous Tokugawa clan. And the Shogun

bothered himself so little about his Imperial Majesty that he spent all his time in Yeddo, three hundred and fifteen miles to the north-east, and they are reported to have paid their homage personally to the emperor only about once a century.

So closely was the emperor confined that his person was never seen by any one outside of his family. In fact, the position was so void of prerogatives, and possessed so few attractions, that it became by no means a rare custom for an emperor to resign his office, and, investing his infant son with the empty titles, retire to one of the superb monasteries in the mountains surrounding Kioto, where he could at least see something of the world.

Thus it was that the Tokugawas, giving but nominal deference to the fountain of honors, grasped the administrative power, and bullied their subordinates to their hearts' content. Like all centralized power, however, their authority over the Daimiates gradually became dissipated. Satsuma, Chosiu, and Tosa, were permitted to do pretty nearly what they chose. And soon each prince, so long as he paid his regular homage and tribute, held almost unlimited sway over his Daimiate. Each one had his palace in Yeddo in charge of some near relative.

Passing now to the respective provinces we find that the administrative power was almost entirely in the hands of the *samurai* class. These are the double-sworded gentlemen that we see so often represented in Japanese pictures. They were, in

theory, bound body and soul to the interests of
their lord. To disobey him was the highest crime.
They were to gird him round with a living wall,
standing betwixt him and every danger. In return
for these services he was to distribute among them
annual pensions of so many bushels of rice apiece.
They never worked at manual occupations. Their
only business was to attend on the prince. They
were the aristocrats of the realm. The swords they
carried were typical of their genteel and chivalrous
breeding. The sons of *samurai*, during their infancy, would carry wooden ones. When fourteen
years old, at which age they reached their majority,
they would receive a pair of genuine ones. This
day was made one of festivity, and all the family
friends sent in their congratulations. The young
man was now admitted to the counsels of his elders,
and was treated with all becoming deference. The
next thing was to try the temper of the blades.
And until this was accomplished the youth was
nearly wild. The first hack would usually find its
way into some luckless dog roaming about the yard.
The bodies of criminals also furnished much practice. The executioners also tested the edges by
taking off heads. Should dogs and criminals be
scarce, however, a night's loafing in the dark streets
generally furnished a victim. When a *samurai*
appeared on the street he must always wear his
swords. It would have been a serious breach of
etiquette not to have done so. The *samurai* were
haughty and brave. They cultivated the most

pleasing politeness. They were very sensitive, and very easy to take offense. They would instantly draw their swords upon any one insulting them. But toward the mercantile people and the peasantry they were very overbearing. A peasant was once slain on the spot for splashing some mud upon a *samurai*. If a peasant laughed at a *samurai* he would be cut down instantly. The lower classes always passed these gentlemen with averted faces and downcast eyes. If one *samurai* was rude to another one a duel followed. Therefore, when two *samurai* met they tried to outdo each other in politeness, so as to avoid giving the least cause for offense. I have seen four of these gentlemen take nearly five minutes to get out of a door. Each one wanted the other one to step out first. The excessive politeness that we notice in the Japanese is the product of feudal times. A typical *samurai* was courteous toward his friends, haughty toward foreigners, vindictive and merciless toward his foes, hasty and furious in his temper, recklessly brave in combat ; sly, treacherous, and cunning in politics ; easy, lazy, and licentious in private life, and a prodigal boon companion, socially considered. He had no well-grounded principles. He was fickle and unreliable. A *samurai* must always avenge insult with blood. If he could not assassinate his enemy he would often slay himself by the famous stomach-cut, or *hara-kiri*. A strong-minded Daimio would have found himself at the head of a dangerous and serviceable body of men, and would have been a most arbitrary dictator. But, as was before intimated, the head families of the clan usually managed to absorb all favor and power, and the Daimio became a myth, while the pampered *samurai* merged into a parasitical condition of willfulness and indolence, having frequent duels, and rendering the immediate vicinity of the castle decidedly dangerous after nightfall. Many a morning has dawned upon the mangled remains of some belated peasant, whose body had served admirably for testing the temper of some lawless blades. Redress in such cases was almost impossible.

It thus became a matter of vital importance for the head families to keep possession of the person of the prince, so as to give legality to all proceedings. As the Shogun guarded the emperor, so these *samurai* guarded the Daimio. And the massive Tenshius were quite as much for preserving this legal seal from sudden factions of rivals as from the unexpected inroads of the enemy.

The legislative and judicial departments, as we understand the terms, can not be said to have existed in the Japanese feudal system. There was no legislative body at all. The law of the land was the will of the prince modified by the influence of his chief retainers. Like most semi-civilized societies, the common law was very simple ; and was not enshrined in elaborate treatises and reports, like our voluminous system, that requires years of persistent application to fully grasp. The principles of the feudal code were decidedly primitive. In the first place, whatever conflicted with the prince's will must be wrong, and was not to be tolerated. In the second place, there must not be the slightest manifestation of disobedience from subordinates, for this would be the grossest of misdemeanors. In the third place, existing customs, when not conflicting with the above, were to be duly respected and adopted as the common standard of adjudication. Finally, the opinion of the presiding Yakunin, or magistrate, must be decisive in all cases left to judicial discretion. And from his decision an appeal was practically impossible.

In this primitive condition of society, where legal complexity could hardly be said to exist,—and where, if it did, it could be easily severed by the will of a single individual,—you can readily perceive that it required no very great amount of accumulated lore to fit a man for passing judgment. Almost any young *samurai* could mete out what little justice there was to be doled forth to the harmless, simple people of the provincial towns and villages. A fair amount of self-confidence—(and these gentlemen were rarely found wanting in that article)—and a knowledge of local customs, quite fitted any young blade for the position of Yakunin.

The term "Yakunin" conveys but a faint impression to the Saxon mind. But to the native intellect it is the embodiment of legal majesty. He everywhere stands forth as the executor of the royal will, the inexorable administrator of the unwritten law. The mountain boor of Mino, or the

mud-bespattered peasant of Echigo, may have but
hazy notions of the invisible power within the distant imperial moats of Yamashiro, but he finds a
tangible something about the ubiquitous Yakunin
that is impossible to be ignored.   The presence of
one of these magistrates is indispensable in all public actions.   It is he that sees that the environ-
ments of the castle are properly cared for.   He
keeps the avenues, roads, and bridges, in repair—
impressing peasants, if necessary, for the work.
He regulates tariffs upon the highways, furnishing
horses and coolies at standard prices.   He collects
the revenues.   He punishes offenders.   He guards
the prisons.   He keeps up a correspondence with
the friendly provinces, and takes endless pains to
make hostile ones as uncomfortable as possible.
He receives envoys and presents them to the prince
with due formality.   He escorts.   He spies out
traitors.   He sponges with consummate grace, and
eats his master's rice with gratitude exquisite to
behold.   By my troth! it will be difficult to find
anything of a public nature of which a Yakunin is
not, in some way, a prime ingredient.   Is there an
obscure mountain village that needs—or rather,
does not need—a magistrate?   Zounds! he again
turns up quite equal to the emergency.   Does my
lord desire to make an excursion to some hot
springs?   It is the Yakunin that arranges all preliminaries.   He goes on ahead to order the people
to remain in their houses when the princely *nori-*
mon comes down the street.   He sees that proper

deference is shown by the coarse-minded masses. He secures all the best rooms in the hotels, bundling out all the occupants thereof. Is there a civil commotion in the streets? Behold! the indefatigable, double-sworded exponent of the royal will comes swaggering along, significantly grasping his hilt, and orders a dispersion of the crowd with a wave of his fan.

If you desire to see the atomic beauties of this apparently indispensable office, go to a little hamlet of two families, near Tsuruga, in Echizen. It is needless to say that the sire of one of these performs the duties of a Yakunin, diligently attending to the welfare of the community and seeing that the public receive no hurt.

But a truce to this. The night is well spent, and our hand wearies. We have taken our glimpse of a state of society that has existed a thousand years. Imbecile figure-heads now no longer are made to spurn the advances of outside "barbarians." Semi-barbaric cavalcades of *samurai* no longer follow their princes in stately procession along the somber avenues that wind through the empire. The horde of parasites that formerly flocked about the palace has been turned adrift, while my noble lord has been summoned to Tokio, where he may be more directly under the imperial eye. His Daimiate has been surrendered to the imperial government; and he is allowed, as a recompense, one-tenth of the revenues of his former province.

The speeding years are dismantling the moated turrets. The water lilies bloom upon the stagnant ponds. Where once the lotus flowers brooded on the murky waters of the moats, the bulrushes and the reeds now afford shelter for the sedgebird's nest. The autumnal leaves have accumulated upon the grassy lawns. The dragons and the bronze fishes keep solitary vigils over the crumbling ramparts. For the lord of the estate has gone forth; the turbulent retainers have dispersed, and the somber pines mournfully communing with the winter gales, regret the pageantry of former years.

Truly yours,

THEOPHILUS PRATT.

OUR POSTAL SERVICE.

LETTER VI.

HIROSAKI, *September* 10, 1874.

DEAR JULIUS MARCELLUS:

IN your last letter you asked many questions about my life here in the interior: how I spent my time; what kind of a house I am living in; what sort of school-buildings we have; and what class of scholars are under me.

Let me begin with a description of my house. It is a well-built, double-storied, Japanese dwelling, that was formerly used by one of the relations of the Daimio. The exterior is not very prepossessing; for your true Jap, however dainty he may be about the interior arrangements of his mansion, appears to have rather indifferent ideas about external show. You can never judge of the affluence of a family by outside finish. One great beauty about a native house is that you need hardly any furniture. The picturesquely papered walls and *shojees*, together with the neatly polished ceilings, make the general appearance so pretty that much furniture would only mar the effect. The house is splendid in summer time. But during

6

these severe northern winters it is very difficult to keep warm. I, of course, have tables and chairs.

My yard is also thoroughly Japanese. It is surrounded by a closely woven reed fence and is quite secluded. I frequently invite my visitors out here. My left-hand neighbor is a *samurai* turned photographer. He learned his profession in Yokohama, and is able to turn out a very fair picture. My right-hand neighbor is a merchant who has bought out the titles and estates of an impoverished *samurai.*

The school-building is some three hundred feet back of my house. It was formerly used by the retainers of the Daimio. In reality it is a long shambling line of barracks; somewhat better, however, than the usual run of such structures. It cost about twelve hundred dollars; cheap enough from our stand-point, but rather expensive from a native's, the cost of whose humble domicile does not often exceed four hundred. The large school-room is furnished with benches, tables, maps, globes, and black-boards. A large stove stands guard at my end of the room. The floor is bare but well polished. Light is admitted through a series of glass windows arranged along the side of the room. Their transparency furnishes an inexhaustible fund of astonishment to the country folks. The adjoining room contains a small library and a few mathematical instruments. Beyond this room is the dining-room, which you will find to be well saturated with the odor of salt radish, rice, and fish.

Beyond this again, extends a long series of rooms for the boarding scholars. Then come the offices of the directors.

On the whole, after seeing the miserable villages that line the road from Awomori, you will be positively surprised at the really academic appearance of the institution. From a native stand-point, these are exceedingly liberal arrangements. The accommodations are the best in the city. The situation is the most aristocratic, being upon the edge of the outer moat, and the furniture seems quite elaborate to a native. The school is supported by the ex-Daimio. You cannot help admiring the endeavors of this people to obtain learning. The scholars number about eighty. They are all the sons of *samurai;* common folks do not yet frequent the school. When you get acquainted with the boys, you find them a sharp set of youths. The first time I entered the school-room they all seemed alike, and I was much puzzled to know how to distinguish them. I found them all very polite and very attentive to their duties. Their ages averaged sixteen. Their style of learning differs somewhat from ours. They adopt the Chinese style of committing everything to memory. A boy will accurately repeat a whole page, and yet have but little idea of its meaning. I have great trouble in breaking them of this habit. In studying they raise a tremendous row. Three or four will get into the school-room, and rock back and forth upon the benches yelling in unison the next day's history lesson. They shout forth sentence by sentence until it is learned. Take such a sentence as "Cæsar, having vanquished Pompey, returned triumphantly to Rome." They first repeat Cæsar half-a-dozen times; then they bawl forth the participial phrase at least a dozen times; and, finally, yell forth the concluding clause with such deafening gusto that you might well imagine the immortal Cæsar and a legion of hoodlums at his heels were triumphantly announcing the fact that the vanquished Pompey had gone below, where fathers-in-law cease troubling.

The foreign teacher in Japan holds rather an anomalous position. He is at first disposed to consider himself merely a pedagogue plying his humble avocation for exceedingly lucky wages. But he soon finds that he holds a highly respectable position. His house is generally the best in the city, and occupies a site where only the relatives of the Daimio were formerly permitted to live, and he finds himself decidedly the leader of fashion. All the scholars pattern after him as closely as possible, and receive no small amount of social distinction from being under the tuition of a foreigner. The head men of the city will be proud to visit and receive visits from him. Should he be under government employ at Tokio he is at liberty to call on the emperor on New Year's Day. The emperor visits the schools frequently. In the early days, before he had begun to feel his importance, he would listen to examinations, present prizes, and submit to long-winded addresses from the masters and directors with commendable patience. And on one occasion, in Kioto, he even condescended to partake of refreshments offered by one of the teachers.

Whenever I go out for a walk the directors send an escort with me. They seem to fear my coming to grief at the hands of some fanatical *samurai*. When I first came here, every time I went out for a walk about thirty of the scholars would turn out with me. They came ostensibly for the exercise, but I think they were possessed with a desire to cut a swell in their native streets. And so the whole crowd would come streaming after me in a long procession, bringing the whole town out by the din of their clogs. To shake them off appeared impossible. I was finally inspired with the idea of lengthening my strides to a regular training gait. All manfully endeavored to keep up. Away we stalked down the main street, across the suburbs, through the fields, and down the long avenue that stretched toward the mountains. Three or four of the stoutest managed to keep up, but we could look back over two miles of straggling squads of demoralized small boys. The stratagem worked like a charm. Thereafter my escort consisted of three stout pedestrians. One day my escort being tardy, I slipped out alone. Upon my return I found the whole board of directors convulsed with consternation. They had sent the whole school in all directions to hunt me up. One squad didn't get back until near ten o'clock, having, as they represented, gone down the extreme length of my most extensive walk; doubtless, however, tarrying by the wayside booths to brush dull care away with a little *sakè* and fish. My return seemed to afford infinite relief. One eagerly inquired whether I had received any injury; another, whether any-one had insulted me; and yet another, whether I wasn't afraid of the dogs. They said they were afraid of my being cut down by some of the discontented old-style *samurai* who were bitter against foreigners, believing them to have been instrumental in the abolition of feudalism. My escort thereafter was always on time.

The avenue just spoken of leads to the east until it strikes the grand avenue that leads over mountain, stream, and plain, until it reaches Tokio and ends in Nihon-Bashi. Along this noble highway swept the trains of the Daimios as they passed down to do homage to the dread power of the Tokugawas at Yeddo. Hither flocked his retainers and subjects to bid god-speed to him on his tedious journey; bowing themselves to the ground as his stately *norimon* (sort of palankeen), borne on the shoulders of attendants, passed between the swaying multitudes. Down where the avenue merges into the winding mountain road among the foothills formerly stood the summer villa of his Excellency. Here his relations and retainers, who were not going to accompany him, took their leave, sipped the farewell cup, and turned their steps back to their quiet city and solemn groves, regretting, perchance, that they were not to visit the wonders of the distant metropolis.

A melancholy recollection will always linger around these stately highways. They are not so well kept as of yore. The small pines are frequently cut down of a dark night by fuel-seekers, who dislike to trudge off to the mountains for their fagots, and who would have atoned for their indolence with their heads in former days, for the Daimios took much pride in their roads.

During the summer afternoons this place forms a popular resort for the citizens of Hirosaki. You frequently come across large picnic parties holding high carnival beneath some spreading tree, or upon some swelling knoll where no passing breeze is lost. As we pass along, some jolly customer, brimful of *sakè* and fish, will rise up from the feast and perform the weird fan-dance, to the delight of his uproarious companions, who applaud and laugh at his tipsy flings. Sometimes one of the party will endeavor to absorb the attention of the company by singing a song or telling a story, wherein his fathomless shrewdness figures conspicuously. These convivial groups frequently remain long after the moon has risen, and in the still hours of the evening you can hear parties returning from some rollicking cruise, hiccough forth barbaric odes that make you dream of Chinese horns and Moorish conches for the remainder of the night. For you must bear in mind that there is nothing like Japanese singing, either on the earth, or in the heavens above, or in the waters beneath. The operator first makes a prolonged hissing sound by drawing his breath between his lips. He then closes his eyes so tight that you fancy he never intends opening them again upon this cruel world. Then a series of groans and grunts begin to wallow up from the depths of his abdominal recesses, finally exploding from his mouth in a succession of fiendish hoots and yells. In the meantime his contorted features loosen and shake themselves out into expressions of the most approving and ineffable serenity; while he occasionally claps his hands as if forcibly appropriating that applause which he certainly ought never otherwise to obtain.

I shall never forget the first time I heard one of these execrable productions of the infernal muse. It was on the trip from Hakodatè to Awomori. As the steamer came to anchor, I went below to get my valise. While picking it up, I thought some one was speaking. Turning around, I saw a raw-boned fisherman in the opening stages of this interesting frenzy, and supposed from his agonized countenance that he was suffering from an attack of seasickness. But he wasn't. He exploded into one of his most impassioned strains, making my ears fairly tingle.

Flute playing is also a popular source of recreation, and appears to instill the very essence of amiability into the savage breasts of this neighborhood. Four patrons of this divine art, in the immediate vicinity of my house, possess as many specimens of these sweet little sticks. The melody is a mournful strain of unvarying monotony that they appear to be never tired of playing. On moonlight nights they and I are particularly wakeful. Singing and flute playing, with desultory strumming on fiddles, completely exhaust the musical genius of this people. The opera, the oratorio, the concert, are utterly unknown. There is no requesting Miss Tomita or Miss Tanaka to afford you the exquisite pleasure of seeing her down to hear Parepa or Rubenstein; no inspection of dashing actresses through binocular magnifiers; no formidable array of claw-hammer parquets; no small boy always dodging between you and the prima donna; no steaming and puffing while trying to get out; and no hagglings with hackmen after you are out. Blissful primeval simplicity! In America the evenings form the favored time for brilliant gatherings, but here they are a perfect blank. With the setting sun, the doors are slid to, and drowsiness or gossiping relaxations end the day.

Between teaching, and walking, and reading my home mail, time is well spent. Should *ennui*, however, steal upon me unawares, I sally forth into my kitchen to refresh my boy's rather hazy ideas of bread-making with a few rather indefinite views of my own, which appear to leave him more hopelessly perplexed than ever. A boy is an indispensable appendage of the Oriental sojourner. It is the boy that cooks, washes the dishes, and waits on the

table.   He makes your bed, and fills your lamps,
and cleans your room.   He looks after your interests generally.   He will not allow any one to cheat
you, but always takes a percentage of all money
passing through his hands, the rate of which will be
proportioned to the rascality of his nature and the
carelessness of his master.

But the specimen that I possess will never be able
to add much to his income, for the simple reason
that he lacks the cleverness for cheating, and barely
possesses the requisite amount of intelligence for
chewing rice.   It was only after much difficulty
that his services could be procured, for the people
here are rather timid about foreigners.   He set his
wages at five dollars per month ; and I made no objection.   From this income, he supports a wife, and
is able to sport a pair of woolen drawers, to the no
small envy of his former associates who are compelled to ply their daily avocations minus that
delectable article of apparel.

My boy has very vague ideas about foreign styles
of cooking.   To begin, he thinks it useless to wash
his hands before kneading up the dough.   I am in-
flexibly of the contrary opinion.   As to ever washing out the dish-wiper, why, that's pure fogyism!
He considers it an absurd piece of foreign fastid-
iousness to beat up the whites of the eggs before
mixing with the sugar and flour.   My own views
as to the necessity of this proceeding not being very
clear, I am not prepared to convict him on this
point.   Therefore I refer the matter for your deci-

sion ; for I am by no means disposed to give slavish deference to the recipe.

He roasts a fowl quite fairly, but he hasn't the least idea as to how stuffing is made. Neither have I. His omelets are passable, that is to say, would not be taken for soap. It is on sponge cake, however, that he prides himself. But it is fair to parenthetically remark that his master is not particularly elated with his proficiency in this branch of cuisine accomplishment. Nevertheless I must modestly intimate that this cake is quite palatable when I chance to assist in its concoction. Otherwise, he appears to exert some fell influence over its proper development. He takes a melancholy satisfaction in having the top sag down like the crater of a volcano. Now I would not be fastidious about the shape, provided this depression did not reduce the interior to the flavor and consistency of leather. I am fully convinced that he slaps all the ingredients together into a dish and then shoves it into an oven.

The first loaf of bread seemed to give his honest heart genuine satisfaction as he came grinning into my study with it in his hands. I told him to cut me a slice. His knife slipped hopelessly off the crust. He finally got it apart by driving the meat knife perpendicularly through the center and bearing heavily against the handle, making some artless remarks meanwhile about its being somewhat *kattai* (tough). The inside was as yellow as a carrot. I intimated that the color wasn't exactly orthodox ; and that adamantine inflexibility was not considered a requisite of the staff of life. I condescended, however, to initiate his unenlightened mind into the mysteries of this science by making three or four loaves myself, and was able, with comparative ease, to turn out some very fair specimens of brick-bats. We mutually agreed to give it up as a bad job, and I fell back upon the crackers in my store-box.

His ideas of coffee-making were also based upon erroneous conceptions of the art. His first efforts resulted in a complicated emulsion that failed to pass muster, or my throat. I told him to put an egg into it next time, for that would settle the grounds. The following morning a long, sooty jet of liquid streamed from the nozzle into my cup. He looked perplexed, and began scratching his head, muttering something about *yukinai* (not right). The cover was lifted, and lo! the unbroken egg, boiled to a flint! Considerable explanation convinced him of the propriety of breaking the egg into the grounds before pouring on the hot water.

I have occasion to feel devoutly thankful that I am not dependent on him for my living. If I allow him to discontinue his coffee-making for three days he invariably forgets the recipe, and brings in on the fourth a mixture much resembling tar, both as to flavor and consistency. If I permit him to discontinue cake-making for a week he produces a batch of cookies that would infallibly bring tears to the eyes of a frisky crocodile. And as to his griddle-cakes! Pitiful Zeus! They are so elastic that the

Supreme Court and Amphictyonic Council combined could sit thereon without leaving the least impression.

About once a month he is smitten with an unaccountable ambition to tickle his indulgent master's palate with some new dish. It is impossible to imagine from what source these combinations of culinary genius take their rise. He usually spends about two hours over these inspired stews. I am invariably forewarned of their *début* by about an hour of deafening hissing and sizzling in the region of the kitchen, combined with a powerful odor, compared with which garlic and boiled cabbage would be ethereal and delicate perfumes. He then slides back the *shojee*, and, with a face wriggling with ecstatic subjective approval, hopes the *danna-san* (master) will condescend to try a trifling variety in cooking that his unworthy servant has had the presumption to innovate. The *danna-san* tries to smile a melancholy approval. But when the inspired prodigy has gone out, the heartless *danna-san* throws half of the mess into the yard to be eaten by the crows, leaving the remainder to be eaten by the precious inventor. The crows eye the mixture with considerable suspicion before bolting it. And for the next two or three hours I fancy myself able to detect a certain listlessness in their deportment, as if they were suffering from indigestion,—if it be possible to conceive of anything disagreeing with a crow.

I would not part with this boy for a number of

reasons. In the first place, it would be impossible
to find another one in the province to take his
place. Secondly, although he knows nearly as
much about cooking as I do, yet he knows more
than the whole province combined. And it would
take at least a year to instill his concentrated knowledge of the subject into a new customer. Finally,
I might go wild with *ennui* had I not his diversions
to amuse me. I gain a splendid idea of the utter
ignorance of this people concerning our civilized
notions of living ; and also a practical knowledge of
their charming primitive simplicity as regards methods of reinvigorating the inner man. His meals
are very simple. He merely throws a couple of
handfuls of rice into some water, and allows it to
boil until cooked. He then falls to, and chokes it
down with a couple of sticks, ever and anon nibbling
a piece of salt-radish. In eating his mouth works
like an ungreased pump, making noise enough to be
heard in my study. And yet his system is undoubtedly more complicated than Adam's. The
revered progenitor of our unfortunate race doubtless never took the trouble to boil his vegetables.
And he probably hadn't the remotest conception of
the chop-sticks used by this portion of his fallen
posterity, finding his fingers quite handy for stuffing down raw chops, and easily cleaned by sucking
and rubbing through his hair. And as to washing
his hands before indulging in culinary freaks, he
would probably have shaken hands with his degraded descendant. And as for beating up eggs

instead of instantly sucking the ends,—ah! it is too evident we have fallen from the primitive style of preparing chow-chow.

But, in addition to my boy, I find my spare time well taken up in defeating the machinations of my neighbors' cat and dog. The former animal, in particular, I view with hostile emotions. One day my boy and I, after uniting our combined skill and intelligence, were able to produce a dish somewhat resembling chicken pot-pie. 'Tis true the resemblance was not remarkably striking; still we flattered ourselves that we had done a pretty good thing, although the pastry did look like distress. While anticipating a second delicious meal off this dish my combination of chief butler and baker suddenly announced that a certain bob-tail cat had entered the cupboard in some mysterious manner, and had feloniously absconded with the remnants. My first proposition was to shoot the cat; and, with the intent of carrying out my deadly designs, I began unpacking the accumulation of dust and rust from the chambers of my revolver. But when the directors heard that I was lying in wait with deliberate intent to annihilate the vile transgressor, they were greviously agitated and begged me to desist, inasmuch as it might frighten the people, and as it was against the local laws. The firing of a shot would probably form an epoch in the history of the neighborhood. The immediate community would take some weeks to finish comparing notes as to the volume and quality of the report, and the inimical

character of the agent. Taking heed of their admonitions, I thereupon inserted some acetate of
lead and white vitriol into sundry pieces of meat,
and, with savage exultation, saw the animal walk
off with them. But to my infinite disgust, the
brute called around next day for more. But he
quit coming after that, and the curtain falls upon
his further history.

The dog lives two doors off. From my first appearance he took a violent antipathy to my person,
and I have never been to much trouble to dissi-
pate that prejudice. Should he happen to be
outside when I appear on the road he instantly
springs into position behind the fence, and commences a furious attack by barking up and down
behind, occasionally venturing to seize it between
his teeth, and shake it violently ; creating the impression, as we poor mortals are sometimes wont to
do, that but for this impediment wonderful things
might be accomplished. On one occasion he unin-
tentionally threw himself against a weak place, and
came tumbling through into the road. It was
interesting to notice the rapidity with which he
resumed his former position.

Another idiosyncrasy of his is to gnaw holes
through my reed fence and tear up the flowers,
and root around generally. My boy then goes out
and claps his hands at him and says "*Shoo!
Chickshaw!*" (Begone! Beast!) Whereupon the
dog wags his tail and continues operations in the
most jocular frame of mind imaginable, until he

sees the ominous shadow of a top-boot sailing through the air, when he suspends operations long enough to carry it off. His partiality to my yard increases in direct proportion to my murderous assaults upon his person. He spends as much of his time here as he can. On one occasion he came near creating a complicated legal discussion by biting another man's pig that had meandered near my veranda. He sometimes invites in two or three of his chums to help him in his horticultural pursuits. He also comes here to fight out his duels. The furious combatants paw up the soft loam, and leave the yard like the field of Waterloo.

All dogs up here have a wolfish propensity for howling at night. They have a great variety of tones, and rising and falling inflections. This dog appears to be a kind of chorister. His companions seem to regard his voice as something uncommonly fine. Now this canine nightingale invariably trains his band just beside my window at midnight, apparently considering night air specially suited for this purpose. His enthusiastic efforts usually rouse ambition in the emulous breasts of two or three other band-masters in the vicinity ; and they rout out their classes and start up opposition. These songsters then exchange challenges, and have a grand fight, and in the morning I wake to find my ink jug and fourteen tin cans lying around the yard, while the boy's clogs have been driven through the fence into the side of my neighbor's house.

" But he still lives. Aye, lives, and confronts me

7

daily " with a knowing wink whenever I appear outside.   After all, his machinations lack the malicious audacity of the cat.   I permit him to exist.   Betwixt him and my unhung chief baker, I shall be able to worry out my contract here.   I shall not renew it.   The loneliness is too sepulchral. Thanks to Fred, I have a good offer at Tokio that I shall accept.   The monotony of life in the interior is extremely wearing.   Up at seven, breakfast at eight, school from nine to three, allowing an hour for dinner, and reading and walking to finish the day.   There you have it in a nut-shell.   To pursue the same routine, to sit down to meals alone, to have no healthy excitement for the mind for months, will be a strong test for the most elastic minds.   In the first six months you finish all your investigations.   The novelty gives you mental tone. But after that, you come to your rope's end, and it will be well for your soul if you possess sufficient moral ambition and elevation of spirit to avoid the foul example of the majority of those living inland, who, when they depart, leave an unfortunate progeny to drag out a degraded existence.

I hope you will not feel shocked at my allusions to this subject in my letters, for it is the chief characteristic of foreign life in Japan.   I shall always handle the subject without ceremony or mercy.   Would that I could blot out this hateful stain upon our civilization !   Write soon.

Truly yours,

THEOPHILUS PRATT.

MAYEBARA; TYPICAL OLD-STYLE SAMURAI; BEHEADED IN 1876 FOR
FOMENTING REBELLION IN CHOSHIU.
(*Native Photograph.*)

LETTER VII.

HIROSAKI, *October* 14, 1874.

DEAR JULIUS MARCELLUS:

Your letter inquiring about the terrible murder of the German Consul at Hakodatè came duly to hand. I shall devote this letter to a description of it. The facts in the case are derived partly from personal observation, partly from my interpreter, partly from Mr. Hawes, the American Consul in Hakodatè, who was present at the trial and execution of the assassin, and partly from the confessions of the assassin himself in court.

During the month of August, the directors allowed a vacation. I decided to spend it in Hakodatè, and consequently set off from Hirosaki in the latter part of July. One of my scholars was to form my escort, for the authorities still seemed to fear for my personal safety; and before I returned to my duties I was convinced that their apprehensions were well grounded. They thoroughly understood their countrymen.

The summers in this province are very hot, so we started off at dawn, while the dew was yet resting on the fields, and when the town was just beginning to stir. The scenery differed much from that of my previous ride in March. Instead of sleet, slush, and a shivering population, we had green fields and a hot and dusty road :—the children were naked; the men had merely a rag around their waists; and the women were stripped down to their girdles. We reached Awomori at dusk. After five months of mediæval existence the sight of telegraphic wires was exhilarating. We went over the straits by moonlight. The water was almost perfectly smooth, being merely ruffled a little by the strong current in mid-channel. In summer this northern scenery is enchanting. The lofty crests of distant Iwa-ki-san, the well-wooded promontories that plow half way through the straits, the chiseled cones of Yesso, and the lights glimmering around the shores, form a glimpse of matchless landscape that I love to conjure up in my lonelier hours. Looking down the vista of the future, we brush away the fishing hamlets and squalid huts, and girt the lovely shores with elegant villas and palatial mansions of millionaires from Tokio and gouty bankers from Sendai, who, as Saturday night comes round, leave the bustling marts and take the Northern Express for Awomori to see their families summering round the bay.

We reached Hakodatè at dawn. This is the last place in Japan to be selected as the scene for a tragedy. From times when the memory of man ceaseth to hold, it has been booked as a place fit for exiles and spirits destitute of ambition. It is vaguely reported that sundry rollicking tars from off Perry's squadron, during its cruise nearly twenty years ago, had a spree and came to blows with the natives. However that may be, Hakodatè now can register one event which, taken with all its circumstances of barbarous atrocity and appalling suddenness, stands without parallel in the history of the Treaty Ports.

There lived in Akitah, the province just south of Awomori, a young *samurai* of a somewhat morose disposition. In the good old days when the Daimios supported legions of retainers, the family of this youth managed to live with some degree of style, being able to considerably elevate their heads above the peasantry. Under this auspicious state of society, our young warrior was duly educated in all that pertained to feudal military lore. He could dream over the charming prospect of future ease, with the prospect of a fat Yakunin-ship looming up beyond. But the foreigner came and brought trouble and revolution. The southern princes warred against the northern princes and prevailed ; and, in accordance with the ideas of the foreigner, the old order of things was abolished and the centralized imperial government was instituted, to the boundless disgust of thousands of *samurai* thus cast adrift. Some of them inherited sufficient property to live in comparative style ; some held sinecures under the government ; while many of the less favored were compelled to resort to manual labor, and the papers would sometimes announce how a whole family had been found starved to death, being too ignorant to perform any kind of mental work, and too haughty to lift a finger at any other. To illustrate the extreme contempt in which labor is held, in my walks around Hirosaki I frequently met men whose faces were disguised with towels. Upon inquiry, I was informed that they were poor *samurai* returning from their work in the rice-fields, and that they were so mortified at their occupation that they did not wish to be recognized in public.

Now, our hero was poor and proud. He earned his living for two or three years by teaching the old native literature, which, by the way, is intensely anti-foreign in its sentiments, and abounds in glowing exhortations to the young men of the country to be patriotic and adhere to pure old Japanese institutions. These exhortations were illustrated by thrilling stories of devoted youth flinging away their lives *pro bono publico*. He brooded over these wild precepts and legends, and thoroughly imbibed their spirit of animosity toward foreigners. This contributed to sour a temper already short of the original allowance of amiability. About this time he caught his first glimpse of a foreigner—a red-headed sailor pumping out a small ship that had put into the coast from stress of weather, whereupon his contempt for the "yellow-haired beasts" from the west increased immeasurably. In addition to this, he was galled by the taunts of his comrades for having sneaked out of the civil

war some three years before, for it came out during the course of the trial that he had shirked the
battles of the revolution by feigning sickness. This
teasing does not appear to have sweetened him at
all.

But the hardest blow of all came when the study
of the English language was introduced into his
native town, quite drawing away all his own pupils.
It was bad enough to be plagued with the foreign
customs that were being gradually innovated, but
to lose his means of support by the introduction of
the barbarian literature, was a stroke beyond his
endurance. Starvation or manual labor seemed to
be the only choice. He would face neither! He
would go to some of the Treaty Ports and slay one
of these interloping dogs, and then die, producing
a sensation at least. He would thus escape a long
life of drudgery and poverty; his town's-folk would
regard him as a patriot,—a true, old-style lover of
his country,—and he would be able to redeem his
not very brilliant reputation as a warrior. The
idea took complete possession of him, and he resolved to carry it out. His entire worldly possessions, when turned into money, amounted to thirteen dollars. With this in his pocket, and his
sword in his belt, he embarked on a junk bound for
Hakodatè. Nobody appears to have been aware of
his intention.

Arriving at his destination in due course of sailing, he took up his quarters in a hotel in the native
part of the town. On the following day he saw a

large, bearded foreigner walking in the streets. As
he carried a stout walking-stick, however, operations were postponed. On the next day he saw
several more, but he considered the odds of war
still doubtful, as they were provided with umbrellas. On the third day he went up to the temple
of the god of war to propitiate success. This
temple is situated some distance up the mountain
side, and commands a superb view for many miles
of all the roads leading out of Hakodatè. His
case was desperate, for he had spent all his money
in debauch. He had nerved himself up for his
work with abundance of rice-beer or whiskey. If
you were to stand beside the swarded embankment
that bounds the courtyard of this temple, your eye
would follow the winding road that leads out of the
city, up by the temple, and, then turning to the
right, passes through a lonely hedged lane down
toward the desolate sea-coast. About half-past five
o'clock in the afternoon, a little man—minus umbrella or cane—walked briskly down the road and
entered the fatal lane. But our warrior has already spied his victim. He waits until he has
turned the angle, and then follows. From his own
confessions, it appears that he had some doubts as
to whether this was a genuine foreigner or simply
a native dressed in foreign style. He therefore
asked two women whether that man they had just
passed was a Japanese or not. One said "Yes;"
the other, "No." He then went nearer and flung
his umbrella at the doubtful party so as to get him

to turn around. The gentleman turned and re-
proved him for his rudeness, and then went on.
The dastard instantly unsheathed his sword and
gave a fearful downward cut upon the shoulder,
close up to the neck. Then the little German ran
down the lane some two hundred yards, and, pushing open a heavy gate in the hedge, ran up the hill-
side some distance. He then fell on his face in a
garlic patch, either from loss of blood or from trip-
ping in a sunken tub containing manure for the
garden. The pursuer was instantly upon him and
hacked him to pieces, cleaving his head into four
parts, severing both arms at the elbows, both legs
at the knees, and inflicting frightful gashes all over
the body. It was the common talk in Hakodatè
that he left a mark for each year of his own age,—
twenty-three. He then ordered the terrified gar-
dener out of his house to dash a bucket of water
over the mangled mass, in order to see if life were
wholly extinct,—as if, indeed, there could be any
doubt! He then commanded the trembling man
to hand him the watch and chain belonging to his
victim, refusing to defile his own touch. It was
now well past twilight, and he went and delivered
himself up to the authorities. He was instantly
bound. The candles were lit in the court-room,
the judges took their seats, and the trial began.
The sword, which was so bent as to be ruined, was
handed over for safe keeping. Crazed with liquor
and frenzy, the fellow began rapidly to tell his
story. The gods had appeared unto him in por-

tentous dreams and had urged him to slay foreigners. In accordance with these behests, he had formed the resolve to exterminate the entire alien breed within the four seas of the realm. He had begun on Hakodatè, intending, after having thoroughly purged that polluted hole, to visit the other ports with his cleansing brand. The visions gave him no peace. While praying at the shrine of the god of war that afternoon, the gods singled out his victim and delivered him into his hands. He wildly gloried over the deed, his fierce eyes flashing with hate. He abused all foreigners in unlimited terms, but was peremptorily ordered to desist by the judges. Somewhat surprised, he became subdued and sullen. After the examination had been concluded he was locked up for the night.

The trial continued for several weeks. The next day the fellow repeated his story with considerable enthusiasm. He appeared utterly indifferent as to consequences. His manner conveyed the impression that he thought the judges would highly approve of his conduct after having heard his explanations. But when the judge coolly informed him that not a word of his story relating to the visions had been believed, the devoted patriot assumed an air of insulted indifference. He denied having any accomplices. He refused to answer any questions about his previous history. The court then adjourned until a dose of torture had unsealed his lips. The method of torture is very painful. The culprit kneels upon the blunt edges of half-a-dozen wooden blades. Heavy slabs of stone are then laid across his lap. The knees are thus crushed and the blades are forced through his shins gradually. In the meantime he is beaten with sticks covered with cord.

In appearance, the assassin was tall and athletic. His forehead was low. Beneath leered a pair of snake-like eyes. His nostrils were broad and flat. The thick, licentious lips had a sulky expression, betokening a passionate and revengeful disposition.

As the news flashed through the Settlement that evening, it was paralyzing. I was dining with a friend of mine, and the report came that the German Consul had cut his throat at a tea-house in a fit of insanity. All manner of rumors went around. The timid ones saw a complicated conspiracy to exterminate foreigners, and slipped their revolvers into their pockets; and the knowing ones confidently intimated that some Akitah merchants, having come out of the little end of the horn in a business transaction with the Consul, had selected a fanatic as an instrument for revenge.

The assassin was finally sentenced to degradation from his rank as a *samurai,* and to decapitation. The sentence was carried out in the harshest manner possible. Only about half an hour elapsed between sentence and execution. He attempted to say something to the judge, but was unceremoniously hustled out of the room. He then requested permission to write a letter to his family. Permission was withheld. Finally, he requested the executioners to make a clean job of it and not haggle. Even this request appears to have been intentionally ignored. One sword struck across his shoulders. As he fell over on his face, the second blow came down upon the back of his head. One of the executioners then grasped him by the hair of the head and cut his throat. The head does not appear to have left his body. He was not executed, but ignominiously butchered—perhaps a fitting punishment for a dastardly attack upon an inoffensive stranger from whom the slightest provocation had never been received. The only foreign spectators of this closing scene were the American, English, and Danish Consuls. From beginning to end the deportment of the culprit was defiantly cool. He, never flinched, nor showed the least signs of terror, although a sickly attempt was made to start a sentimental tale of final collapse of pluck just at the last moment. He died as the majority of criminals die.

And now I hear you asking whether such cases are common; whether or not this occurrence is likely to be repeated? To which I reply that such cases are not common, and that I think it will never be repeated. Although there are many in the interior that bear no good will toward the foreigner, yet few will be found to face so ignominious an ordeal. It is but just to remark that the majority of *samurai* are highly mortified at this affair. There is considerable chivalry among the respectable members of this class, and these

notions of feudal honor will always act as a retard-
ing force. During the last decade, assassinations
were quite frequent. In some cases a conservative
Daimio would order a retainer to steal off to a
treaty port and kill a foreigner in order to annoy
the Shogun and bring on a complication with some
foreign power wherein opportunity might be presented for overturning the Shogunate and expelling
all aliens. In such cases, although the deed might
be cowardly, yet the delegated party was bound by
the highest sense of honor to carry out the injunc-
tions of his lord at all hazards. Another frequent
cause of assassination resulted from a certain overbearing superciliousness on the part of a certain
portion of our community that I forbear designat-
ing by name. A quarrel at a brothel over a favorite
girl has, on one occasion at least, led to slashes.
Had foreigners been all they ought to have been,
from their first entry into Japan, the record of
bloodshed would be less humiliating to contemplate.

But times are changed. Daimios no longer command hundreds of devoted desperados. The customs of outside nations have become better understood. And the isolated fanatic, deprived of
the moral support of a sympathizing clan, and finding but scanty inspiration from the ancient legends
that are ignored by his companions who now admire the foreign literature, must eke out his inspired
motives from some extraordinary source before he
will venture upon the career of an assassin. In

addition to this, the Japanese Government now
frowns so severely upon this custom, and takes
such extreme measures in degrading the assassins,
that there will be few who will venture to brood
over such schemes. Formerly an assassin was
allowed to retain his rank, and he was also allowed
to perform the *hara-kiri* before having his head
taken off. The government has now issued decrees
over the whole empire threatening to visit such
offenses with the heaviest penalties. This settles
the question, for this now makes this species of
gaining notoriety decidedly unpopular.

Truly yours,

THEOPHILUS PRATT.

STREET SCENE IN HIROSAKI.

LETTER VIII.

A FEW REMINISCENCES.

DEAR JULIUS MARCELLUS:

I HAVE been much amused lately by the proceedings of a Roman Catholic priest who has recently come to Hirosaki. As I think the facts in the case will be interesting to you, I present them in full.

Some weeks ago I was sitting in my room, when the directors and several of my senior pupils were ushered in. They appeared to be in considerable trepidation and excitement. It was some time before I could get a connected story. I finally made out that a Jesuit priest had entered the city and intended to commence proselyting. Now, to you, this statement may seem harmless enough. But I can assure you that it was a startling episode here. The Japanese have by no means a pleasant recollection of the Jesuits. They can well recall how, some three centuries ago, a company of these priests came with petitions and humble manners; how they ingratiated themselves with the Daimios of Kiushiu and gained a favorable hearing at court;

how, as they rapidly increased in wealth and numbers, they changed their tones from meek request to arrogant demand, daring even to ignore the will of the great Hidèyoshi, the generalissimo of the realm ; how, as years of prosperity increased their pride, they defied the government, built churches in Kioto against the imperial decrees, and taught the people to disobey their rulers and give allegiance to a foreign potentate at Rome ; how they bitterly persecuted the Buddhist ; how they resisted the temporal authority and plunged the nation into a frightful civil war ; and how, before the obstinate sect could be extirpated, it became necessary to swell the royal ranks to a hundred and fifty thousand warriors, and forty thousand lives had to be sacrificed. You can hardly wonder that a storm of fear and hate sweeps through the native breast when such facts are recalled. It is from the Jesuits that the Japanese gained their ideas of Christianity. And it is the Jesuits we have to thank for the closing of the country so long to civilization. You can now readily see why the advent of this priest caused such a stir among the authorities. To their imaginations, this individual possessed some power by which he could gain a hold upon the ignorant and the superstitious people of the town. If he were to make a disturbance in the town the displeasure of the government might be visited upon them. The case was a novel one and left the authorities involved in inextricable bewilderment. But what brought the fellow to

Hirosaki in particular, said I? A very interesting disclosure was the result of this question.

It appeared that a low-grade *samurai* had left Hirosaki and had gone to Tokio soon after the revolution. He was shrewd and calculating, and was seeking to better his financial condition. In Tokio he ran across this priest. He soon became a proselyte. He was keen enough to detect here a fair method of gaining a livelihood with but little exertion. Now the fathers were on the outlook for a good opportunity for gaining a foothold in the interior. Here was the chance. The young convert could be immediately available. Application was made to the government for a passport to permit Mr. A. to teach English in the Toögu-Gakko in Hirosaki. The man was a Frenchman and understood almost nothing of English. But what mattered that? He was a foreigner, and the proselyte testified that he had been engaged to teach in Hirosaki. That was sufficient. The passport drawn up for a six months' sojourn was duly delivered, and the couple started off overland. You can well imagine the surprise of the directors to receive a notification from Tokio informing them that their teacher had started out and would be due in about twenty days. The communication was profoundly mysterious to them. After a long discussion they wrote back that there must be some mistake, for they already had their teacher.

In due time Mr. A. arrived and took up his quarters in a hotel on the main street. The au-

8

thorities called upon him and informed him that he must instantly return. He presented his pass. " Oh ! but you obtained it upon a false statement of facts," was the reply. " I shall not say how it was obtained," said he, " but there is the legal permit to stay here six months. And in this paper the government commands that I be treated with all courtesy and due respect. It is not for you to go back of the passport and send me back. That is for the government to do." Here was a dilemma indeed ! In vain did they endeavor to extricate themselves. And so they spent many weeks in corresponding with head-quarters, smoking innumerable pipes of tobacco, and holding consultations with the other teacher, who puzzled them sorely by advising that the father be sent back regardless of passport.

In the meantime the fellow had rented a house, and went around calling on his neighbors. He gave medical advice. How much he knew about doctoring I am unable to say. In this way he insinuated himself into quite a large circle of acquaintances. All this time he did not openly declare his real profession. He wore citizen's clothing. His servants, however, let out the fact that he was a Jesuit priest. His intrusive impudence knew no bounds. He visited our school and gave advice about teaching English. He button holed the scholars and talked about foreign literature. He told the directors that I was not going to return from Hakodatè. Much to the consternation of the directors he called upon me one Sunday morning. I was taking my bath. I could hear him in noisy dispute with the scholars in the audience room. One of them had been converted in Yokohama by a Protestant missionary. He began operations upon him in the vernacular : " So, you are a Christian, eh? Don't you know, my friend, that you are breaking the laws of your country by doing this? Don't you know your head is the forfeit of your act ? "

Scholar : "Ah! But that is the ancient law against Roman Catholicism, which was mistaken for true Christianity. But—— "

Priest : " Hold on! Not so fast! There are no ' buts ' in the case. You forget that, although the edicts have been taken down from the public gaze, yet the laws have not been repealed. Therefore you are under penalty of death."

Scholar : " But the laws were made against the corrupt Roman Catholic Christianity, not against the pure Protestant Christianity. Therefore—— "

Priest : " Now, just wait a moment! You must not display such ignorance upon so important a subject. Even if the edicts had been more directly leveled at Roman Catholic Christianity, yet they were not specifically so worded and promulgated to that effect. They were sweeping decrees against *all Christians.* Now, the Protestants are also Christians, and must come under the exterminating clause of the decree, as well as the Roman Catholics. And although the edicts have been taken down, the government is still silent on the point, and makes no public repeal and no public discrimination between Protestants and Catholics. Therefore you are unprotected."

My entrance interrupted this conversation. The man evidently possessed great cunning and adroitness. Although dressed in citizen's clothing, his leering eyes and sneering lips reminded one of the ideal inquisitor. His English was barely intelligible. Nevertheless, he launched forth into the most enthusiastic conversation. He made particular inquiries about cooking arrangements. Would it be too much to request the loan of monsieur's boy for a few days, in order to instruct his own boy, who knew absolutely nothing about cooking? The impossibility of the inspired subject in monsieur's happy possession being able to give any instruction was then discussed. Was monsieur an Englishman? No? Ah! An American! America was a cold country, and had a sparse population, he had been informed. By the way, he had a friend over there. Possibly monsieur might be acquainted with him. He lives in Panama. Thus we conversed. The directors felt positively relieved when he took his leave. They plainly did not wish any intimacy to spring up between us.

All the strenuous efforts of the Hirosaki authorities to get rid of him seemed to be fruitless. He was an elephant on their hands. He was asked how long he intended to stay. He replied that it would probably be all his life. It was then ordered that he should hand in a written account of himself, specifying where he came from, what his occupation was, and what he purposed doing in the city. To which he wrote that he came from a French province. For proof of this he referred them to a specified page of the register at the French Consulate in Yokohama. As to his occupation, that had been sufficiently specified in his passport. And as to what his future movements might be, he was unable at the present juncture to definitely state. This harmless reply was all they could get from him. It was finally agreed to wait till the expiration of his pass, and then send him home. But Jesuitical cunning was quite equal to the emergency. About two months before his time was to expire he made arrangements to teach chemistry in some obscure school in the city. His salary was to be one hundred dollars per month. And he was to pay it out of his own pocket! Two or three persons were then posted down to Tokio to make the arrangements. Of course there could not be the slightest chance of success. But the time spent in going overland and in protracting the negotiations would take him much beyond his time. When notified that his pass had expired, he would reply that he was negotiating another agreement, and must remain for some definite answer. In fact, he had it in his power to protract his stay to an almost unlimited period. Sometimes it was an agreement for teaching chemistry. Sometimes it would be for surgery. Sometimes astronomy.

Truly the man thoroughly understood the weak side of Japanese character.

Now, to you, brought up amid our free institutions, it will appear utterly incomprehensible why a body of public-spirited citizens did not wait upon the obnoxious brother, some dark night, and show him the inside of a tar barrel. But you must bear in mind that there is no such thing as individual public action in this land. The people look to the government to do everything. It is the government that builds the railroads, puts up telegraphs, runs steamers, directs labor, makes farms, introduces machinery, imports cattle, makes all improvements, starts schools, and sends students abroad. It will be difficult to find what the people do not expect the government to do. The simple reason is, that the people are hardly able yet to do these things for themselves. Besides this, the government does not yet feel safe in trusting too much power with the people. The agents of the government, in the shape of Yakunins, transact all business of a public nature. Such a thing as the people sending a stray sheep back to treaty-limits would be an unheard-of assumption of executive power, utterly bewildering to contemplate. This country has yet to learn our decisive methods of severing complicated festoons of red tape. In the northern portion of the empire, in particular, the people are backward about assuming any responsibility in public matters. Being distant from the central power, they are watched very jealously.

Therefore, for five or six stout citizens to bind the reverend gentleman, neck and heels, and post him off in a *kago* (sort of palankeen) for Tokio, would be a combination of officiousness and hardihood, the bare mention of which would daze the average native imagination. A native up here shrinks from assuming responsibility in such matters. An individual reckless enough to assume it would be an anomaly. The people are simply to implicitly obey orders. A subordinate must be a machine incapable of subjective volition as regards taking the initiative in public action. He must give absolute deference to the commands of his superior. Bad luck to him should he presume to modify orders with individual opinions. In the native mind, obedience is the consummation of duty. Disobedience is a most serious offense. These two points have been drilled into their very being. As a child, obey your parents, even though by so doing you be bartered away to lead a life of shame in the brothels of the Yoshiwara; as a wife, obey your husband, even though he be unreasonable and cruel in his conduct; as a servant, your master; as a vassal, you lord, even unto death, for this is the most commendable of acts; as a younger brother, your elder brother. And this not with mere halfway obedience, but absolute, that asks no questions.

You can, therefore, easily perceive how, when a case of unusual nature arises—a case that does not chance to be covered by the specifications—great

perplexity ensues.   The Yakunin easily comes to
his wits' ends, not because he fails to see what
ought to be done, but because he trembles to assume authority, lest he lay himself open to the
charge of insubordination or carelessness. He, therefore, holds long consultations with his colleagues,
and finally sends a letter to head-quarters begging
for further instructions.   So long as he implicitly
obeys every word of command he has but little cause
to fear.   I will, at this point, give you a characteristic story told me by one of the scholars.   A Daimio ordered one of his generals to make a particular
disposition of his forces, and to attack the enemy
at a given point on a specified day.   The general,
however, seeing that disaster would result if the
plans were carried out, saw fit to make his own disposition of the forces, attack the enemy after his
own fashion, and thereby gained the victory.   But
in so doing he had deliberately disobeyed.   And on
his return, as he bowed his head down to the *tatamis* in presenting his respects, his enraged lord held
his head down, and beat him with his clenched fist.
And this was considered mild punishment !

Centuries of such training have produced a universal disposition to shirk responsibility.   In this
country a man who can act decisively, and can successfully amalgamate orders with a discreet amount
of individual opinion, is a genius.   Now in the case
of this priest the regular course of action would
have been for the officers to have arrested the ad-
venturous apostle, and to have handed him over to

the mayor of the city.   He would then have sent
him to the Governor of Awomori, who in turn
would have forwarded the parcel, right side up with
care, to Tokio by steamer. But, zounds! The man
held a passport from the emperor! True, it had
been obtained under false pretenses, but the man
puzzled them by his cool and defiant attitude. The
case was a novel one. The officers, fearing to
make an arrest that might precipitate a diplomatic
complication, referred the matter to the mayor.
The mayor referred it to the governor, and the
governor appealed to Tokio. And Tokio hesitates
to make an arrest, per force, because it would be
mortifying to make a public exposure of the fact
that a foreigner had thus " done " the government
out of a passport. And then a disclosure might
imply that there had been careless management in
the Foreign Office; and this might make it very
disagreeable for some high Yakunin in that department, who (I suspect) clogs the whole transaction
by trying to hush up the affair. So his Grace, the
governor, waits for definite orders. The mayor re-
fuses to act without them. And the badgered officers
assume an air of indifference, wash their hands of
the entire matter, and mechanically wait for further
developments. While the people, with a mixture
of astonishment at the audacity that dares to beard
a Yakunin in his den, and a strong feeling of admiring curiosity at having a foreigner to study at
leisure, look on with a morbid *sang froid* that
drives a republican half wild. And so the matter

hangs. The Jesuit in the meantime is making himself perfectly at home. He calls on his neighbors; distributes medicine to invalids; teaches English; and preaches to small gatherings at his house. How long he can successfully play his game I cannot say.* I don't think the government will ever let another one slip off in this manner.

As this letter seems to be composed mostly of anecdotes, I will conclude with one giving the experience of an eccentric friend of my acquaintance. It shows how far a foreigner with a bold front can browbeat the natives. And this story is very characteristic of a certain class of bullying Saxons that one meets in Japan. Mr. B. was very fond of rambling over the country. On one occasion he happened to stray beyond treaty limits. Not in the least disturbed at this occurrence he took up his quarters in a hotel, and ordered a bath. The landlord asked him to show his passport. Of course, he had none. He said, however, as the exigencies of the case did not seem to be imperative, he would spend the night in the hotel, and return to treaty limits in the morning. This satisfied the landlord. Our friend then went down to the bath. But he was much surprised to find it occupied by a strapping *samurai*. Our friend then told him in language more forcible than elegant to "piggy" out of that. The man replied that he was quite willing to remain where he was, as he felt quite equal

---

* He remained nearly two years, and then left of his own accord.

to the position, and, moreover, had not yet finished his ablutions. The gestures and tone of our irascible friend now became so offensive that the recipient thereof bounced out of the steaming tub, and rushed forward with the avowed intent of chastising the intruder. But about three feet off he was met by a left-hander under the chin, which caused him to step back through the *shojees* into the next room with a rapidity of motion that could hardly be characterized as graceful—an abrupt proceeding that terrified in no inconsiderable manner two old women who chanced to be there watching the progress of the misunderstanding through the crevices of said *shojees*. As the victim showed no disposition to come after his soap and clothing our friend pitched them out after him; for the stage at which he had arrived in the arrangement of his toilet when interrupted could hardly have been designated as presentable to the condoling crowd of sympathizing acquaintances gathering around him outside. Our friend then occupied the field of combat. He barricaded the doors, and spread himself out in the domain so lately occupied, and so hastily abdicated by the unhappy predecessor. After bathing to his heart's content, as he was going up to his room he saw quite a crowd in the yard listening to the explanation of the man who hadn't time to finish his bath, and who appeared to be illustrating his points with considerable warmth. Soon after the landlord came upstairs in considerable trepidation, and said that the *samurai* (who, by the way, was a Yakunin

from the next village) had found out that the foreigner had no passport, and that he was going to
have him carried back to treaty limits that same
night. Our friend said that he would see about
that. He ordered up two *hebachis* (braziers), with
pots of boiling water.

In a few minutes he heard steps on the stairs.
Presently about a score of holes were punched
through the *shojees* and as many sparkling eyes
looked through. A through reconnoisance, however, of the premises seemed to convince the outsiders that a six-footer, stripped down to a pair of
drawers and a pair of invulnerable hob-nailed dry-
docks, and armed with a ladle and two pots of
scalding water, was not the most eligible belligerent that the occasion called for. So they retired
for further discussion on the ways and means of
capturing the Philistine. And Mr. B. finished
his dressing. As the crowd below began to be a
source of annoyance, he went down in a high
temper. He fiercely demanded what they wanted.
They said he had no passport and must return to
treaty limits instantly. He then demanded if there
was any one in the crowd authorized by the government to take him back. To which answer was
made that there was not. "And who is that big
samurai making all this row?" "Oh! He is a
Yakunin from the next village." "Then," said Mr.
B., "why is he making all this disturbance? I
must report him at Tokio. What is his name?"
But the fellow had vanished like smoke! If you

had looked down the next street you would have seen him. clogs in hand, racing for the next village, utterly oblivious of the fact that he had left his towel and soap upon the veranda.

" And what's this crowd doing here, I should like to know ? What are you blocking up the entrance for ? Has the government authorized you to be annoying the people in this hotel ? I must take a few of your names in this book of mine and report the affair at Tokio," said he, drawing forth his pocket-book. But there wasn't time to get a single name ! With one impulse, the frightened throng rushed forth into the street and scattered in all directions, leaving the vicinity as quiet as you please. And that ended the matter. In the morning he returned within treaty limits.

All this sounds very strange to you, but it is still a very characteristic description. In a few years, however, I think the Japanese will become more self-asserting. When that time comes this letter will amuse the natives themselves.

This will be my last letter from Hirosaki. To-morrow I start for Yokohama. My next letter I hope to date at Tokio. It is with feelings of considerable regret that I bid farewell to the Toögu-Gakko and the scholars. They have been my companions for eight months. They have been kind and obliging in escorting me about the country. They have been diligent in their lessons, and extremely polite in their deportment in the school-room. I would much enjoy teaching them for another year. But the lonely life I am leading is beginning to wear me down. My successor is already on his way here. He brings his family with him. He will, no doubt, be able to remain here several years. With a wife to attend to your house, you can live very comfortably here. I must be about my packing.

Farewell,

THEOPHILUS PRATT.

P. S.—I am writing this at a little village outside of Hirosaki. We left at daylight this morning. There was a slight fall of snow, and the road was very slushy. The scholars followed me two miles out of the city. They then stopped, and one of them stepped out and made a speech in English. He thanked me in the name of the school for my kindness and care in instructing them ; said that they were sorry the place was so lonely ; but that they had all tried to make it pleasant for me, and hoped that my journey would be a pleasant one. I was not prepared for this speech. But, turning in my saddle, and looking down upon the upturned faces and moistened eyes, I was really touched. I shall never forget that scene. There they stood in a semicircle, ankle deep in the mud, and shivering with the cold. Each face was touched up with an expression of genuine sorrow; for they had all been my companions in my loneliness, had all taken their turns in escorting me in my walks, had all been my faithful pupils. Under the inspiration of

the moment, I spoke for several minutes in reply,
" Boys," said I, " we have now taken our last walk
together. I shall now journey on to Awomori;
but you must return to your native city. I thank
you for your many kindnesses to me during my
stay in Hirosaki. Without you, my stay would
have been very lonely indeed. I thank you for
your diligence in your studies. By your diligence
and kindness you have made my stay very pleasant.
Perhaps I may never return to Hirosaki. Perhaps
I may never see Iwa-ki-san again. But I can never
forget the school and the scholars of the Toögu-
Gakko. Should you ever visit Tokio or the United
States, I shall always be much pleased to see you.
In the meantime, diligently continue your studies.
I hope we shall meet again in this world. If not, I
hope we shall meet in the next. I hope you will
all meet with great success. Farewell." They all
bowed low, and my horse bore me down the road.
I looked back several times, and there they stood.
I can see them now, almost, as I write this. I really
did not know there was so much feeling in the
Japanese nature. When you have once gained
their confidence, they are very affectionate. But
their enmity, when once roused, is implacable.

Yours in haste,

THEOPHILUS PRATT.

Awomori, *November* 19, '74.

DEAR JULIUS MARCELLUS:

Before sending off my last letter, I met with a

delay that detained me in this place nearly a week.
I take this opportunity to send you a copy of
the farewell address presented to me by the directors and scholars several days before starting.
It will serve as a kind of third postscript.

ADDRESS. .

Since you came, last spring, to the school of
Toögu, sailing over the waves, crested with foam,
and taking no care of the uncivilized waste, you
have taught the scholars for eight months, with
your patience and industry. The fruits growing
abundantly on the scholars, they made greater progress, having compared to the last year.

The effect was chiefly brought about by your
wonderful energy. For the association, thus re-
ceiving your kindness hitherto, I have no words to
express the gratitude. Hereafter, I wish to reward
your trouble of teaching, with the perfection of
their study, with all my heart.

Up to this time, you are living in the lone place
without any friend to speak each other, save a few
scholars. As you know, I being silly, not only I do
imperfectly all that is required, but as I cannot
speak the English like a dumb, have no means to
comfort you, though I know your weariness and
loneness.

Moreover, other disagreement to your wishes are
not few, but as these proceed from my being stranger
to the English, I cannot hope to pray anything but
the clear inference and forgiveness.

The lacquer wares and silk threads are not, in reality, excellent things, yet as these are the manufactures of the city of Hirosaki, I will offer these to you as the parting presents. I pray you to receive these.

9 Sagaki.

LETTER IX.

TOKIO.

BEING A CONFIDENTIAL CHAT ABOUT THE METROPOLIS.

TOKIO, *May* 31, 1875.

DEAR JULIUS MARCELLUS:

YOUR letter from Naples came duly to hand. You ask me many questions about the situation and general features of Tokio ; about the geological aspects of the surrounding country ; about its history, its inhabitants, the methods to which we resort for amusement, the present system of schools, and the social features of the place in general.

Although your questions appear simple enough, yet, to transfer my ideas accurately to your mind through the clumsy *media* of pen and ink, will take no little time and paper. Written descriptions rarely convey accurate impressions to the reader's mind, and it is correspondingly rare to find a knight of the pen who does not regard his version or description of place, character, or thing thoroughly correct. It is amusing to notice how the same question will be answered by different persons. Ask a dozen residents of Tokio or Yokohama whether gratitude should be considered an element of Japanese character, and you will find yourself in

AINOS.
(From a Native Photograph.)

possession of a vast and entertaining variety of affirmation, negation, and invective. Be it therefore understood that we are only going to state our own views upon the metropolis.

As the day is warm I shall lay myself out systematically for my work. In the first place, I have ordered the boy to put a couple of bottles of lemonade down the well so that I may refresh my pen betimes. I have ordered all the *shojees* to be taken out, thus throwing parlor, bedrooms, and dining-room into one vast, airy apartment. So I am sitting in a kind of pavilion opening out on all sides into the garden. My chum has gone out for a day's shooting in the paddy fields beyond the Sumida ; so that my only companion is a little bull terrier that divides its time between sitting on a chair watching me write, and occasionally furnishing periods by bouncing out through the shrubbery at my neighbor's children who come peeping through the bamboo fence at the *ejinsan* (foreigner). Please excuse my shirt sleeves, for it is hot notwithstanding the bay breeze that is playing through the rooms.

Now I feel prepared for that first question of yours. Let's see, what was it? Boy! bring me that letter on the bed. Ah! here we are : "General features of Tokio and the geological aspects of the surrounding country."

In answering, we will omit the usual exordium which begins by positively announcing that Tokio is surely to be found transfixed by such and such a

parallel, and has never been known to be otherwise
than astride such and such a meridian.

The city of *Yashikis** and conflagrations is flanked
on the east by a lovely bay, on the north by an extensive stretch of level territory, and on the west
and south by miles and miles of undulating country
exquisitely diversified with picturesque ranges of
hills. This is the most extensive piece of low country to be found in the empire. It is the paradise
of the ubiquitous *jinriksha* man, for he can trundle
his establishment as far northward as Sendai, a distance of about two hundred miles, before he must
give way to the *kago* (palankeen) and the pack
horse; to the north-west, he can meander peacefully
for ninety miles until the Nikko range impedes his
blissful course; and to the west, and south, the tra-
ditional even tenor of his way will meet with but
few obstructions for sixty miles. A fair geological
inference would be, that this rolling hill country
and plain is formed of the *débris* washed off from
the mighty spinal range during the floods of pre-

---

* A *Yashiki* was a style of feudal architecture peculiar to Yeddo.
The central feature was a palace of vast proportions. Around this,
on all sides, were gardens, lawns, and court-yards, covering frequently many acres of ground. All this was then hemmed in with
an unbroken line of barracks arranged in a quadrangle and having
heavily barred windows and iron-bound gates of massive proportions.
Each Daimio had his *Yashiki* in Yeddo wherein he and his army of
retainers resided during their long visits under the Tokugawa *régime.*
But few of these grand structures remain; many were burnt during
the revolution; and some of the finest, having been turned into government offices, were set on fire and destroyed by stoves improperly
set up therein.

historic ages. The extensive rice flats of Echizen,
Kaga, and Echigo, on the west coast of Nippon,
show that the turbid streams were also busy on the
other side of the range. Mixed up with all this al-
luvial drift will be found large quantities of lava
from Fuji-san and Asama-yama. So much for the
geological features of the surrounding country.

The features of Tokio are various. The stranger's
impression of the city will be materially modified by
the time of the year, the state of the weather, the
moral tone of his *jinriksha* man, and the importunity of the Shiba priest. It is all very well, should
he chance to strike a day when the fickle metropoli-
tan climate chances to be smiling, and hit upon a
team of amiable bipeds, to make the columns of
that paper for which he is acting as foreign corre-
spondent beam with vivid eulogies on the divine
temperament of the native disposition, the tran-
scendent salubrity of the Japanese climate, the
beauty of the mausoleums, and the courteous deportment of the priesthood. But let him come up
on a day when the piercing gales from off Nantai-
zan are raising every available atom of dust and
pouring them down the streets in unremitting
clouds ; just let him try to view park and temple
with half-shut eyes and frozen liver ; just let him
drive like a hurricane to the station to catch the.
last train, and then have a grand fight with the *jinriksha* men ; have them push the money back in
derision ; have them follow him all the way to the
slip bawling in vociferous unison at the incompati-

bility of the pay with their gigantic exertions ; have
them grasp his clothing and bawl in his ears as he
is attempting to pass the slip ; and have a recollection of a sudden cessation of hostilities as a boot or
cane goes off into a promiscuous assemblage of ribs,
shins, and top-knots, and then a gloomy tinge will
be imparted to the columns of that public instructor.
The peruser thereof will gather the impression that
the word beastly but inadequately expresses the
Tokio climate ; that the temples are barracks ; and
that a *jinriksha* man is a combination of vicious
balkishness and unutterable avarice, to be ranked
below the vilest of the vile.

Let us take a ride around the city. Visitors
have reduced the " doing" of Tokio down to a
science. Let us suppose we are new-comers, and let
us go over the beaten track. Here we jump into a
jinriksha at the station and merely say " *morrow-
morrow* " (slang for go sight-seeing), and the faces of
the crowd instantly become electrified with a beam
of intelligence ; and four happy top-knots (only
two are necessary) immediately spring into position
fore and aft of the vehicle, and away they go yelling like Modocs until we reach Shiba, in the south-
west portion of the city. Here we can well spend
a full hour in examining the mausoleums of the
Shoguns (Tycoons) ensconced upon the gentle
slopes of a deeply wooded hill. The elegantly
lacquered floors, the richly frescoed ceilings, the
pillars with exquisite arabesque designs, the massive tombs of stone and bronze, the carved and

gilded walls, the bronze lanterns that look like
dwarfed minarets, and the cool, melancholy avenues
winding through the groves, will delight you exceedingly.

We now go through the castle grounds to
Asakusa, some four miles off, in the northern portion of the city. Here we find an extremely large
and unromantic Buddhist temple. In the immediate vicinity are all manner of shows. From
morn till dewy eve the place swarms with sight-
seers. Peasants, corporals, gaping military recruits,
and crowds of women armed with babies, loom up
from all quarters of the metropolis to inspect the
miniature Barnums.

We now leave this uproar and confusion, and
make off for Uyeno, about two-thirds of a mile
north-east of Asakusa. This is a pretty park upon
a bluff. Scattered through the grounds are a few
temples of rather indifferent quality. Several of
the Shoguns were buried here. At one time this
park was the prettiest part of Tokio, and its temples were far-famed ; but the Imperial Revolution
of 1868 worked sad havoc with the shrines, and left
only a few inferior buildings and some bullet-
spattered gateways, which are rapidly disappearing. From the tea booths that line the brow of
the hill, you obtain a lovely view of the city. The
pretty panorama stretches for miles to the west,
south, and east. And sixty miles to the south-
west, you see Fujisan lifting its flattened crest far
above the Hakonè range.

Leaving Uyeno, we drive down the Ginza, across *Nihon-Bashi* (the center from which all distances in the empire are computed), and reach the station in time to catch the five o'clock train.

Regarding the history of Yeddo, or Tokio as it has been called since the Imperial Revolution, you will find that it does not date back four hundred years. When the Pilgrim Fathers were clearing away the timber from the cheerless shores of Massachusetts Bay, the site of Tokio was waving with tall grass and was tangled with under-brush. A few hamlets of fishermen and peasants were scattered here and there. The wild geese from Yesso could, with rare impunity, frequent the marshes of the Sumida. *Tokugawa Iyeyas*, while campaigning in this vicinity, noted its rare adapta-tion for a commercial metropolis, and his suc-cessors made it the permanent capital of the *Tokugawas*. The great feature of the city is the castle. The citadel was built by *Ohta Dokan*. The two outer systems of circumvallation were subse-quently added as the grandeur of the dynasty grew apace. The circumference of the entire castle is now eleven miles.

Scores of *yashikis*, or palaces, sprang up all over the city in order to accommodate the Daimios and hordes of vassals that trooped with tithes and homage from more than a hundred provinces. Then, as a matter of course, merchants and trades-men came in immense numbers and built up the lowlands around the bay, beside the river, and

along the base of the bluffs. It did not take long
for the glory of Kamakura to depart, and for
Yeddo to become the metropolis. Every favorable
breeze now brought fleets of junks scudding up the
bay, gliding up the Sumida, and creeping off into
the numerous canals that cut up the city outside
the moats. Rice, salt, charcoal, fish, oranges from
Kiushiu, sea-weed from Hakodatè, and lumber from
Chiba, were some of the cargoes. This was the
great epoch of commercial prosperity in Japan.
For three centuries a profound peace reigned
throughout the empire.

But Yeddo itself was always a scene of bustle
and excitement. Between conflagrations, earthquakes, processions of Daimios coming in from the
provinces, and brawls between members of hostile
clans, the mildew was not allowed to settle so
thoroughly as it had done in other parts of the
realm. New Year's Day was the great festive
occasion. Friends exchanged visits and feasted.
There is but little doubt that New Year's calling
was introduced into America from Japan. The
Dutch at Desima carried it to Holland, and the
Knickerbockers then carried it to New York. The
custom does not prevail in England. On this day
the Daimios in Yeddo presented their respects to
the Shogun.

The next event would be the annual visit of the
Dutch delegation from Desima. After their chief
had, on his hands and knees, crawled into the
presence of the Generalissimo of the Four Coasts,

prostrated himself, and then crawled back again; and after his companions had sung Dutch songs, danced Dutch jigs, and kissed Dutch kisses for the entertainment of the royal household, they would be sent back with a few presents to Kiushiu (*vide* Kaempfer).

Then some powerful northern Daimio would for several days pour his retainers along the Oshiu-kaido, and another army of *samurai* would stream up the Tokaido from the south. Bustle and excitement would follow until they were settled down in their *yashikis*. How the children and the women tried to catch glimpses of the lords through the chinks in the doors!

But Yeddo wanted variety. So some windy night an incendiary, or careless waiter girl, would set fire to a house, and away would go about a quarter of the city. These vast conflagrations occurred about every two years. They usually began beside the moat and would lick up everything down to the bay. With the exception of the castle, the city was rebuilt about every eight or ten years.

At another time the community would be entertained with a grand street duel between hot-headed *samurai*. Then some high officer, who had rendered himself obnoxious to his subordinates, would be hacked in pieces in broad daylight by a sudden dash of assassins rushing upon him at some unexpected point. Japanese in feudal times had to use great care in addressing each other. A word, a gesture, an uncourteous expression of voice, has frequently given offense that has been avenged after years of nursing. The rude official was surrounded with scores of thirsty blades awaiting some dark night or unguarded *yashiki.* The extreme politeness of the Japanese is the product of feudal etiquette.

Next, perchance, would occur a social tragedy. Some Daimio has insulted one of his vassals. Feudal etiquette stigmatizes any *samurai* who raises his hand against his lord; so the fiery vassal calls his friends together, settles all accounts, and immolates himself on the shrine of honor by performing the *hara-kiri.*

And now nature steps in and a violent earthquake sends the city scampering into the streets. These shocks were generally quite harmless. On two occasions, however, since the founding of the city, the greater portion of Yeddo was thrown down and burned. As many as twenty thousand people perished on one of these occasions. But these episodes were never allowed to interfere with trade. A Japanese merchant is not so easily disconcerted. With only five dollars in his pocket, he will set up shop again, while the embers of his former establishment are still smoldering. The whole burned district will be rebuilt in a month. The center of every merchant's house is a fire-proof *go-down* (warehouse). When a fire-alarm is raised, he hastily puts all his valuables inside, seals up the cracks with clay, leaves a lighted candle inside, securely bolts

the door outside, seals it also with clay, and takes
up his clothing and bedding and leisurely goes to
the nearest open piece of ground and camps out all
night.   The next day he builds up a frail, tem-
porary domicile around his *go-down*.   No attempt
is made to fight the fire.   The Yeddo merchant is
emphatically a man of business.   Accustomed to
handling money, he has acquired a reputation for
energy and liberality.   Accustomed to bustle and
excitement and to variety in customs, he has become decidedly cosmopolitan in his tastes, and fond
of all kinds of innovation.   Accustomed to a thriv-
ing business atmosphere, he has acquired a brisk-
ness of action and a recklessness in speculation that
quite take the breath out of a north countryman,
and instill a mingled feeling of contempt and admiration into the effete being of a victim from
Kioto.   It has been his lot to deal too frequently
with impetuous *samurai*, who often settled bargains
with their swords.   And this experience has given
him a finished politeness of manner, which renders
him a fit model for some of our home clerks, and
an obsequious pertinacity in adhering to prices that
renders him an object of disagreeable comment at
times to his European victims.

But old Yeddo has passed away.   The arrival of
Perry marked an epoch in its history.   Consternation filled the court when it was known that a foreign fleet rode at anchor only a few miles below the
capital.   They must be instantly ordered off.   But
they refuse to go without delivering an important

letter to a high official! Are they then unlike the
Dutch? Aye, and are persistent in their demands.
Terror spreads from the court to the city. The
merchants begin to carry off their valuables to
places of safety. A general exodus appears immi-
nent. Old *samurai*, who had been lamenting the
decline of chivalry, now begin to snuff carnage and
breathe vengeance against the intruders. But the
pressure is too great, and a treaty is reluctantly
made. Dissatisfaction seizes the *samurai*. Angry
mutterings come from the north, the west, and
the south. The political sky grows black. Nevertheless, the foreign trade prospers. The merchants
become opulent. The prices of silk, rice, and tea
become trebled. And all the pressure falls on
the *samurai*, who alone derive no benefit from this
outside traffic. And, as if infatuated, the Shogun
makes treaties with other nations, and opens other
ports. This must surely be stopped. The Shogun
is favoring the barbarian beasts and is betraying
the national interests! He is urgently petitioned
to expel the intruders, but replies that it is beyond
his power. Then the discontented *samurai* transfer their allegiance from the Shogun to the Mikado,
and, for the first time in centuries, the tide of
power sets from the east toward the west; the
chrysanthemum begins to prevail over the mallow
leaves, and the imperial voice commands the Shogun to annul the treaties and expel the barbarian.
The answer is that things have gone too far. No
power can annul the treaties. Heavier and darker

hangs the political sky over the house of Tokugawa. Influence rapidly deserts Yeddo and flows
steadily toward the Gosho and the Phenix car. The
Shogun, unable to carry out the imperial decrees,
is commanded to lay down his office. Unwilling
to raise the standard of revolt against the son of
heaven, he retires into voluntary exile, after a vain
attempt to wrest the imperial person from the
grasp of the hostile and powerful Satsuma clan.
The Aidzu and Tokugawa clans, however, bitterly
continue the struggle unavailingly. They are
driven from Kioto, pressed steadily backward upon
Yeddo, fight desperately for a few days in the
Uyeno grounds, are driven slowly northward, and
are finally vanquished in their last furious struggle
at Hakodatè in Yesso. And the Mikado, who has
been ruling by proxy for more than a thousand
years, comes to Yeddo and rechristens it Tokio.
And now out with the barbarian! But hold!
What means this sudden change? Has the Mikado
gone mad? Was not the rallying cry of the revolution, "Down with the Shogun! Out with the
barbarian!" Yet he is far exceeding the Shogun
in his liberality! More favorable treaties are made!
Additional ports are thrown open, and foreign
civilization is introduced!

This singular transformation must rank as one of
the most extraordinary changes in history. The
new government clearly saw the folly of struggling
against foreigners, and, as only Japanese can do,
gracefully bowed to the force of circumstances.

Arrogant and haughty when in power, they well
know how to be humble and obsequious when
under power. And so, not without a pang of regret, we bid farewell to Yeddo.

Tokio is quite a new city. The castle has been
much dismantled, so that the people may more
speedily forget old times. Almost all the *yashikis*
have been destroyed. Houses patterned after European models have sprung up everywhere. Just
accompany me for a short time and we will note
the main points of interest.

Let us begin, then, at Tsukidji, the foreign concession. It is down on the bay. In former times
it was a snipe-pool, but it has been sufficiently filled
in to make a fair piece of property. The location
is not very healthy. At ebb tide, three or four
.miles of mud-flats are laid bare under the very
noses of the community. The wells are brackish.
In some parts dampness and malaria render the
ground floors unsafe for sleeping purposes. For
foreign commercial purposes it is a failure, as the
water is shallow for eight miles into the bay. The
merchants, therefore, have pronounced anathemas
upon the place and concentrated their forces at
Yokohama. The place is at present almost entirely
occupied by missionaries, who have made it one of
the most presentable spots in Tokio. Like Desima
at Nagasaki, it is an artificial island hemmed in
with broad canals. But unlike Desima, no Yakunins stand guard at the bridges to prevent egress
and ingress. The Tokugawas little dreamed that a

Dutch legation would ever be built within a mile and a half of Nihon-bashi.

Tsukidji is also dangerously situated as regards fires. The northerly gales carry all the conflagrations down in this direction, so that it has on one occasion been burnt out, and badly scorched on another. On such occasions the creaking of well-ropes, the roar of the multitudes streaming by, the blinding clouds of glowing cinders, and the blazing *tatamis*, borne along on clouds of dust, render the scene interesting, and hot for the fire volunteers. Tsukidji has four churches, two legations, three seminaries, a hospital, a hotel, a butchery, an orphan asylum, and half a dozen parsonages.

Half a mile southwest of Tsukidji is the Naval College, an institution with an able staff of English instructors. Beyond this is the Sei-O-Ken, a hotel upon foreign ideas, kept by the Japanese. In building it the chimneys proved a failure, so they have run innumerable stove-pipes through walls and windows, until the institution resembles a huge soap-boiling establishment. They, however, serve up a capital *table d'hôte*. They have also introduced the civilized institutions of bar-room (patronized almost entirely by Europeans) and billiards. The reading-room has a fair assortment of foreign journals, including some of the indecent illustrated literature of New York city.

Another half-mile brings us to the railway station, a building that would do credit to any country. Another half-mile brings us to Yamato-Yashiki, a

THE UBIQUITOUS JINRIKISHA.

pretty bluff covered with fine European houses for the use of foreigners in the employ of the Survey, Telegraphic, and Engineering Departments. Under the old *régime* this was one of the aristocratic portions of Yeddo. Here we also find the Ko-bu-sho, the Department of Public Works. It is a massive *yashiki* turned into offices. Near this stands the Engineering College, which possesses the finest group of buildings in Japan. They are substantially built of brick and stone, and would be a credit to any country. It has a large staff of European instructors, and is in a most flourishing condition.

We now cross the moat, and turn to the west. Upon a bluff that skirts this part of the city we find the Mining Department. It is a magnificent old *yashiki*. This institution seems to accomplish but little beside giving employment to a horde of *samurai*, whose prime occupation seems to be drawing pensions, and meeting every day to annihilate endless supplies of weed in discussing ways and means for—for (does anybody know?)—for a continuation of the present order of things perchance. The natives are so jealous about the mineral resources of their country that they grudgingly allow any outside inspection. Once in a while an engineer will be sent through the provinces on a tour of inspection. His reports are then duly considered and ignored, until lapse of time renders it necessary to organize another expedition to keep up the delusion that something important is being done by the Mining Department.

10

Passing northward for a mile along this pretty bluff we come to the British Legation, an immense "compound" surrounded by a substantial brick wall. In the center rises the huge residence of Her Majesty's Minister. Scattered through the spacious and pretty grounds are small brick houses for the Consul, the student interpreters, and a host of underlings usually connected with an English legation in the East. In fact, the emperor himself does not live in such style. These magnificent legations, found wherever the cross of St. George unfurls to the breeze, are truly indicative of the power of the British Empire. But their immense cost, taken in connection with the prolific capacity of the house of Hanover-Brunswick, makes it rather disagreeable for the common run of English taxpayers. My experience is that Americans, behaving themselves, are just as much protected and just as well received abroad as Englishmen, even though our people do not lavish money on their legations. The American citizen does not seem to need so much protection as a British subject. He behaves himself better toward the people of a foreign country, and consequently has less collision. Englishmen have been frequently cut down in Japan. I do not know of any *native-born* American so dealt with. There have been one or two naturalized ones assassinated, I believe. When the British subject learns to deport himself like a gentleman upon all occasions toward inferior races he will be disposed to dispense with the expensive luxury of being too much governed.

This entire bluff is known as Ban-Cho, and in old times it was highly favored by the aristocracy. Many pretty villas are scattered all over it. At the end of the bluff we find a light-house and a race-course. Rather an odd place for a light-house, you will say, and so it is. It was built in honor of the braves who fell fighting for His Majesty during the revolution. There is a weird superstition that it serves to guide the departed souls, should they chance to be hovering near during the cheerless hours of night. However that may be, 'tis surely a fine beacon for belated travelers who have not been so happy as to fall in the Imperial service.

This vicinity is a sort of Campus Martius. Several times during the year races, wrestling, fireworks, and sports of various descriptions take place here. Hither swarm all classes of natives, and fill the boxes and scaffoldings that have been thrown up around the race-course. These are occasions of thrilling interest to the youth of the city. The horse-racing is the funniest portion of the whole programme. Each race is contested by half a dozen specimens of slab-sided horseflesh. At some uncouth signal the startled animals rush forward ; at the first turning at least one pair of shanks describes a cycloid over the nag's head ; at the second turning another candidate for glory prosaically measures his length in the mud ; and at the finish two or three demoralized nags come shambling down the home-stretch amid a feeble cheer, being kept from loafing up against the fence to rest by the vigorous use of tongue and stick.

Passing down the hill we come to an extensive level district filled with the houses of the common people. Near the moat is the "compound" of the Kai-Sei-Gakko, the Imperial University of Japan. The buildings are not so elaborate as those of the Engineering College, but it is in quite as prosperous a condition. It furnishes a good curriculum of studies, and has an able staff of foreign instructors. The location, however, is low and unhealthy.

Crossing to the northward we come to Tsuruga Dai, reputed to be the highest bluff and the healthiest locality in Tokio. Here we find many fine houses in European style, also a large Russian church, and an extensive female seminary. The atmosphere is very pure, and the view is lovely. The city stretches away for miles. Yonder is the tall roof of Mitsui's Bank, rising like a tower above the general level of houses around it. There lies the terraced, thrice-moated castle. There stretches the Ginza like a streak of snow, its modern style strangely constrasting with the surrounding architecture. And nearly four miles to the southeast you see the spires and gable-ends of Tsukidji; while far down the bay you see the forts built across the Shinagawa Shoals at the limits of the suburbs.

And this is Tokio, with its five years of modern improvement, its schools and colleges, its twenty-eight square miles of animation, bustle, and trade.

As to your question concerning the climate of
Tokio, a few words will suffice. January and
February are cold but clear months. But little
snow falls; and the ponds, canals, and river are
rarely frozen. A penetrating northerly wind makes
you feel the cold to be trying. The gusts are very
fickle. You will first have three or four days as
balmy and as lovely as May, and you allow your
fires to burn very low. Then your blinds begin to
rattle, and a freezing gale rushes down from Nikko-
san and takes the city by storm, making it misery
to go out, and making it almost impossible to keep
warm should you chance to be living in a native
house. The month of March is even more change-
able. About the middle of April you begin to drop
your overcoat and bank your fires. The flowers
now begin to come out. Crowds of people daily
flock to Uyeno and Asakusa to see the beautiful
groves of cherry trees buried in floating masses of
pink and white blossoms. May is usually as lovely
as can be desired,—although a little fire is agreeable
in the evenings and on a few days when the fickle
blasts of winter suddenly return as if loath to be
exiled in the northern solitudes. The month of
June is rainy and muggy, and everything becomes
sticky and moldy,—an occasional fire is sometimes
in order even in this month. July and August
settle down to clear weather and steady heat, which
is usually moderated by a typhoon near September.
The last-named month is rather inclined to be
rainy. October and November are simply perfec-

tion, and December is almost as good. You start a low fire about the middle of October. For at least five months a steady fire is essential to comfort. It is reported, however, that certain Scotchmen go nearly the whole winter without any artificial heat. This does not, however, indicate the average capacity for enduring cold of our community, for to chill the blood of some of these Caledonians would require the windward exposure of an iceberg. The climate is healthful on the whole. The grass is green all the year; and the camelias bloom all winter. The drinking water of Tokio is bad, especially in the low lands. The immense above ground drainage in gutters is thought to infect the springs. Filtering and boiling are resorted to. Much water is also brought from more favored localities in wooden pipes. The natives always drink tea, and are therefore not much annoyed in this respect. From December to March small-pox is an epidemic. The natives pay no more attention to it than we do to the measles. Almost everybody has had it. It does not seem to take violent hold of bodies nurtured with vegetable food. Foreigners are not much troubled with it, however. Cholera is an anomaly. Rheumatism and consumption are the prevailing ailments. The peculiar leg dropsy is very fatal to many. This is a malady unknown to us; it always begins at the knee and travels upward and attacks the vitals.

The conflagrations form the most disagreable feature of Tokio. They have a regular season,

which almost invariably commences in the middle
of November and lasts all winter. They are attributed to poverty-stricken incendiaries ; carpenters, clothing merchants, and lumber dealers being
the popular scapegoats. But the fact that fires are
coincident with the approach of cold weather and
the consequent use of *hebachis* (braziers), argues
that they are the result of carelessness on the part
of the natives, who are notoriously heedless in carrying shovels full of blazing charcoal all over the
house to different *hebachis*. You frequently find
the *tatamis* in a Japanese house scored with charred
holes,—silent witnesses of the shuffling carelessness
of a free-and-go-easy waiter girl, who invariably
laughs and says " *narahodo* " (indeed) when you call
her attention to them.

Life in Tokio differs much from that in Yokohama ; the latter place, in fact, is not Japan at
all. The European society is composed of professors, missionaries, employés in the different
departments, and a few of the intelligent Japanese
who have been abroad. The teachers of the engineering colleges and the employés of the Ko-Bu-
Sho live at Yama-to-Yashiki. The teachers of the
Kai-Sei-Gakko live partly in the vicinity of the
university and partly at Kaga-yashiki, two miles
northward. Quite a number of clerical and secular
people live at Suruga-Dai, while the missionaries
have monopolized Tsukidji. You will see, therefore, that distances of at least two miles separate
the five branches of the Tokio community. It is

a hard day's work to make the round on New
Year's Day.   One is surprised when he hears that
the directory has six hundred names down as residents of Tokio.   Many are scattered around in obscure places.   Many are in the employ of the
Mitsu-Bishi Steamship Company and are only
nominal residents of the place.   Others, whose
names are down, are in the employ of the Kitakushi,
and Mining Department and are off in Yesso or
Akitah.   So that it is safe to say the average community does not exceed three hundred.   And as
educated Japanese return from abroad and fill
positions now occupied by foreigners, this number
will rapidly diminish.   The native population is
about eight hundred thousand.   In the days of the
Tokugawas, however, when armies of retainers
filled the numerous *Yashikis*, it exceeded a million
and a half.

Our leisure hours and business hours are variously
employed.   If you are adviser to a department of
government, you dole forth the requisite amount
of admonition (which may or may not be heeded),
invest largely in curios, drive around in a carriage,
keep your temper when interfered with by officious
Yakunins, wisely let the department take its own
course, and set an example of heroic intrepidity
and commendable punctuality in drawing your
salary as the appointed day rolls around.   Even if
you do not chance to be an adviser to a department
but hold some subordinate position, you will also
find pay-day to be an interesting season of much

unction. If you are a missionary you will find
your time well taken up with studying the capricious language, teaching, preaching, and a few
social duties. If you are a teacher in one of the
government schools, you will find your life singu-
larly unique. Your first move on coming to Tokio
is to get a house, provided the government has
not already furnished one for your accommodation.
This undertaking usually assumes ponderous proportions before success crowns your efforts. Natives
do not like to let good houses to foreigners. They
abhor the tracking of muddy shoes over their
tatamis. And then the *ejinsan* is so rough in handling a fragile Japanese house. He thrusts the pipe
of his stove through a wall and thus greatly increases the risk of fire. Then he knocks down a
partition so as to have a large dining-room, and
makes a big hole in the wall by backing his chair
against it after a hearty meal. He drives about a
hundred and fifty nails into the posts all over the
house in order to hang up a multitude of pictures,
guns, fishing-rods, hats, boots, trowsers, and a
myriad of other things indispensable to his ideas
of comfort. On sundry occasions he spits tobacco
juice and an occasional mouthful of hot soup upon
the *tatamis.* And he invariably keeps a brace of
dogs that are perpetually jumping through the
shojees, measuring their heights against the nicely
papered walls, or when not thus engaged, are pur-
suing botanical investigations by tearing up the
shrubbery in the garden and digging tunnels

through the artificial *Fujisans*. As I just remarked, you will find it difficult to get a house at all. You finally succeed in renting one on Ban-Cho or Suruga-Dai for about ten or twenty dollars per month. You usually have a long bicker with the landlord, who wishes you to insure the premises against fire. He tells you that this is a regulation of the Tokio-Fu (city government), and that all *ejinsans* must comply with it before taking a house. Steering clear of this imposition, you finally secure the premises upon your own terms. For twenty dollars you can get a fine house with a large yard. You then invest in about thirty dollars' worth of furniture, set up your stove, and paper up all the crevices. A few panes of glass along the *shojees* looking out into the yard complete your preparations. You generally get some other gentleman to take a part of the house, and you keep bachelor's hall together. Your next step is to get a boy. You walk over to Yama-to-Yashiki to see if Peak's boy can recommend one. To be sure he can, he has a friend who is an excellent cook, and happens to be out of employment because his master's contract was not renewed by the Ko-Bu-Sho. He shall come around to-night. His wages? Well, his late master had a large household and gave him ten dollars per month. Ever get drunk? Never! His credentials? Oh, he shall bring them with him to-night. All right. Send him around this evening. Promptly he comes in his best clothes and well-polished top-knot. You and your chum then

form yourselves into an imposing inquisitorial committee upon character. Albeit you consider his
appearance somewhat " fishy," and feel morally certain that he has borrowed or rented his credentials,
you nevertheless engage him on trial, and he begins
operations by blacking your boots on the spot.
Next week he brings his family around and stows
them away out of sight in some of the back rooms.
Thus you are thoroughly started in house-keeping.

As a matter of course, for the first two months
you are deeply engrossed in your classes. You
teach from four to five hours per day, Saturday
and Sunday being free. You find the students
quite different from scholars in the interior. They
are more forward in conversation, being not so
modest or timid as north-countrymen. Some of
those who have been under inferior specimens of
instructors are rather inclined to be insolent and
intractable. They possess little of the deferential
politeness found in boys who have never come in
contact with the libertines of the Treaty Ports.
Having access to libraries, you frequently find them
plagiarizing their essays. Considerable vigilance is
required in detecting these frauds. The convicted
party usually laughs and says he was in a hurry
last Sunday to go off with his friends and see the
cherry blossoms at Uyeno. In my next letter I
am going to give you some specimens of these
compositions. I shall also give you a fuller account of the schools in Japan, as space will not
permit in this letter.

The only punishment allowable is "imposition" after school hours. After sentencing a precocious youth to copy out ten pages of his reader before going home to dinner, you find him very industrious for a fortnight or so thereafter. The most annoying experience connected with teaching is trying to secure punctual and regular attendance. They are frequently absent from recitations, so that you have to be very exacting with them. Their elastic excuses have to be rigorously reduced to proportions of probability. After a few weeks' experience, you find yourself compelled to fix a definite limit to their decimation of relatives. You begin to insist that parents are to die but once a year; grandparents, but once in six months; and immediate relatives are to be sparingly used up, as occasion may require. And the ubiquitous plea of important business is never to be tolerated without specific definitions in writing.

As in the interior, the scholars are all the children of *samurai*. No restriction is actually placed on the admission of the children of the lower classes; but, partly from the lack of appreciation of the value of education, and partly from social antipathy resulting from centuries of prerogative, the children of the lower classes are unable to derive much benefit at present from the schools patronized by young bloods. This, of course, makes it pleasanter for the teacher; for the *samurai* are not only more cleanly in their habits, but also much superior as regards breeding and intelligence.

This is the result of centuries of superior advantages.

As a rule, the scholars dress in native costumes, and they look much better this way. The first appearance of a small boy in coat-tails and tight trowsers is quite paralyzing.

Nevertheless, you soon become really attached to your class. You find many excellent specimens of young men. Some of my most intimate acquaintances have been among my scholars. While freely associating with them, I have never known them to presume upon my friendship.

Outside of school hours, the time of the foreign instructor in Tokio is variously spent. In winter, he will hurry off home, toast his feet at a stove, and read until dinner time. After this, perchance, he will go over to Yama-to-Yashiki and play chess with Peaks; or he may possibly prefer to walk down Ban-Cho, and have a delicious season of gossip with his colleagues respecting the probability of getting a "rise" at the end of the year. An occasional evening spent in solemn conclave with his chum in investigating the boy's accounts, and blowing him up roundly for cheating, seems to give much zest to one's mental tone.

About once a week he gives a "stag" dinner or attends one. Should time, however, be still hanging heavily, he can go down to Tsukidji and call on the latest arrival of young ladies; and should his taste for this species of diversion be strong, he can occasionally journey on to Yokohama and shed his beams on the most radiant localities along the Bluffs.

As spring comes on, he begins to spend his afternoons in visiting places of interest. He will first go to see the pleasure gardens of the emperor within the second moat of the castle. A Saturday afternoon becomes well merged in the gloaming before the lovely lawns, the bamboo groves, the picturesque tea-houses, and the shadowy cascades have been sufficiently admired. Another afternoon can be profitably spent at Hamagoten, the Imperial Gardens on the shores of the bay. These are smaller than the former, but are more finished.

When the cherry groves and the avenues of Mukojima are in full bloom, he can take a boat up the Sumida, and spend a delightful afternoon in walking down vistas of swaying blossoms that overhang the river banks for nearly a mile. Hither flock the *élite* of Tokio upon every sunny afternoon, and spread themselves out for an unlimited treat of tea and cakes upon the verandas of the tea-houses that line the river, or upon the stone seats amid the box-wood copses.

It is also considered the "correct thing" to visit the native theater at Shimabara two or three times during the season. The play commences at eight o'clock in the morning and closes at six o'clock in the afternoon, frequently requiring many days to render a single tragedy. The natives take their dinners along with them and eat in the building. The Japanese are consummate actors. Their

farces and comedies are capital. The tragic acting,
however, I can not say so much for. There is so
much sameness and bloodshed connected with it
that you never care to see much of it. The
enunciation is very clear and distinct. The gestures, from a Japanese stand-point, are certainly excellent. The tragic portions of their plots are very
monotonous. It is usually the same old story. A
hot-blooded *samurai* becomes insulted in some un-
pardonable manner—although as to what constitutes an insult in the eyes of a young top-knot
thirsting for glory is by no means clear. A solemn
gathering of friends then takes place, and the
frightful provocation is duly discussed. After the
regulation amount of " *narahodoing*," the wrathful
Don Quixote furiously announces his determina-
tion for blood, b-l-l-o-o-d! Nobly said! Blood must
be had! Sticking his vengeful blade into his belt,
he then swaggers off to find his enemy, who is
usually accommodating enough to be asleep, or up
to his chin boiling in a bath-tub. An amount of
promiscuous chopping and scientific hacking then
ensues that is supposed to thrill the soul of chivalry
with the very essence of admiration. Arms, legs,
thumbs, ears, slices of calf and thigh strew the
stage, to the unbounded approbation of the enrapt-
ured house. And during this scuffle the stage-boy
(supposed to be invisible) comes out and removes
the clogs that have been kicked off by the furious
combatants, so as to have them ready for the next
scene. After this, the hero himself becomes the

victim, to the unfeigned grief of the old ladies in the pit, for the friends of the minced man take up the quarrel, and arise in wrathful indignation and smite the slayer some dark night, make an elaborate example of him as he had done with his enemy, and then tumble the remains into a river represented by a painted board; while the moon, represented by a round paper lantern, is let down from the roof, and the scene looks melancholy enough amid the tolling of the monastery bells. So the quarrel, thus thoroughly inaugurated, is taken up by the relatives, and mutual extermination horrifies the house for weeks to come. The tragedy usually ends at three or four o'clock in the afternoon. Then a farce is acted, so as to restore cheerfulness to the house before breaking up for the day.

We Americans here usually celebrate the Fourth of July. We sometimes have a ball at the Legation, or have a dinner at the Uyeno Park. These occasions are always exceedingly jolly.

Our summer vacations we usually spend in traveling. I will make this the subject of a future letter.

After a stay of two years in Tokio you begin to find the time hanging very heavily. You have exhausted all the pleasure to be derived from wrestling, horse-racing, and theatricals. Your study of the native literature has reached that point where you find it destitute of elevating thought. You settle down to reading the history of the country and keeping up with the news of the day. You do

everything mechanically, and it becomes difficult
to entice you out of your den. A kind of indolent
mental torpor seems to settle down upon you.
You derive infinite comfort from loafing on your
veranda, dozing over the last home mail, and discussing the latest scandal. Old residents here are
rare gossips. But thanks to the letters I have to
write to you, I hope not to drift into this imbecile
method of thought. I trust that I shall not develop any remarkable keenness in becoming con-
versant with the private affairs of the community
at large.

I certainly shall not become a member of that
"outside committee" that sits in judgment on
every breath of scandal, and constitutes a most indefatigable agency for the propagation thereof.

I think I have answered all your questions.
Resting assured that I have endeavored to do so, I
am,

Truly yours,

THEOPHILUS PRATT.

LETTER X.

TOKIO, *July* 10, 1875.

DEAR JULIUS MARCELLUS:

IN my last letter I promised to tell you a little more about school-teaching here.

In no part of Japan are the schools so thoroughly organized as they are in Tokio. The foreigners connected with the schools in Japan number about a hundred. Of these, at least fifty are here in the metropolis. The highest salary paid is nine hundred dollars per month. This sum is paid to the heads of the engineering and educational departments. One of these gentlemen is a Scotchman, and the other is an American.

The professors in the colleges receive between two hundred and fifty and four hundred dollars per month. The usual salary for teaching English is about two thousand dollars per year.

Of course these high salaries will not last many years. As educated Japanese return from abroad, the number of Europeans in government employ will be gradually reduced, and in twenty-five years I doubt if there will be a dozen Europeans in the schools here.

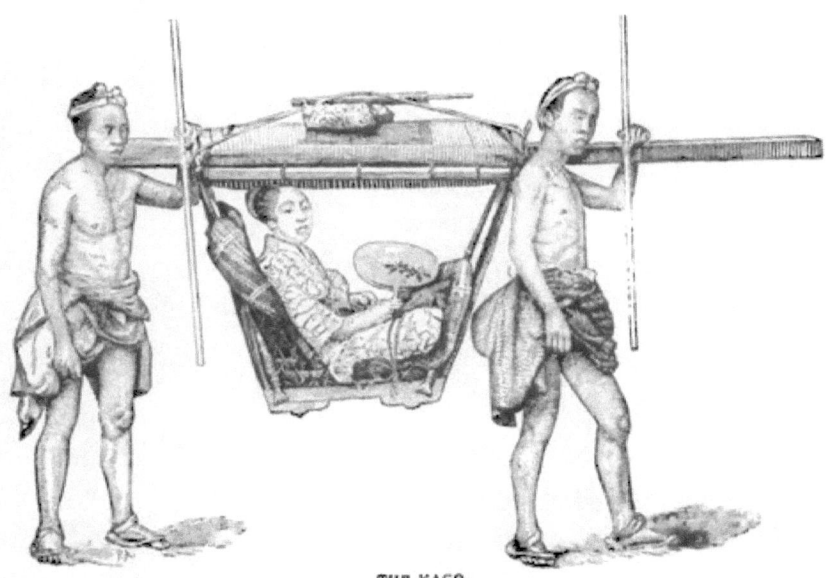

THE KAGO.

The government has also established schools in Yokohama, Nagasaki, Osaca, Niigata, Kioto, and a few inland cities. But the number of European teachers in each of these places will not exceed six; and in some of them only one is stationed. This estimate, of course, does not include private schools and mission schools.

The expense of keeping up this school system cannot cost the government less than half a million dollars per year. All the books, charts, globes, ink, pens, and the usual school apparatus are imported. They are furnished to the scholars at almost nominal prices. The tuition is free. A Japanese student pays from seventy-five cents to two dollars per month. There is but one school that charges two dollars, for very few can afford to pay this sum outside of their personal expenditures.

Instruction is conducted altogether in English. A new class will at first have some difficulty in comprehending you. But after a few weeks they master the phraseology and technical terms of each branch of study so as to be able to recite and converse very intelligently. Conversation here is made a special study. Text-books have been prepared containing English idioms and phrases. Some of these books have been compiled by native authors; and some of the expressions therein used are very amusing.

In teaching, you will find the scholars very tractable. The teachers are not allowed to chastise.

This method of suasion, in fact, is a species of barbarism that they have not yet copied from our
civilized home schools.   It never pays to lose temper or patience with Japanese.   They have a thorough contempt for any one unable to control himself.   In managing your classes, the most effective
instrument is a mild touch of irony or sarcasm
judiciously administered.   They are as sensitive to
this as mettlesome horses are to the touch of a
lash.   But if too often used, you will soon find the
tables turned, for they also are expert at this kind
of thing.

When a boy is incorrigibly lazy, you will find it
an excellent idea to keep him standing an hour or
so at the map trying to find obscure places.   Should
he attempt to lean against a desk, gently call his
attention to the fact that government property was
not made for such purposes.   Should he attempt
to lean against the wall, intimate that both his person and the wall will become thereby soiled,—a result not to be desired, because of the financial condition of the country at large.   The unhappy youth
then continues his work with great melancholy and
lack of enthusiasm.

The ages of my scholars average fifteen.   They
are all of the *samurai* class.   As a rule, they are
very polite and docile.   They are particularly clever
in mathematics.   In grammar and analysis they
stand well.   In applied English they are fair.   In
Japanese and Chinese they are instructed by native
teachers, and, as a rule, are good.

They do not board in the school, but come from considerable distances. Some of them live four miles off, and most of them live at a distance of two miles. They always walk back and forth. At a quarter to nine every morning you hear the ceaseless clatter of about two hundred pairs of clogs coming through the massive gateway. Their lunch is a ball of cold rice with the inevitable salt radish and fish. They are hard students, but I do not think their diet will allow them to stand as much continuous hard study as our students at home can stand. They are much troubled with weak eyes. They use candle-light mostly ; some use kerosene lamps.

I find it very interesting teaching them applied English. They have innumerable questions to ask about our institutions and customs. They also ask very many questions about Christianity. I never knew how thoroughly saturated our literature and history were with Christian thought and sentiment until I began to teach these people. Some of the pages in a poem or review will require so much explanation that my teaching almost becomes a Bible lesson. The use of the term Creator, or nature's first cause, will suggest a line of inquiry that will take up an hour easily. Why do the books speak of a Creator? Because the average reasoning community in Christian countries accept the fact that there is one. Can they prove this? They can prove it so as to satisfy reasonable belief. How? By the theory of probabilities. There are two suppositions. Either all things came by chance, or they came by design. Now is it more probable that the vast machinery of the universe came by chance or by design? By design, of course. Then does not design betoken intelligence? And does not intelligent designing betoken a Creator? Yes. Then is it not the most probable and reasonable theory that the world was made by a Creator? To this they readily assent. But then comes a flood of questions about Christianity. Why should Christianity be called the true religion? Because it contains the most perfect code of morality. If the Creator made man with such vast powers for good and evil, is it not reasonable to suppose that he would give him a law whereby to regulate his thoughts and actions? And does not Christianity answer this purpose perfectly? Can you compare Buddhism and Brahminism with it? Compare those countries that have been under Buddhism and Brahminism with those that have been under Christianity, and will you not find the Christian ones much more elevated? Then is it not reasonable and probable to suppose that the Creator gave the Christian religion to man? And when the Bible itself calls it the true religion, why should we not believe it?

They are so ready to ask questions on these points that you sometimes are obliged to check them. Some of them have read Mill and other infidel authors, and are well up in all the hackneyed objections. They are very quick to see

single points, but they do not follow a succession of points down to a conclusion tenaciously
or logically. They are clear and bright, and
can suggest difficulties about as easily as they can
breathe. But they are always ready to laugh at
their exposed fallacies, and are very good-natured
under rough handling. They possess any amount
of self confidence, and are always ready to enter
upon the discussion of any subject that may arise.
The *nonchalance* and eagerness with which they
discuss weighty subjects is interesting. If they
fail to carry a point, they are rather amused at having made as good a fight as they did. When a
hard lesson is on hand, some of them are rather
inclined to talk against time.

During the midday recess, they are as noisy as
you please. They romp all over the school-yard
playing tag. With their petticoats on, they look
more like a lot of girls at play. Some of the pleasure-loving ones are apt to slip off and cut the
afternoon session. They dearly love to go with their
friends to the tea gardens at Mukojima and Uyeno,
where they can discuss tobacco and foreigners with
endless comments. It takes a long time to break
them of this habit. They are puzzled to know why
the teacher should care about this regular attendance so long as he is paid anyway. One of the
boys was incorrigible on this point, and as a punishment he was sentenced by one of the teachers to
stay after school and write a composition on idleness. The youth evidently never exerted himself

to do justice to the subject. Here is a verbatim copy of this remarkable document:

" IDLENESS.

" I have a very great refuse for the letter, Idleness, which now I made up the composition; because the idleness prevented for a task of all the people, and he was persuaded to induce in his idle party, but was never fall on his hand. When I was learning in any private school at last year, any idle came to my room, how do you not swing in a play place? 'he saies.' Yeas' I reply and I did so that with he. how do you not take a walk in a street? again, yeas I reply, and soon, how do you not see a spectacle? he " saies " too again. no ! then I reply. how do you not go an eating house? he " saies " too more. no ! reply I. when all pupil recite a meaning for each lesson, he saies always I cannot, or I did not prepare ! " why do you not so study " I asked, because I can not endure heat or cold " he saies, I dleam all saies thus, therefore he spends the gold hour in vain, and he could not succeed his purpose wherefore I was very refused to describe it.

" Diligent men were overpower on a poverty, heat, cold."

Another naughty boy produced this on the same subject:

" IDLENESS.

" There are an Idleness and Industrious in the

world and Idleness is more than Industrious, but in
the uncivilized countries is not so much because
this would studies for several lesson—and to discover for several thing and food which is very good
for bodies and shall not become to Idleness but
while is very Idlemen I supposed that it shall become & industrious from their character if their
father and mother shall be right character and also
right conscience. In Japan the food is very as you
know—and Idlemen shall never move and go to
play to and for when they finished to eat food, as
soon shall sleep therefore in Japan Idleness are
there great but Japanese commenced to civilization
therefore Idlemen becamed to little number and
their begun to go to school.

"This composition is bad and mistaken to not
know the meaning of Idleness and I was sick therefore can not so good but I think always, it is
wrong."

Every Monday morning the whole school must
bring in compositions. Some of the scholars are
very nice writers. The penmanship usually is very
fine. Some compose as well as boys of a corresponding age at home. They are, of course, not always idiomatic, but the pleasure-loving ones do
not make a very brilliant success at this essay
writing. Saturday and Sunday they spend in having a good time with their companions, then
they get a book and craftily plagiarize some sentences hurriedly selected. I send you literal copies

of some of these essays sent in by the notorious truants of our school. They should serve as a terrible warning to lazy boys through all time to come.

NO. 1.—COMPOSITION ON THE BENEFITS OF POLICE.

" Police is a warlike and brave man and he have big and long stick with which he defenses a blow of a robber. Activity of a police is alway noticed in every newspaper. The most warlike and bravest fights eighteen robbers who were drest with the drawn swords and he defenses himself with a stick and at last, he takes them as prisoners. When there is a fire a police works like a fireman and tumbles down a houses with his stick. A police goes before a person who carries baggages at a fire in order to drive away the spectators so that he carries them easily and quickly. If a person prevents a police's or a fireman's work, the police beats him or uses him to carry the water or to push a pump, therefore I cannot stand heedlessly by seeing a fire."

———

No. 2.

Another one sent in the following poetry, highly eulogistic of the policemen :

" We can't think their hardships in walking when
　　snowing or raining without rest.
When the midnight storm disturb our dream,
We see them in watch under nature's dome :

When the sun begin to rise in his majestic light,
We meet them walking regardless severe cold or
   heat." (! ! !)

No. 3.

" Police is the regulation of city or policeman is
one of the constabulary force, who is officer in
Japan : the rule are make very hard to him, because in the among them like an idle rosal, (?) but
half of their are study, and so I think so that. The
police man is very much necessary for the people,
because he is defeat in city for every days and
night, when the policeman saw the thief or bad
man, he is soonly taken prisoner and bringing to
the station of police then they are wants the investigation ; also here is a foolish man, who is fall
down into the river to die, it is very scarcely in
Japan ; and all thing of street engage to the police ;
the number in the station of police are about one
hundred and number of about eighteen one thousand, among them *Satsuma, Jesso* are nearly above
them engaged to him, because they are savage and
warlike countries people in Japan, and so they are
strong men ; then the foolish man or thief man
less than the an ancient time, so that people are
glad of it."

NO. 4.—HISTORY.

" History is most important for a human to remember a past condition of ancient world, and the

history is one kind in the part of a science, therefore when a man learned the history would he animate his intellect ; and the history has remarkable worth for a education that is led to goodness a people, the reader imargin Napoleon, Washington & Taiko they how do that do, and practice their good conduct, and they would not take a·double wrong for a old instance.   But have no history in barbaric country, therefore they knows nothing but savage or fight ; therefore I think that all the science would had been led from the history."

NO. 5.—USES OF THE ENGINEERING COLLEGE.

"College of Engineering which put in a Japan that it is used for countries if it would not be there people can not have mean to dig gold, silver, iron and other metals in the mountains & there are several way of the science, in the College of ingineering. Now shall not describe of name & mean of the science for have no time because I had my father business.   We shall wish to enter in College of Ingineering ; great examination for next year."

In closing my letter, it is but fair to remark that but few compositions are so atrocious as the foregoing.

Truly yours,
THEOPHILUS PRATT.

THE TOMB OF TOKUGAWA IYEYAS, NIKKÔ TEMPLES.

LETTER XI.

TOKIO, *September* 10, 1875.

DEAR JULIUS MARCELLUS:

I SPENT my last vacation in making a tour through the interior. This is about the only way we have of spending our holidays. During August there is a general exodus of foreigners from Tokio into the interior. Some of us journey over to the west coast. Some of us go down the Nakasendo (Inland Road), or Tokaido (Coast Road) to Kioto. Others roam through the mountains of Shinano and Mino. While the majority visit Hakonè, Fujisan, and Nikko. We do not have any great centers of fashionable resort like Saratoga and Newport, where the sultry summer days can be spent in sipping mineral waters and lemonade upon cool verandas and shady lawns. Our summer recreations usually consist of a long tramp through the mountains. These trips require much preparation and planning. The selection of a route occupies at least a week. Then you must lay in a supply of canned fruits and vegetables, and some ham and dried beef ; and you must look up a traveling companion with whom to have a few animated discussions upon the road. The natives have a great advantage over us in making these excursions. They merely pick up their heels and walk. A handkerchief will hold everything they need on the road, and they are the best-natured companions imaginable. Being very fond of pilgrimages to places of religious note, they also swarm through the country during the summer. The objects and places of veneration are varied. Sometimes it is a volcanic cone that has become the residence of a goddess; sometimes it is a shrine overlooking a wild ravine; or, perhaps, it is a cave by the sea-shore, the haunt of some water-witch; or it may be a lake romantically embosomed amid some lofty ranges where a *gongen*, or mountain spirit, plays the mischief with the winds and the rains, sending them storming across the plains with fearful fury unless properly propitiated with yearly offerings.

When the snow has melted from Fujisan, thousands will scale its stupendous cone, place their offerings beside the shrines near the crater, worship the sun as he rises from the waves, and gaze upon the clouds floating thousands of feet beneath. While the rice is yet green upon the stalks and the crops are maturing for the autumnal gleaning, the worthy peasant, with about three dollars in his pocket for traveling expenses and religious contributions, grasps his filleted staff and sets out upon a tramp of about two hundred miles, visiting all places of sacred interest on the way; and in about a fortnight he returns with sufficient unction to

last a year,—for you must remember that the
masses are devout. Some have visited all the
noted shrines in the empire, taking a couple of
years or so for the undertaking. These pilgrimages, however, were almost entirely confined to the
lower classes. The *samurai* rarely felt inclined to
go tramping and sweating over the country at the
beck of sleek, oily priests that might chance to
have empty coffers. These gentlemen were disposed to be fastidious in their tastes, visiting only
the most fashionable places, taking their own time,
and abundantly consulting individual comfort.
Their favorite resort was the celebrated shrines of
Nikko, situated in the heart of the central mountain system of Japan, about ninety miles north of
Tokio. The locality is a tangled maze of glens,
wild ravines, cascades, woods, temples, and mountain torrents. All the streams of the neighboring
ranges seem to meet in the vicinity, forming a delightfully cool summer retreat. Ancient superstition has fixed this as the abode of certain *gongen*,
whose patronage is greatly to be desired, and whose
wrath must be assiduously appeased. The uneasy
hurricane winds that dwell in the misty caverns beside Chiusenji Lake hard by, and which often im-
petuously sally forth, tearing the thatch from the
roofs and flinging the grain prostrate in the mire,
are a source of grievous complaint, and need frequent exorcisms and secret ceremonies to secure
them within their dripping chambers.

The shrines of Nikko are unparalleled for symmetry of proportion, elegance and variety of design, and richness of lacquering.

As these temples were on my summer programme, I will now allow the pages of my journal to describe my visit to them. I also hope that you will get something of an idea how we spend our vacations here.

July 23.—Not yet daylight. We must be off so as to avoid the heat of the day. Have routed Jack out of bed. We send the boy on ahead so as to have dinner ready for us at midday. Our clothing and provisions are stowed in a separate *jinriksha*. Off at last! We are far beyond Uyeno before the chill has begun to leave the morning air. A few early risers are sliding back their doors and rendering the premises vocal with their stentorian yawnings. We run along the Oshiukaido for about eighteen miles. The road is flanked by paddy fields as far as the eye can reach. Take dinner at a village. The butter and the currie powder got hopelessly mixed up by the breaking of the bottles. We sit on the mats and dine off bread, roast chicken, and cheese. Small boy is watching us through the fence. Jack asks him if he is hungry. Boy wilts. Jack wonders why foreigners can not make a living off rice. He tries some. Jack ceases to wonder. Jack tries to eat with chop-sticks. Landlady laughs. She wants to taste the pickled cabbage and crackers. Pronounces them *kekko* (splendid). Boy then washes the knives and forks, and we are ready to start again. Call for the bill. It is four times too much. Jack mildly expostulates with the landlord. He replies that all foreigners pay such prices. Jack says he is not a fool, and advises the landlord not to be one. The landlord then comes down one-half. Jack then says that he is a *Mombusho* official of the seventh grade, and threatens to report the extortion at Tokio. Landlord then comes to terms. We prepare to depart. The landlord and his family then escort us to the street and request us to patronize them on our return. Continue our journey. Road much the same as in the morning. Villages numerous. The summer costume of people similar to that prevailing around Hirosaki. The men have only three feet of narrow cloth about the waist. Only the lower classes are thus exposed. At dusk we reach a large village on the banks of the Tonègawa. Cross in a flat-bottomed boat. Spend the night at a small village on the other bank. Sleep under a net. Find the native pillows very hard. Are much bothered with a bad odor from the drains. We request the rain-doors to be left open all night. The landlady says she is afraid the dogs will come in. But we carry our point. At midnight I am awaked by the foulness of the air, and find she has slyly shut them. Open them again.

July 24.—Breakfasted at daylight. The road merges into a cool and lovely avenue of pine trees. The country is becoming more interesting. It undulates gradually toward the distant mountains.

12

Wheat fields and wood lands take the place of rice
flats. Our road is now a stately vista that winds
like a serpent across the fields and through the
woods. With but trifling interruptions, it continues
for fifty miles until it loses itself in the mountains.
We walk and eat water-melons. The swarded
banks beside the road make lovely seats. It's
getting warm. We reduce our toilette down to
trowsers and singlets. Every mile or so we quaff
hot tea at little booths beneath the trees. Jack
keeps up his smoking. Japanese dogs are spoilt.
They lie right in the road, and never think of
getting out of the way. The kind-hearted coolies
never think of hurting them, and always pull
their vehicles to one side. Then they scold the
dog, and he wags his tail. Jack takes a load of
pebbles and keeps distributing them in advance.
Effect good. One pampered hound, however, re-
fuses to stir. The coolies turn to one side. But
the wheel of Jack's vehicle passes over the gently
wagging tail. Dog went to the top of the embankment at one leap. Seemed to be completely demoralized and discouraged. Everybody regards it
as the best joke of the season—dog excepted.
Reach Utso-no-miya at dusk. Only fourteen miles
from Nikko. We wait a couple of hours for them
to change the water in the bath-tub. While this is
being done, we hear a tremendous row downstairs.
A large party of foreigners from Tokio are having
a row with their coolies. They are not fluent in
the vernacular, and the coolies are trying to impose

upon them. Thus it is the world over. Cheat the stranger! Fleece him! Consider him legitimate plunder! Curtain falls.

July 25.—The landlord says we are twenty-two miles from Nikko. Distances in Japan are elastic. The avenue becomes yet more imposing. Its deep shade is cooled by the streamlets bubbling along the roadside. Meet a couple of colleagues returning to Tokio. We reach the village by midday. The shrines are beyond it. The village is situated upon a long slope, and in itself is not interesting. A stream from the mountains comes tumbling down through the middle of the street. It forms a convenient reservoir for the town. Quite a number of fox, hare, and deer skins are exposed for sale in the shops. Our pretty hotel is some distance up town. The terms are seventy-five cents a day. A native would pay less than half this sum. There's no help. All the hotel keepers are in league. Civilization is gradually striking in.

July 26.—We start off to see the far-famed temples. They are buried in deep forests about a mile up the mountain side. Passing up to the end of the long, straggling street, we come to a wild ravine through which fiercely rushes a frothing torrent from the highlands. Two bridges span the chasm. One is intended for common use. The other was intended for the *Shogun* and his envoys. It is finished off with the finest red lacquer. The guide book (I wish all journals would specify what portions are derived from guide books) narrates a

curious legend about this gorge.   Shodo Shionin, a
Buddhist priest of the eighth century, chanced to
pass this way with his disciples.   He saw no
bridge, and found it impossible to ford the boiling
rapids, rendered doubly dangerous by the timber
plunging amid the eddies.   While supplicating the
gods to extricate him from this dilemma, he indis-
tinctly beheld through the mist the god Shinsha .
Daio, on the opposite shore, holding two green and
red snakes which he cast over the abyss.   A long
bridge instantly spanned the flood " like a rainbow
floating among the hills."   The bewildered priest
was inclined to doubt his senses, but seeing the
grass growing between the planks, he was convinced, and passed over.   Immediately after crossing they were astonished to find that the bridge,
the grass, and the god had vanished !

From this sacred bridge many paths branch
away in all directions, leading to numberless romantic spots hidden away in the deep gloom of the
groves.   For miles around, wherever a cascade
dashes down some sequestered ravine ; wherever a
mountain stream, widening in the glens, gives
glimpses of unusual beauty; wherever some spring,
slipping from the oozy fissures beneath some crag,
comes tumbling down the vale—there you will find
fantastic shrines in honor of some saint or *gongen*.
Weeks could be spent in following up these various
paths.   Following the road up for some distance
through the woods we come to the temples of
Iyeyas.   They are built upon four terraces on the

mountain side. The terraces are about fifteen feet above each other, and are connected by flights of stone steps. Cryptomeria groves of superb proportions cast a deep shade over the place. The entire premises are surrounded with a wooden wall lacquered in red and capped with bronze tiles. There are ten main buildings scattered over the different terraces, besides many smaller ones. All are built of *kayakc*, the finest hard wood in Japan. All are roofed with thin bronze tiles, and all are so elaborately lacquered and gilded that none of the underlying wood-work is to be seen. The natives say that it took a boat-load of gold from Sendai to furnish the gilding. However that may be, it is certain that the resources of the empire were placed at the disposal of the builders.

The first terrace is approached by a long, sloping vista. On this terrace we find an elegant vermilion-colored pagoda. It is covered with the gilded crests of Tokugawa. A large granite *torii* (bird-perch) and some tea booths constitute the remaining structures.

We enter the second terrace through a handsome gateway. Before us are three structures of exquisite proportions and finish. In them were stored the paraphernalia and Sanskrit literature of the temples (*Guide Book*). Also, when the Shogun came to worship the shades of the great Iyeyas, his retainers tarried therein, while their "barbarian exterminating lord" went up to the private chapel on the fourth terrace. But the building that invariably excites the stranger's keenest interest is the very stylish stable used by my lord's horse. It is elegantly made. Each rafter is tipped with ornamented brass and stamped with the royal crest. It is so thoroughly exhausted by the guide-book that I shall not describe it. My only regret is that such sumptuous accommodations should have been provided for a knavish *betto* and a vile, hammer-headed pony.

Passing under a massive bronze *torii* we enter the third terrace. On either hand stands a graceful, airy belfry, faultless as regards symmetry and shape. Several bronze lanterns are arranged along the side. During the summer festivals, when the ceremonies were prolonged beyond twilight, they were lit up. Here also are some massive bronze candelabra presented by the Dutch. The guide-book suggests that they were sacked from some Roman Catholic cathedral in the Spanish Netherlands during the wars between the Catholics and the Reformers.

The fourth terrace is enclosed by a paneled wall about eight feet high, abounding with decorations. Before us stands the famous Yomei gate. (See frontispiece.) It has exhausted the art and ingenuity of the architect. It is a bewildering maze of tracery. For beauty of design and prodigality of decoration, it is matchless. It is equally lovely whether glittering in the sunlight or shimmering in the moonbeams. The railing of its balcony is supported by dragons' heads. Just above the portal

are two white dragons linked in terrific combat.
Underneath you see groups of children playing.
Beneath these are clusters of Chinese sages in various philosophical attitudes, such as only Chinese
philosophers can assume. The dragons, upholding
the massive roof, with their flaming eyes and gaping crimson jaws, seem to be on the *qui vive* for
evil spirits.

Going through the gateway we enter the court-
yard where stands the chapel of Iyeyas. It is an
architectural gem. Gable-ends, ridge pole, eaves,
rafters, and the very planking of the floor, exhibit
the consummation of native skill. For a full description of it, I refer you to Satow's *Guide-Book*
which I send you by this mail.

The tomb of Iyeyas is further up the mountain
side. We ascend a long flight of moss-grown steps.
At the top, in the melancholy woods, is the weird
bronze monument that marks the spot where rest
the ashes of the great law-giver. It is somber and
plain. I cannot think of anything with which to
compare it. The historic interest, however, forms
a sufficient attraction. The martial pines stand
around in close array as if to guard Gongen-Sama
in his long rest. He was the heart and soul of
Japanese feudalism. What the tomb of the Proph-
et is to the Moslem, such was the sepulcher of
Tokugawa Iyeyas to the *samurai*. Antiquity bears
testimony to the reverence that has ever been paid
to the memory of the dead. Mausoleums, pyra-
mids, and pillars, built at prodigal expense, com-

memorate the deeds of ancient heroes. The pride
of Halicarnassus, the surpassing glories of the Taj,
and the matchless beauty of the Nikko shrines
equally testify to the appreciative character of
mankind in widely separated countries. During
the days of the Shogunate, swarms of *samurai*
flocked hither to worship the shades and propitiate
the favor of the departed with becoming offerings
and ceremonies. But the great dynasty has fallen,
and the pageantry that formerly streamed along
the great vista, exacting cringing deference from
the wayside folk, has faded away forever; and the
beauties of the place only excite unpleasant mem-
ories in the minds of those who love the good days
when the trusty sword was the "*samurai's* living
soul."

July 27.—We visit the shrines of Iyemitsu, grand-
son of Iyeyas. They are about half a mile from
those described yesterday. A long avenue through
the woods connects the two. As they resemble
the shrines of Iyeyas in almost every particular, I
shall not describe them.

July 28.—Visited several shrines of minor importance scattered through the forests. Some of
them are of rare beauty.

July 29.—We followed one of the paths that
twists off from the Sacred Bridge and goes winding
through the thickets. We follow it up to where it
madly hurls itself through a narrow gorge. Here
we find upwards of one hundred and twenty large
stone images of Buddha in Nirvana. They are ar-

ranged along the shady bank in an extended line facing the water. With dreamy eyes they seem to watch the spray that floats from the foaming current. The *Guide Book* asserts that in counting these images, no two persons will return the same figures. Jack and I made an elaborate attempt to get the same result. He began at one end, and I began at the other end. While counting we placed our canes upon each figure. "What do you make?" said I. "One hundred and twenty-seven," said he. "One hundred and twenty-five," said I. We try again. "One hundred and twenty-four," said he. "One hundred and twenty-two," said I. We then appealed to a Japanese, and he said the correct number was one hundred and twenty-three. He then counts them himself in order to show us, and comes out one hundred and twenty-one! We give it up as a bad job. One gets confused at the similarity of the faces and at the noise of the roaring torrent. Besides this several of the small images are overgrown with grass, and you are almost sure to overlook some.

July 30.—We decide to visit Chiusenji Lake and the cascades, seven miles or so further up the mountain side. We get off early. The road leads through gorges and ravines of the most savage grandeur, where the foaming torrents from the lake thunder at the feet of dizzy cliffs and shiver themselves into spray against the massive bowlders that have fallen from the heights above.

A steep climb up the side of the mountain brings

us to an elevated plateau about four thousand feet
above sea level. On the right rises the volcanic
crest of Nantaisan, looking out upon the distant
Pacific nearly eight thousand feet beneath. In the
plateau is embosomed lovely Chiusenji Lake, encircled by densely wooded hills. It is seven miles
long, and is very deep. It is said to contain no
fish. Upon its border is a village, which is occupied by thousands of pilgrims during the summer.
But when the winter has settled down upon the
mountain, freezing the lake and filling the glens
with snow, then the houses are utterly deserted.

The cascades in this vicinity are of peerless
beauty and pleasing variety. The outlet of the
lake, after winding through several hundred yards
of woods and tangled underbrush, falls seven hundred and fifty feet into a fearful abyss. The width
of the cascade at the top is about fifteen feet. But
it spreads out into a comet-like cloud of spray long
before it reaches the bottom. You can but faintly
hear it as it falls whispering into the dark pool beneath. On three sides the rocks descend sheer,
thus encircling the boiling gulf and presenting an
appearance of hideous grandeur. A tea booth
perched upon the brink of the chasm furnishes a
superb outlook. The dense woods grow up to the
very edge, as if the monstrous shaft had been sunk
with precision and care. It is called the Kègeon-
no-taki—*taki* meaning cascade. We lunched on
the border of the lake in a native hotel. There are
quite a number of pilgrims in the village.

GLIMPSE OF CHIUSENJI LAKE.

It is very cool up here. The breeze rippling the lake is really chilly. In the afternoon we walked through the woods bordering the shore up to Umoto, at the upper end of the lake. About five hundred feet above the level of the main lake is a much smaller one that discharges its overflowing waters into it by a series of magnificent cascades. The lowest one is called the Cascade of the Dragon's Head. The upper one is that of the Boiling Waters. It comes sliding down an inclined plane of black rocks, and plunges into a gloomy pool beneath. The scenery here is enrapturing.

As we were dallying around these lovely places, a heavy shower overtook us, and the path became ankle-deep with mud. They say that it rains every afternoon up here during the summer.

By nightfall we had waded through the last puddle, and had crossed the little bridge into the village of Umoto. Here are innumerable sulphur springs, celebrated for medicinal qualities. During the summer the place is filled with invalids. It is, in fact, a village of hotels. Here I saw for the first time that common institution of former times— promiscuous bathing. Persons of both sexes, utterly regardless of apparel and modesty, flock out from the baths to look at the strangers.

We found considerable difficulty in finding rooms, for the hotels were full, but finally succeeded. We soon donned Japanese garments lent us by the landlord while ours were drying. It is fun to watch the people from the veranda. Many

of them have never seen foreigners. They were
very respectful in their observations, however.
They were all engaged in amusing themselves:
some in playing chess on the verandas of the
hotels ; some in boating on the lake ; some in reading aloud so as to be heard over half the village ;
some were boiling in the mineral vats in the street ;
but the majority were sipping tea, smoking, and
gossiping. This is a most popular place for soak-
ing out rheumatism and impurities. The springs
are far-famed. And a dreary place it is. Impenetrable woods, steaming pits, and three or four hours
of rain every afternoon. Everything was saturated
with the fumes of sulphur. The bed clothing,
mats, food, and the very knife with which the
melon was cut, were thoroughly impregnated with
the disagreeable odor. The little streams pouring
into the lake were fuming with it.

In the winter time the springs of Umoto are
deserted, all the hotels are closed, and the place is
as silent and as desolate as the grave ; while the
streets are banked with snow and the sleet drives
through the crevices of the houses. Late in the
spring the place is again opened. Only people
with considerable means can afford to come, for all
the provisions have to be brought from a distance.

Much game abounds in the fastnesses of the un-
frequented glens, where the profound silence is
only broken by the music of the *takis* (cascades)
and the cries of the deer and wild boar.

In future years, when the neighborhood has been

pruned off, and a few modern institutions for con-
venience established, the place will doubtless become a fashionable and elegant resort.

July 31.—We bade farewell to Umoto. The
landlord escorted us to the bridge and said good-
bye. Returned to Nikko.

Aug. 1.—Spend in writing up my journal and in
revisiting the shrines.

Aug. 2.—Stroll up the valley and call on several
of the Tokio folks who are spending the summer
here. They have rented a house for the season.
We have an animated discussion over the Presiden-
tial election.

Aug. 3.—Visit a number of other friends who are
scattered through the village. Some have brought
their families and servants and have rented houses.

Aug. 4.—Having visited the main points of interest, and, intending to visit Nagasaki this vacation, I start back for Tokio.

Aug. 5.—Spend on the road.

Aug. 6.—Reached Tokio about 6 P.M. We
were so dusty and dirty that we went sneaking
through all the back streets so as to avoid meeting
any acquaintances. Shall start for Nagasaki to-
morrow. Jack is going to Hakonè.

Aug. 7.—Went down to Yokohama and procured
my ticket. Under the P. M. S. S. Co. it would
have cost a hundred dollars to go and return from
Nagasaki. But under the Mitsu-Bishi Company I
can go and return for thirty-six dollars. This company has bought out the Pacific Mail on this line.

It bids fair in a few years to be the great maritime power of Asia.

Aug. 8.—Started this afternoon for Nagasaki. Fine sail down the bay.

Aug. 9.—We are steaming along finely. The coast is only a few miles to larboard. Late in the afternoon we saw a distant waterfall in the province of Kii. It is said to be about five hundred feet high. It must be very fine, for we can see it at a distance of twenty miles. Shall visit it the first chance I can get. We have a great number of passengers aboard. In the steerage there must be five or six hundred; in our after-cabin there must be at least a hundred. Two-thirds of these saloon passengers are Japanese. They appear to enjoy foreign travel and food immensely. Some of them speak English and are very sociable. All the officers of these steamers are foreigners. The sailors are natives.

Aug. 10.—Arrived at Kobè at daylight. It is situated near the entrance of the Inland Sea. Respecting its commercial prospects, it has seen its best days as regards Europeans; but it will see better days as regards the natives. When the port was opened eight years ago, European merchants came in with a rush. They were going to coin money without stint; and a good many, no doubt, did so, and they lost it again. The place was simply overdone, and the native merchants soon began to take a large portion of the business. The European population of Kobè at present is about two hundred, and this number will probably grow less as time rolls on. The Japanese population, however, has rapidly increased, and in a few years will number over four hundred thousand. This place is a center of trade. The steamers from China and the Inland Sea stop here, and the produce from Osaca, Kioto, and the central provinces is sent here for shipment. The climate is almost perfect.

Aug. 11.—We started down the Inland Sea. This is one of the lovely spots of earth. Three thousand little islands are strewn broadcast through a narrow channel. Shall not attempt to describe it. It takes about a day to steam through it, and it is a trip never to be forgotten. Many of the islands are under high cultivation. The villages on some of them are extremely picturesque. In future years, when wealth has rolled into the country, these islets will make magnificent places for villas.

Aug. 12.—We passed Shimonosekè, the far-famed Shimonosekè of diplomacy. It guards the western entrance to the Inland Sea. When properly fortified, it will be as formidable as Sebastopol. The situation is lovely.

Aug. 13.—Arrived at Nagasaki last night.

It is a singular fact that persons who have had only a glimpse of a place can usually tell a vastly more entertaining story about it than can the oldest inhabitant. I believe no less than a dozen writers have remarked that Nagasaki is very pretty. I make the same remark. An equal number have advanced the indisputable proposition that it is encircled by most picturesque hills, and has a most lovely harbor. All true, every word of it. And, moreover, the vegetation on the surrounding hills is heavy and almost tropical. The climate differs much from that of Tokio. The winter is very mild : the spring is lovely ; the summer is hot ; and the autumn is equal to what we have in Tokio. I am going ashore to find the house of Mr. D., my missionary friend, who has kindly invited me to stop with him during my stay here.

Aug. 14.—Spent in " doing up " the place. Trade here is very brisk. The business is mostly in the hands of Japanese and Chinamen. There are but few foreign merchants ; and, as in the other Treaty Ports, there is but little chance of their increasing.

The products of this port much resemble those of the other ports, with the exception of tortoise-shell work, which may be considered a specialty of the place.

The native character is rather blunt. The people lack the extreme politeness of the Japanese in general. Centuries of commerce with the Chinese, the Portuguese, and the Dutch, have tended to make them brusque in their manners.

The foreign community is smaller than that of Kobè. It is so limited that considerable freedom of social intercourse exists. In Yokohama there is an upper circle arranged on the decimal scale. A clerk, a storekeeper, or anybody in the lower paths of mercantile occupation, is pronounced unclean and unfit to bask in the same sunshine, or breathe

the same atmosphere inhaled by beatified snobs, who are not above occasional sprees down to Kanagawa. Social life in Nagasaki is apt to become rather monotonous after a year or so. The arrival of the steamers and an occasional party help somewhat to enliven things. Boating, canoeing, and swimming are the favorite pastimes. The hilly nature of the country spoils driving and riding. An occasional regatta is the chief recreation of the amateur oarsmen. One lately came off between Shanghai, Kobè, and Nagasaki. Shanghai came prepared to row, to conquer, and to brag. But the other crews also displayed a remarkable proclivity for rowing. One of them conquered, and the other did an amount of bragging that must have shocked the vanquished.

Aug. 15.—We took a boat and went down to Pappenberg. Those who doubt the capacity of the natives to be sincerely converted to Christianity will find it interesting to visit the cliff on this little island, where, centuries ago, hundreds of martyrs were flung upon the rocks beneath. This is a famous place for picnics.

In going around the harbor, it is interesting to notice the ruins of the many batteries that formerly swept the waters of the bay. Each promontory, each commanding bluff—even the melancholy crest of Pappenberg itself—give abundant evidence of the solicitude of the government to discourage foreign intrusion and a reoccurrence of the bloody scenes that seem to have accompanied Romanism

13

into all lands. This country would have been civil-ized by this time had the meddling monks ab-stained from dabbling in State affairs.

Aug. 16.—We went down to the coal mines in Takashima, a small island at the entrance of the harbor. The supervisors are Europeans. The place is worked by a joint company of natives and foreign merchants. It pays well. At present they are flooding it. It took fire in some unknown manner some months ago, which could not be put under by ordinary methods. It is supposed that the earthquakes created sufficient friction to cause combustion in some of the obscure strata, and that it had been smoldering for months, for a strong odor of gas had been noticed for many weeks. On this occasion the native workmen displayed admir-able pluck. They crept up as close as possible to the fire, and held their ground until the hose drop-ped from their hands and they were dragged away insensible. On resuscitating, they would insist on returning to their posts.

Aug. 18.—We made an excursion over the hills. Country lovely. The natives have some excuse for calling this the land of the gods.

Aug. 19.—Played croquet. Ate water-melons. Drank lemonade. Very hot. No breeze. Hills cut off the sea air. Nagasaki is built on the wrong side of the bay.

Aug. 20.—Began to think about returning to Tokio.

Aug. 21.—Continued thinking.

Aug. 22.—Decided to start.

Aug. 23.—Started.

And now I must shut up my journal. I have given you in this letter a specimen of our methods of spending vacations and keeping journals.

Don't criticise severely. Remember everything is strictly *entre nous.* In traveling, I can assure you it is a most wretched bore to make daily entries. Japanese houses never have tables. I lie flat on the floor when I write.

I am very glad to see that Columbia has won the inter-collegiate boat-race. Harvard seems to have hard luck. I don't wonder at her desiring close communion races with Yale. She is doubtless tired of getting annually thrashed by " one-*hoss* colleges."

Keep me posted on all home news.

Truly yours,
THEOPHILUS PRATT.

LETTER XII.

TOKIO, *May* 18, 1876.

DEAR JULIUS MARCELLUS:

I HAVE been much interested in the missionary question lately. Many of my most intimate acquaintances being missionaries, I have been favored with an excellent opportunity for obtaining a close insight of all their labors. Knowing that you feel interested in everything pertaining to the present condition of Japan, I will now give you the results of my observations respecting this highly prominent factor in its civilization.

The evangelizing of this country may be said to have been begun by the Jesuits three hundred years ago. But properly speaking, the mission work in Japan has sprung up within twenty years. Nay, accurately speaking, earnest, thoroughly organized, and efficient work has hardly been in operation more than six years. And its growth during this period has been really wonderful, when we consider what it has had to contend with.

The first Protestant missionaries came to Japan about eighteen years ago. For the first ten years their force was very small, and was limited to

Yokohama and Nagasaki. The early comers, as a matter of course, had to spend most of their time in making dictionaries, translating catechisms and doctrinal literature, and in trying to get a clear comprehension of the new language—a language that is difficult to master even under the most favorable circumstances. The times were also very unfavorable for their operations, as the natives were yet bitter in their hate toward Roman Catholicism.

In 1867, however, this feeble force began to increase, and the natives, beginning to discriminate between Romanists and Protestants, became more disposed to listen. In 1870, the Imperial Revolution being ended, the work became firmly rooted, and spread rapidly. New missions were established at Kobè and Osaca, and those at Yokohama and Nagasaki were reinforced. But it was reserved for the year 1873 to witness the grand influx of all denominations, for the Presbyterians and Dutch Reformed were the pioneers.

This year forms an epoch in the mission history of Japan. New stations were established at Hakodatè, in Yesso, in Niigata on the west coast, and in Tokio, just then thrown open to foreigners. And recently missionaries have been employed to teach English in the interior, with the understanding that they may teach Christianity outside of school hours to all those disposed to listen. So that all of the empire may be said to be embraced within the scope of mission work.

Of course the force in each place is very limited. Hakodatè has but two families; Nügata, two; Hirosaki, one; Nagasaki, three; Kobè, five or six; Kioto, three; Osaca, four: and Tokio and Yokohama form the great centers, as a matter of course. In each station the families are located in comfortable but not expensive houses, built upon European plans; and in each, the general plan of carrying on the work by preaching and teaching is the same.

Beginning with Tokio, we find here about fifteen families, besides an almost equal number of single workers of both sexes. In this number I have not included the Roman Catholics; I would guess their force at about ten. They are indefatigable workers, but I do not think they will ever be very popular, because of their previous history. Nor have I included the small body of Greek priests connected with the Russian Legation.

Almost every Protestant sect is here represented. We find Methodists, Canadian Wesleyans, American and Scotch Presbyterians, Congregationalists, Baptists, and American and English Episcopalians, all working harmoniously and independently. It has been calculated that two thousand people hear the Gospel every Sunday in Tokio. Places for Christian worship are scattered all over the city. There are three chapels in the foreign concession, and an elaborate Greek church on Suruga Dai. Here there is preaching on Sunday. Then three or four times during the week services are held in rooms

rented in various parts of the city, when the Scriptures are freely discussed and distributed, and the
superiority of Christ's teachings held forth. It
is the policy of the missionaries to avoid ridicul-
ing or abusing the pagan forms of worship as much
as possible. In addition to this, many young
Japanese go to the missionaries to learn English,
and, of course, receive much Scriptural instruction
with it. There is also a fine mission hospital, under
the able and energetic management of Dr. Faulds
of Scotland, and the ladies have erected two
large and well conducted female academies for
educating Japanese girls. In addition to all this,
the zealous missionaries take turns in preaching to
the English-speaking residents every Sunday morning, and it is to be hoped that this will form a permanent feature of their work here; for an able ex-
position of the truth certainly benefits the community by creating a healthy moral tone on topics
common in pagan countries.

Nor is the work confined to Tokio. The members of the various missions travel off into the
suburbs, into the distant villages, and even beyond
the mountains, preaching and giving instruction in
hotels, in private houses whose masters have invited
in their friends to hear the mysteries of the foreign
religion, and to the folks at the wayside inns.

In Yokohama the work is yet more extensive.
There are at least twenty families, with fully an
equal number of co-operative single workers. In
addition to abundant teaching and preaching, much

good is accomplished by a well organized medical dispensary. There are also a number of seminaries and foundling asylums. In no part of Japan is there such an abundant distribution of religious literature. In various ways, at least three thousand people must hear the truth every week. Places for preaching and instruction are rented in many of the villages surrounding Yokohama, and there are places in the country where weekly or monthly visits are paid. And occasionally a Japanese from the far interior will request a missionary to accompany him to his native village among the mountains to expound the Scriptures to his friends, who are too poor to come to Yokohama. Much good seed is thus cast. When the missionary reaches the village, he puts up at a hotel. He then informs the landlord that he wishes to preach in his lower room. Permission is generally easily obtained. The *shojees* are then removed, thus throwing all the rooms into one. The talking then begins in a conversational way, and the crowd begins to gather until the streets and yard are packed with listeners. The exhorter then steps out on the veranda and preaches to a respectful gathering for a couple of hours at a time. The people are champion listeners. They wear an ordinary man out. They are insatiate. They come three or four times a day urging a continuance of the speech. I knew one missionary who began at four o'clock in the afternoon, and when he was exhausted his native helpers carried on the exhortation until nine o'clock at night. Of course sermonizing is not resorted to. Simply the barest recital of the life, the work, and the agony of our Redeemer seems to chain their attention. The people then disperse. Very few of them, perhaps, will be baptized. But curiosity has been awakened to know about this extraordinary religion; books are bought; and when the missionary makes his next visit, he will find a number of earnest inquirers after the truth. The good that will result from this kind of circuit work is incalculable.

Nor are the missionaries in Yokohama negligent of their own countrymen. Through their influence, a temperance hall and reading-room have been established. They preach on Sunday in English at the church in the Settlement, and they are interested in other good works. In the other Treaty Ports the missionary operations are of a similar character, but are on a more limited scale, owing to the smallness of the forces. Each Treaty Port has become a center from which radiates Christian influence.

Of course the direct fruit of this labor is comparatively small. The actual number of converts to the Protestant faith is but one thousand; but the number of inquirers and listeners much exceeds this. And the good that has been done and will yet be done by these devoted men and women will never appear in figures,—nor can it.

I can assure you that the lot of the missionary in Japan is by no means an enviable one. In the

first place, while the native is an incomparable lis-
tener, yet he is possessed of such an amount of good-
natured indifference on religious subjects that it is
very difficult to get him thoroughly in earnest.
The people are usually fickle and capricious.   The
samurai laugh at Buddhism and its gross supersti-
tions.   They readily admit that Bible morality is
perfect and far superior to their own teachings.
But they do not like to put it into practice because
it interferes with sensual pleasures.   They, like
many of our own people, do not object to contemplating Christianity from a purely theoretical stand-
point, but they cannot endure a practical illustration thereof.   They handle religious topics with an
easy-going, slip-shod spirit, quite inconsistent with
the ideas of thorough-going Westerners.   Intense
and sincere earnestness on spiritual matters is certainly not one of their characteristics.   Although
frequently childishly superstitious, yet they possess a strong natural tendency toward atheism.
Charmed with the novelty of the new religion,
affected with the unselfish life and the tragical
death of our Redeemer, cordially admitting the
matchless purity of his precepts, yet they are indis-
posed to adopt what appears to them to be a severe
and rigorous code of morality.   The theoretical
"*ought*" pleases their fancy, but the practical
"*must*" lengthens the visage and elicits the request
to be excused.   They do not like to commit themselves to a regular and strict course of definite action on such subjects.

Their love of novelty is another serious obstacle
to thorough and effective missionary work. They
delight to remodel and tamper with whatever falls
into their hands. This develops itself into a remarkable fondness for modifying religious creeds
to suit their own views. As they have modified
Buddhism, as they have rendered their own language and literature an inextricable muddle by repeated innovations, so would they tamper with the
Bible and its doctrines. It is really bewildering to
consider the number of amendments that the native
intellect could suggest to the Ten Commandments.
In the first place, it would ease up somewhat the
strictures on carnal pleasures. In the second place,
while freely admitting the general principle that
truth is a jewel, it would modestly intimate that
an awkward statement of facts should always be
avoided ; and that the capacity to "take in" a
brother man, instead of arguing moral degenera-
tion, rather denoted mental acumen of a high philosophic order. In the third place, the Sabbath
should be a jolly good holiday. Then they would
indorse, without amendment, the commandments
respecting idolatry, profanity, theft, homicide, and
filial respect. The tenth commandment would be
considered as a moral curiosity, theoretically prac-
ticable, but entirely too high-flown for human nature. The eleventh commandment, whereon hang
the law and the prophets, would be left to individual
discretion ; coupled, however, with the suggestion
that should a neighbor chance to be too intense for

the locality, the combined community should adopt measures for rendering the premises too hot for his comfortable sojourn thereon. Thus would there be a happy amalgamation of Buddhism, Shintoïsm, Confucianism, and Christianity,—an amalgamation, in fact, that would suit the pagans of all lands,— civilized or otherwise.

But it is not from the natives that the missionaries have to meet their greatest discouragements. It may seem strange to you, but all the persecution they are ever called on to endure comes from the foreign community. They are hounded by the press and by social scandal to an extent absolutely libelous. They are the conventional target for insulting editorial wit and comment. Should one of their number chance to be indiscreet, this is the signal for a cowardly attack upon the entire body of this most refined and respectable portion of our community.

I know of no subject connected with our social cosmos which the people here seem to feel themselves more competent to discuss. Now, if a person not familiar with law or seamanship were to attempt to instruct us upon those subjects, he might find himself the subject of considerable pointed advice from legal gentlemen and weather-beaten skippers. But lawyers, merchants, captains, editors, under-strappers in the Hongs,—men who have never read a missionary journal, or have never had ten minutes' conversation with a missionary, and who know absolutely nothing about their operations,—discuss this missionary question with great warmth and with the most profound and complacent stupidity. They seem to assume that, because a man has lived in Japan, he knows all about missionaries! Because a man runs a tea firm on Water Street, and has never attended a native service, he is, therefore, competent to pronounce evangelization a failure! Because a seaman drops into port about four times a year, has never seen a native chapel, and confines his investigations entirely to Kanagawa, he is able to pour into the ears of passengers stories about missionary shiftlessness and idleness!

The cause of all this hostility is easy to see. The presence of missionaries is a continued rebuke to the greater portion of the foreign community, who are leading lives they would not think of leading at home. The natives are soon taught that these foreigners are living beneath their duties and privileges. They soon learn to point this fact with cutting and contemptuous observations, which gall the recipients thereof exceedingly. They naturally say that the missionaries must be of a higher caste. And they soon begin to draw a line between the two portions of the community; one portion is bent on gain, it is selfish and grasping, it abuses its servants, deals harshly with the natives, and is licentious; the other portion acts justly toward all, so that servants are anxious to secure them as masters, and the merchants are always on the *qui vive* to open accounts with them. They learn the lan-

guage accurately and elegantly, and instruct the
people carefully and thoroughly, and the people
soon begin to love and respect them.

It seems to be a universal feature of human nature that conscious inferiority excites envy and
hate.   This is manifested prominently here.   This
bitter spirit, however, is slowly disappearing; at
least it does not strive to make itself so conspicuous
as it did four years ago.   You must not infer that
the missionaries have no friends at all in the foreign
community, for there are a few who do sympathize
with them, and fully appreciate the difficulties
under which they labor.

Then, again, our missionary friends frequently find
themselves annoyed by their well-wishers—people
who have abundance of advice to offer respecting
the carrying on of the work.   Some people have
such absurd notions on this subject both here and
at home!   One advises all missionaries to live in
native style.   One wants them to farm in civilized
style, and thus impress the people with the superiority of our machinery.   Some of them are
surprised if one happens to return, after an absence
of several years, with his complexion still fair, his
manners still civilized, his tongue still able to articu-
late the words of his native language, and his hair
still disposed to part on one side and not possessed
with an irresistible inclination to wriggle down over
his shoulders in a pig-tail.   And should one return
after an absence of twenty-five years and exhibit no
outlandish manners, still prefer a roof and bed to a

tent and mat, exhibit no ravenous appetite for
rats, be able to tie his cravat and to put his shirt
on beneath his vest, and still be able to preach
without mixing in heathenish quotations from
Confucius, there will be found those who will be
smitten with incredulity, and will express serious
doubts as to the ultimate evangelization of the
heathens. A friend of mine told me the following
story, which is certainly characteristic: A returned
missionary was invited to dine with one of the
"pillars" of the Church. While said "pillar" was
pompously carving a leg of mutton, he patroniz-
ingly condescended to ask a few questions about
apostolic diet in pagan lands. "I presume, sir,
that in the distant realms of barbarism and mediæval obscurity from which you have so lately
emerged, that the article of food now before us is
unheard of?" "By no means," was the reply.
"We occasionally have a joint of it for variety."
The "pillar" dropped his knife and fork and sat
back aghast. "What! A missionary eating mutton! And we only affording it twice a week!
Great heavens! I'll never give another cent to the
cause as long as I live!"

Numberless are the objections raised against the
evangelization of the heathens. In the first place
we are met by the hackneyed question, "Why
don't you keep your clergy at home to labor among
their own degraded countrymen, and not be sending them off to waste their labors in foreign lands?"
For two very substantial reasons, my friends. You

already have enough churches and preachers at home to dispense the truth to every man, woman and child disposed to listen ; and if you were to double the force at home, I seriously doubt whether the results would be proportionately greater. Those who will not be reached now, will not be reached if a delegation of a dozen clergymen were to wait upon each individual of them. Therefore, let this portion of our civilized countrymen, who are too philosophical to be affected by a " Jewish myth," not act out the principle of the dog in the manger by keeping the truth from the Gentiles while ignoring it themselves.

In the second place, the nationalizing and localizing of Christianity is directly opposed to the genius of the Gospels. This course would be human and selfish. Christianity is divine, and is intended to conquer our selfishness. All the woes of humanity, with but few exceptions, spring from selfishness. Eliminate selfishness from our nature and you will eliminate sorrow and misery to a large extent from the list of human woes. The eleventh commandment is a direct and deadly thrust at human selfishness. The Jews rejected this commandment with Christ. And may we not truly say that selfishness is to-day a strong Jewish characteristic? Against this peculiarity of our nature, Christ was inexorable and uncompromising. His command was " Go ye forth into all the world," not " Remain forever at Jerusalem wasting breath and exertions upon a perverse and stiff-necked generation." And in parable he clearly intimates that many must be called because so few are willing to be chosen. Therefore, my friends, you who now wish to keep Christianity at home are acting out the same selfish principle that has been the curse and main impediment to human progress in all ages. No community or people can consistently act out the teachings of Christ without making efforts to give to others the rays of the same light. *When a community ceases to be evangelical, it ceases to be truly Christian.*

Again, it is urged that the expense of the work is great. Of course it is. Do you expect it to cost little or nothing? Where, then, would the opportunity for you to show a self-sacrificing spirit come in? I have generally found that those who are loudest in raising this objection are those who contribute little or nothing to the cause of evangelization. Would it not be more dignified for such to proportion their advice to their liberality? It is a fact that the bulk of missionary contributions come not from the rich and the noble, but from those in moderate circumstances, and from the poor. If evangelization had to wait until millionaires were ready to furnish the funds, it would, in common parlance, have to hang its harp up under the willows (a position in which not a few would like to see it).

Again, it is loudly urged, the native Christians sometimes back-slide. But back-sliding is by no means common. And if it were, this phase of relig-

14

ious experience is not unknown in *our own* lands of glorious civilization and enlightenment. It is more becoming not to advance this objection.

Again, it is urged, the native Christians are not really and truly converted ; they are insincere ; they will not stand fast should persecution arise. Facts prove the contrary. Let the cliff of Pappenberg, and the crucifixions and tortures of Shimambara testify. It is safe to say that they will stand persecution as well as some of our fat deacons that take such Pharisaical satisfaction in classifying themselves among the perfections of the nineteenth century.

Again, it is urged that with such an outlay of money and labor, evangelization should proceed more rapidly. No doubt there are many who think that more tangible results should appear. Let us consider some of the difficulties. Are we not too sanguine when we expect thirty millions of people to be acted upon in so short a space of time ? Are not we, who so rigidly proportion results to time and money, apt to be a little conceited about the progress of Christianity in our own country ? Let us examine a little. Let us begin with Great Britain. There, for thirteen centuries, you have had thousands of ministers at work. And, at the present moment, the force at work in the shires and cities of the United Kingdom can be numbered by the thousands. And what are the results? Is Great Britain completely evangelized ? Is she what she ought to be, after all her centuries of

Christian teaching and advantages? By no means. Nowhere in Japan will you find viciousness of so vile a character as you will find in the iniquitous dens of London, Edinburgh, Glasgow, and a few other civilized foci.

These same remarks are applicable to America, and to France, Spain, Italy, and Germany. Do not, then, expect so great results from the small force in the field. Consider, also, that they have to contend with a difficult language. This language is not well adapted to express the profound and varied ideas of Christian theology. Terms and forms of expression have to be almost invented in order to present many of the ideas of the Revealed Religion. The natives have to be taught the meaning of the innovated phrases. All this, of course, much cripples the effect of eloquence and dialectic discourse. And, in addition to all this, the dissolute behavior of the foreign community terribly injures the cause of Christianity. It is hard to answer the frequently propounded question: "If your religion is so very superior, why do such foul wretches come from your country?" And the explanation that they are not Christians, but sinners, wantonly living below their duties and destined to much severer punishment for so doing, is but half understood by a people accustomed from earliest time to nationalize religion, and who have no ideas of a spiritual kingdom and of an invisible, yet real, communion of the redeemed with Christ.

Finally, it is urged with great gusto that native

Christians do not bear favorable comparison with our Christians at home. It is triumphantly asserted that they retain many of their heathenish propensities after baptism; that to eradicate these qualities, if not an impossibility, will be the work at least of several generations; that they do not possess the high-bred Christian sentiment of Saxons; that a strong alloy of inherent superstition runs through all their nature; that their moral perceptions are positively obtuse when viewed from our stand-point; that a well-balanced, sensitive conscience is a rare thing among them; and that even after years of labor but few can be considered as examples worthy of imitation. Now just permit us to inform you that your comparison is sophistical and unfair. Is it legitimate to draw a comparison between the first converts of a heathen country and our carefully educated Christians who have had every moral advantage from infancy, who have been reared in the midst of every circumstance tending to promote elevation of character, who have derived every possible benefit from centuries of accumulated instruction, who do not have to face the fierce prejudice and bitter persecution of friends and neighbors, and who are assisted intellectually and morally by many generations of inherited tendencies? Certainly not. You should compare them with the first converts of the Saxon and Celtic races. We must bear in mind that the early inhabitants of fair Albion did not become paragons of excellence as soon as they were bap-

tized by Saint Augustine. They retained for many
centuries their barbarous and cruel customs.

Nor can we speak in more flattering terms of
sweet Ireland. For even at this day, after centuries of cultivation, but little of the fruit of Saint
Patrick can be characterized as *sans pareil.* And
coming down to later times, we must remember
that his most gracious Majesty, Defender of the
Faith, &c., King Henry VIII., would bear very unfavorable comparison with modern Christians. Nor
would it be fair to cite as a specimen of modern
Christianity that bellicose queen who was accustomed to slap her courtiers in the face, to lie and
dissimulate without stint, to swear at her noble
lords " by God's blood," and to publicly interrupt
sermons by telling clergymen to " quit their un-
godly digressions." Nay, more, it would not be
very gratifying to national pride to sit in inquisitorial committee on the moral tone of the entire
Elizabethan age. And, bringing the question right
home, could we candidly advise Japanese youth of
to-day to pattern their actions after the naughty
example of the future Defender of the Faith? Ah!
My conceited scions of the Imperial race, are you
all you *might* be and *ought* to be after thirteen
centuries of Christian teaching? Be careful, then,
how you criticise the product of only seventeen
years of labor. Look to yourselves when you dog-
matically clamor that a country which, for twenty-
five centuries, has had only the dim light of natural
religion to guide it, should bring forth characters

fully competent to comprehend and practice the precepts of our revealed religion as our most noble Christians do.

But, incredible as it may seem, the most powerful auxiliary of the missionaries is the Japanese Government. You may rest assured that the government never dreamed of rendering any assistance to the Christian faith when they began to introduce civilization. But they are now beginning to realize the fact that the foreign civilization that they have been so carefully importing during the past six years is the product of Christian principles, and that by introducing our civilization they are introducing Christianity itself. This fact astonishes them immeasurably, and it is a fact that we ourselves do but dimly realize ; yet such is the case.

A prominent counsellor, imported from England by the government, said that all Japan needed was civilization and beefsteak. The gentleman furnishing this advice was an infidel, and evidently did not realize the fact that whatever was good in the civilization of Europe and America was based upon Christian principles. The religion and the civilization of a country go hand in hand. Show me the Druidical mysteries, the fetiches of the African savages, and I will show you a degraded civilization. Show me the nonentities of Shintoism and of Buddhism, and I will show a civilization characterized by social and intellectual stagnation, and by spiritual and political degradation. Show me the

sensuous creed of the Turks, and I will show you
the vilest civilization of to-day. Show me the
comic mythology of the Greeks and Romans, based
upon the vagaries of childish imaginations, and I
will show you a civilization possessing many excellent qualities, but uninfluenced by any deep moral
undercurrents, and characterized by selfishness and
cruelty. In short, give me the general features of
any religion, and I can show you, with reasonable
certainty, the nature of the civilization prevailing
among its votaries. These terms denote correla-
tive conditions of society. Religion is the cause,
civilization is the effect.

And the Japanese, who have been so assiduously
introducing our civilization, are now startled with
the discovery that they have been but pioneers for
Christian missionaries. They now see that the intellectual qualities, the animal passions, and the
selfish desires of nations under Christian influence,
are controlled and curbed by some moral power
that they had not noticed. And they also see that,
but for the checking force of these moral principles, the tremendous faculties of Europe and
America would be dangerous to the world. While
they have assiduously cultivated the intellectual
powers of their youth, are intensifying their appetites and passions by nourishing and stimulating
food, yet they have put no guide on the road, have
put no brake on the wheels, have introduced no
moral power to restrain the undue exercise of these
mental and physical powers. They find Shintoism

and Buddhism quite powerless to do so. Nor can the copious and bitter draughts of infidelity, already freely imbibed, accomplish this end. Nothing under the sun but the Gospel of Christ can do it.

This fact was most whimsically acknowledged by the Japanese when the Mitsui Bank was started in Tokio. This is a national bank, and is backed up with the money of the government. Young Japanese had been specially educated abroad to carry on the banking system on approved foreign principles. They were intelligent, capable, and shrewd. They made excellent cashiers, tellers, book-keepers, and clerks, so far as the merely executive qualities were concerned. They possessed every intellectual requirement necessary for carrying on a bank. But they were *too* intelligent! They were so thoroughly acquainted with financing that they understood many little methods of deflecting cash from the treasury into their own pockets. And there was no power except fear that could prevent their doing so; and fear had but little effect, as there was hardly any danger that the capitalists, composed of effete Daimios and of government officers unfamiliar with banking, could detect how the cash disappeared. In this predicament, one of the bank officers, with great candor and solicitude, came and explained the situation to one of the missionaries. He frankly admitted that he did not believe in any religion whatsoever. He claimed that the Japanese intellect was of too philosophical a nature to accept the Jewish myth called Christianity. "But," said he, " your religion does something that our religions cannot do. *It makes men honest.* Now, we wish our employés at the bank to be carefully instructed in these principles, so that they may learn to discharge their duties with scrupulous integrity."

This story is thoroughly characteristic. Frequently have I met men in America who have candidly admitted that, though not professing Christians themselves, yet they would not care to live in communities where business was not influenced by Christian principles, and where they could not deal with Christian people. And if it were not for the factor of absolute integrity that lies at the foundation of the banking system of the nineteenth century, where would be our immense fabric of commercial exchange? Were it not for the fact that Christian sentiment had made fidelity in commercial affairs to be of paramount importance, the international transactions of the present day would, indeed, be of a limited nature.

At one time the government insisted that Christianity should not be taught in their schools in any shape whatsoever. They even went so far as to insert in some of their contracts a clause to the effect that no instruction should be given upon this subject. Yet it is impossible to explain the sentiment and the illustrations of our great writers without teaching much concerning Christianity. The vast bulk of our literature is so impregnated with Christian sentiment that it is absolutely impossible to eliminate or to avoid it while teaching this sub-

ject. A great part of my teaching in the government schools of Japan has been pure missionary
work.   It was necessarily so.   It would have been
impossible for it to have been otherwise.

But I must close this letter. I could write a
volume tracing the growth of our literature, our
social customs, and our political institutions from
the principles of the Gospels. But time forbids. I
can only state in brief my candid conclusions upon
this subject, derived from several years of close observation. I shall not attempt to argue the matter,
to quote voluminous authorities, or to make a tedious demonstration by clumsy logical methods.
But, in the language of Greenleaf, I will close by
saying that the truth of any hypothesis is established by its coincidence with existing phenomena.

Yours truly,

THEOPHILUS PRATT.

THE CITADEL OF OWARI CASTLE.
(*Native Photograph.*)

LETTER XIII.

A TRIP THROUGH CLASSIC JAPAN.

KIOTO, JAPAN, *August* 3, 1877.

DEAR JULIUS MARCELLUS:

I SHALL start to-morrow on a tour through the provinces that lie north, east, and south of Kioto. This is the classic part of Japan. Our route will be northward across Lake Biwa into Echizen; then, turning to the south, we will pass through Mino, Owari, Isè, and Kii; and then we will cut over the mountains in a north-westerly direction into Yamashiro. My traveling companion will be Mr. Yanagashima, one of my scholars. He is well versed in Japanese history, and is very intelligent. I intend to carry no provisions along. I want to try the experiment of living for a month on Japanese diet, and see how it works. Good night.

Aug. 4.—Left Kioto this evening at seven o'clock, and arrived at Oatsu, on the southern end of Lake Biwa, at ten o'clock. Distance seven miles and a half. Scenery very mountainous. We were stopped three times by the vigilant police. The war makes them active. Even natives have to carry passports. Put up at a hotel. Hotel-keepers charge for best accommodations about sixteen cents per day; for inferior, they charge about twelve cents per day. Oatsu is a town containing about thirty thousand inhabitants.

Aug. 5.—Took one of the little steamers that ply across the lake. The trip to the other end of Lake Biwa is very fine. This is the largest body of fresh water in Japan. Many of the historic events in native history were enacted on its shores. Many of the legends and myths that are most popular cluster around it. On the right is a hill around which a gigantic centipede is said in ancient times to have entwined itself seven times, and then buried its head beneath the waters under the bridge that spanned the river. On the left rises a lofty range of mountains, where lived the famous priest, Benkè, in his monastery. He was noted, the tradition says, for his vast power. On one occasion he stole a large bell and carried it off up the mountains. But the unhappy bell kept saying: "Carry me back! Carry me back, Benkè!" Night and day it ceaselessly cried out, so that the people all heard it. It gave him no peace until he complied with its request. His other exploits would fill a volume.

At four o'clock in the afternoon we reached Shiotsu, at the extreme northern end of the lake. Take dinner *à la Japonnaise*. At half-past five we started for Hikita, some seven miles northward. The first four miles lead through a series of rice plateaus, picturesquely flanked by lofty hills. This was evidently the ancient head of the lake, as the pebbly nature of the ground fully attests. At the end of the four miles we came to the boundary post between Omi and Echizen. The scenery now became grand. We descended into Echizen through a rugged pass. Put up at a hotel.

The productions of the province of Omi are bleached linen, tea, crape, *moxa*, edges for *tatamis*, porcelain, pepper, velvet, silk, fish called *gengoro-funa*, eels, and carp. The productions of the province of Echizen are silver, lead, copper, coal, sulphur, paper called *hosho* (the best paper in Japan, and used in ceremonial documents), mosquito nets, silk, trout, salmon, codfish, mulberry trees, hemp, tea, and lacquer. The word *Omi* means "near the river." The word *Echizen* means "over the pass."

Aug. 6.—Called for our bill. Here it is :

1. For night's lodging, supper and breakfast for two, 30 cents.

2. For sugar, 2 cents.

3. For peaches, 8 cents.

    Total, 40 cents.

Took *jinrikshas* at half-past six. Rode for five miles through a lovely country to Tsuruga, on the Japan Sea. The harbor is shut in by lofty mountains. The place is enchanting. This is the port that will probably be the next to be thrown open to foreign commerce.

Aug. 7.—Hired a boat to visit Jogo, a place some six miles up the western side of the bay. The boatman says that on one side of the bay the people gain their living by hunting and farming ;

on the other side they live by fishing. He also says that the long pine beach at the extreme lower part of the bay was made in one night.

The temple of Jogo is beautifully located at the base of a mountain. Within a mile of it the people are forbidden to catch fish. Jogo is the popular name for the Empress Jingo, who went from this port on a raid into Corea many centuries ago. Her other half has a temple in his honor about half a mile off. Popular tradition says that he makes a visit to Jingo about once a year. Beside Jingo's temple a pretty cascade casts itself into a shaded pool. If you bathe in this water you will be free from sickness for a year—provided you have handed over to the priest that attends the shrine the full allowance of money. Here we found an old woman and a maiden under the water endeavoring to obtain the desired blessing.

We then, on our way back, visited the ubiquitous shrine of *Benten*, picturesquely located on a little promontory.

Then we pass a stone slab rising out of the water; upon it is an image of Jiso, the Buddhist priest. Those who are unable to swim are called stone Jisos. Through its breast is a small hole. The story goes that during a great battle fought five hundred years ago between Nitta and Ashikaga, a stray shot pierced it. The clumsy matchlocks of the thirteenth century could never have done such execution at a distance of three miles. The yarn is charming, nevertheless.

Aug. 8.—Have been out on a tramp through the town of Tsuruga. We first visited the site of the ancient castle of Nitta. It was built on a steep cliff outside of the town. The position is very strong, but Ashikaga led his legions right up the face of the hill and stormed the place. No trace of the castle is left, but the peasants in the immediate vicinity say, that in digging about the underbrush on the steep hillside, they sometimes unearth charred rice, which must be the *débris* of the burnt store-houses of the ancient castle. This was the last battle between Nitta and Ashikaga. Near this spot is the grave of Takayoshi Shinno, a great friend and defender of the ancient Mikados. His melancholy fate excites pity in the breast of every true *samurai*. He fought against the Imperial enemies in Kaga, Mino, Echigo, and Echizen. He died prematurely, and was buried here. For centuries his sepulcher was unknown, but after the Imperial restoration the spot was discovered and marked. Some ancient families in the vicinity treasured up the fact and imparted it to the government. Climbing up the path and pushing aside the underbrush, you see merely an insignificant bamboo fence. Upon a square wooden post is written the name of the hero, the date when the name was written, and a strict prohibition against entering the inclosure.

In the afternoon we went to Matswara, beyond the other end of the town. Here is the place where some three hundred and seventy-five *samurai* were decapitated and buried about twenty years ago. These gentlemen were led by the Prince of Iga, whose head also fell on this bloody occasion. They were bitterly opposed to the introduction of foreigners, but the Bakufu did not sustain their views. Then Takada, the prince, went roving with them through the provinces trying to stir up revolution against the Shogun. They came over the mountains into Echizen. But here they were stopped by the Kaga *samurai.* They delivered up their swords and bodies to the Kaga gentlemen and awaited the decision of the Shogun. The answer was decapitation to a man. The spot is marked with stone monuments.

Aug. 9.—At 10 P.M. we took the steamer that goes fifty-five miles up the coast to Mikunè, the sea-port of the capital of this province.

Aug. 10.—Reached Mikunè this morning. The population is about fifteen thousand. Took *jinriksha* for Fukui, twelve miles to the east. Arrived at 11 A.M. Fukui is built in the center of an extensive stretch of rice-growing country. At half-past eleven we took *jinriksha* for Togu, six miles and a half to the east. The road led through rice and hemp fields. From Togu we walked five miles to Okubo. The road led through a pretty mountainous country. Hotel passable. People kind and attentive. Only one foreigner has ever been in the place.

Aug. 11.—Left Okubo and walked twelve miles to Ono. Our road led through a long stretch of

lovely mountain scenery. Hemp and trees producing lacquer are extensively cultivated. Ono is
situated in a gem of a valley. The lofty mountains
abruptly rise on all sides. The city contains about
forty-five thousand inhabitants. It is well built.
Everybody seems to be reeling silk from thousands
of cocoons. Takada, in his tramp, passed through
here, but was not very warmly received.

From Ono we continued our southerly course,
climbing a mountain covered with verdure to its
very summit. From the summit the view was superb. Behind us lay Ono, the variegated fields,
the sandy streams, and the engroved villages scattered through the glens. While in front of us,
down in the rugged depths of the mountains, lies a
sublime valley. A torrent pours through it. On
its further slope lies a thatched village. Surely
nothing can surpass this in beauty ! Hunting and
fishing are good. Only two foreigners have ever
visited this section of country.

The people are painfully polite. When you
pass along the peasants remove their head-bands.
Should they chance to be driving a large ox that
compels you to step aside, they beg your pardon.
The school-boys in the thatched temples, that have
been turned into school-houses, come out and stand
before the door. Their leader then gravely steps
forth before his constituents and makes a low bow.
This expresses the sentiments of the crowd.

In this vicinity is an antiquated Shinto temple.
The people about it are greatly troubled with

15

wolves. One of the voracious animals destroyed a man down in the hemp-fields last summer. Wild boars also do much mischief by rooting in the fields. Robbers also are a source of much annoyance. At this old temple is a caged wolf of huge dimensions, and both robbers and wild boars greatly dread the wolf. Therefore, the people pray to the wolf to be delivered from their enemies. They pray that three wolves may stand guard over the premises of each one of them. Although these sentinel wolves have never been seen, yet the people believe that invisible ones are actually guarding them and exert a mysterious influence over depredators.

We spent the night at Nakashima, ten miles from Ono. Takada and his gang of *ronins* burnt this place in the most brutal and unprovoked manner during their raid.

Aug. 12.—We left Nakashima and followed the road through fine mountain scenery. At ten o'clock we crossed from Echizen into Mino. We now have wild and rugged mountains. The country is uncultivated and much resembles the Adirondacks. The lofty mountains are covered to their summits with groves of walnut, oak, chestnut, beech, and horse-chestnut. A thick underbrush fills in all spare ground. Wild boars and deer abound. Here is also found the *kamosishi*, a kind of ibex. Legions of monkeys run wild everywhere. They sometimes descend into the regions of rice-fields and make sad havoc with the crops. We made twenty-five miles to-day; the last ten miles were indescribably grand; the scenery was majestic; the road went around the mountain side many hundred feet above the torrents; sometimes it passed over dizzy chasms; sometimes over scaffoldings built along the face of precipices; sometimes over frail bridges; and sometimes over planks that trembled as you crossed the chasms they spanned; the mountains have been packed together in the closest possible order, and they are about as steep as it is possible for them to be without letting slide the immense mass of vegetation that covers them. In fact, in some places, the face of a hill has slipped away, carrying the thundering avalanche of trees and rocks into the torrents below. We passed two lovely cascades. One is three hundred feet high. In one place we had to creep along the face of a cliff where a wrong step would probably have plunged us down fifteen hundred feet. At one place the ravine is spanned by a swinging bridge. It is said the architects derived their idea of the plan by seeing hundreds of monkeys join hands and form a cable from side to side. Old Takada came over the greater part of this road on horse-back. He was eighty years old. He must have possessed considerable vigor, for the road is really a rough foot-path. At ten o'clock we reached Tenjin. While Yanagashima was taking his bath, the floor fell out of the room and precipitated him into the yard, to the unfeigned horror of the land-lady, who was profuse in explanations and apologies. He, however, resumed his ablutions undismayed. Tired? Rather. But he is developing into a first-rate walker.

Aug. 13.—We made thirty-five miles to-day. In the morning we again passed through some magnificent scenery. The rocks indicate the presence of iron and coal. The geology of the country is very interesting. There has been much erosion and drift. In one place the water has worn for itself a deep channel through the rocks. By midday we struck the foot-hills, and were again in the region of pine trees. We passed extensive fields of *taro*, beans, millet, and rice. We found the people very inquisitive, but respectful. By three o'clock we reached Inozoka. From this point we took *jinrikshas* to Yorotaki, a pretty cascade about one hundred and twenty-five feet high. It is a famous resort for picnic parties. It is beautifully located in a glen filled with trees. The sparkling spray combines beautifully with the sunlight and the shadows.

Aug. 14.—From Yorotaki we went through a long stretch of level country to Gi-Fu, the capital of Mino. It is in a favorable location. Place is well built. The productions of the province of Mino are silver, copper, lead, wood for carving and engraving, melons, persimmons, tea, hemp, pepper, rice-beer, crape, cloth, porcelain, carp, trout.

Aug. 15.—Spent in Nagoya, in Owari. This is one of the five great cities of Japan. Its castle is one of the finest. Upon its Tenshiu (citadel) were formely two immense fishes plated with pure gold. They adorned the gable ends, and for miles you could catch their glitter. We spent a day in inspecting the castle and Tenshiu. This Tenshiu rises some three hundred and fifty feet from the waters of the moat. It is five stories high. In the lowermost story you can place two thousand soldiers. The timbers used in its construction are most massive. From the summit your eye takes in the waters of Owari Bay, the rice-fields of Owari Province, and the distant mountains of Shinano and Mino. From this lofty place the movements of an enemy can be accurately inspected miles away. This Tenshiu was almost impregnable against feudal assaults, but against modern weapons it would be useless. It would present a splendid target for artillery practice.

The general features of this castle much resemble that of Hirosaki. It is, however, more extensive. It was one of the strongest outposts of the Tokugawas. Being only three days journey from Kioto, it was most conveniently situated for watching Yamashiro and the central Daimiates.

Nagoya is the great center of inland commerce. The productions of Owari Province, of which it is the capital, are crystals, agate, silk, cotton, earthenware, ironware, and fans. Porcelain, of course, forms a vast article of manufacture. The city is built on a little rising ground that gently slopes down to Owari Bay, a few miles off.

Aug. 16—To-day we left Nagoya and continued

our journey due southward into Isè, the long, narrow
province that borders Owari Bay on the west.
This is one of the oldest portions of Japan. Our
road is level, and we travel by *jinriksha* entirely.
Two-thirds of Isè is a rice-field. The mountains
on the west separate it from Iga, the track of
whose prince we have been tracing. We covered
thirty-five miles to-day. Spent the night at Kambè.
The productions of Isè are tea, oil, wax, cotton,
dyed paper, crabs, clams, lacquerware, tobacco,
garden seeds, hydrangeas, copper, coal, and porcelain called *bankoyaki*. The productions of the adjoining Province of Iga are coal, sulphur, sand for
polishing, and earthenware called *Iga-yaki*.

Aug. 17.—We covered thirty-five miles to-day.
We spent the night at Yamada (mountain-field).
In this vicinity are the shrines of Isè. They are
ranked among the oldest temples in Japan. The
place is about five miles from Futami, where the
sun is said to have first risen between two rocks
that rise from the sea. Around Isè cluster all the
myths and legends of Shintoism, the primitive religion of Japan. This religion was a pastoral religion. The aboriginal hunters and tillers of the
soil offered up the fruits of their toil to the unknown powers that controlled nature. The early
temples were probably like wigwams, built of poles
crossed at the top and covered with skins or thatch.
Then more elaborate structures were built, but the
original form was retained, and even to-day you
find the roofs of all Shinto temples disfigured with

the projecting rafters that cross each other like the original poles twenty-five hundred years ago. And the heavy beams that resemble cannons laid across the ridge pole probably represent the logs that weighted down the thatched roof of some primeval shrine. Into this religion has become welded the doctrine of the divinity of the Mikado. Pure Shintoism is not idolatry. It was the worship of the Invisible by a simple pastoral community. It had no code of morality, no literature expounding doctrines relating to pure life, and no teachings that can compare with the teachings of other great religions. All its temples are built in a style of severe simplicity. No idols are to be found in any of their temples. The only ornament is an enshrined steel mirror about a foot in diameter. Before this they bow and pray: "as the mirror reflects our faces, so may the Invisible reflect upon our minds our sins and duties." Shintoism is doubtless a vast improvement on some forms of idolatry to be met with in Asia. But its great weakness is, that while it recognizes the fact that men should be good, it utterly neglects to tell them how to be good. It fails to give a single commandment or evolve a solitary principle of morality. It is utterly inefficient to raise men even so high as Buddhism has done. If you believe the Mikado to be of divine descent and obey him, you can not fail to be a good Shintoist. It must always fail as a religion. The experience of four thousand years has shown that men need very minute and careful instructions in the very difficult carrying out of so very simple a thing as being good.

The temples of Isè are prettily located in spacious grounds, but in themselves they are not remarkable for architectural beauty. The present buildings have stood about a century.

A lengthy description of these shrines would take us much beyond the limits of our letter. For further information in regard to Shintoism, I refer you to the paper on the " Revival of Pure Shinto," by Mr. Satow, in the Asiatic Reports for 1874 or 1875.

Aug. 18.—We continued our southerly course. We intend to visit the province of Kii and the cascade of Natchi, near its southern part. This is the cascade that steamers coming along the coast can see at a great distance. This section of the country has never been explored by foreigners.

After going ten miles we had to leave our *jinrikshas* and walk. The country was very pretty and hilly. Owing to the uncertainty of the distance between the last two towns, I am unable to say how much I walked to-day. Each traveler we met gave a different figure of the distance. Very few people anyway will give the same answer to the query as to how great the distance is. But the elasticity of this afternoon's walk ranged all the scale between four and fifteen miles.

Aug. 19.—Walked seventeen miles to Nagashima. Then we walked over the mountains to a deep inlet, and took a boat from Furusatto to Shirora.

Distance, six miles.   Then we walked a mile and a half over the hills and struck another inlet.   Took boat again for Owashi.   Distance, seven miles. Our entire journey to-day has been along the sea coast.   On the right hand, the lofty mountains rise in indescribable grandeur.   Panthers, deer, and wild boars abound in the valleys.   The entire southern and eastern portions of this province are exceedingly mountainous.   As the natives say, the mountains are literally placed side by side.   In all eligible localities, the hamlets are nestled.   This province produces crude camphor, tobacco, cotton, pepper, lime, candle-wax, umbrellas, round fans, little egg-shaped oranges, and lacquerware.   The fishermen along the coast also bring in an occasional whale, which Yanagashima classes among the productions.

Aug. 20.—Left Owashi and walked seven miles over very steep mountains.   Striking another inlet, we again took boat some five miles.   These inlets are lovely.   They are full of fish.   Fishing-boats are scattered everywhere.   Some are gliding in from the Pacific well freighted with spoil.   Some are in the deep shadows of the headlands.   When the fish will not bite, the anglers beat the water with a switch, so that the denizens of the deep may fancy it is raining.   Should they then refuse to bite, they are well scolded.

We then walked thirteen miles to Kinomoto. The walk was severe.   The population of this place is four thousand.   We hadn't been five

minutes in the hotel before two policemen bounced
in for our passports.

What interested me most to-day was the universal habit of smoking cigars.   Even the women and
children smoked.   They take a camelia leaf and
roll it into a cornucopia.   This they fill with tobacco, and go puffing along as if they had tin fun-
nels in their mouths.   Bundles of camelia leaves
are sold all along the roadside for two mills per
bundle.   I have never seen this anywhere else in
Japan.

The people here are hearty and healthy.   Their
noses are really Jewish in shape.   In these mountains you will find the people as they have been for
two thousand years.   The place is out of the way.
Foreign elements have never mixed in.   Here you
find the pure Japanese race.   The fleets of Javanese
junks that probably drifted up here on the Black
Stream during the past centuries would find this
promontory convenient for landing.   When the population increased, it could pass over the mountains
into Owari, Isè, and Yamashiro, and mix with the
Ainos.   But it offered no inducement with its wild
mountains for immigration in return.   The people
are certainly an improvement on the Japanese I
have hitherto met.   The corruptions of feudalism
also had less scope here among the rugged cliffs.
And so the people of these mountains are about
the same as they have been for many centuries.
The climate along the coast is very delightful at all
seasons.

Aug. 21.—Left Kinnemoto and went twelve miles by *jinriksha* along the sea shore. The road led through pine groves, across hills, and through much varied and beautiful scenery. Then took *kago* at Atawa and went fourteen miles to Hama-no-mia (shore temple). This place is within three miles of Natchi-no-taki. We spent the night at a Buddhist temple that has been turned into a hotel. Since the Revolution, this sect has become very much impoverished. Many of the monasteries have fallen into decay. We found two very valuable relics at this place. One was a piece of camphor wood with an inscription upon it. The abbot said that it was thirteen hundred years old. We wanted to buy it, but he said money was no inducement to part with it. Another relic was a little bell heavily alloyed with gold. It produced a very sweet note. This was a thousand years old. It was well authenticated. It had been handed down for fifty generations from abbot to abbot. It was brought from China by the priest Ji-kaku Daishi. This relic he was induced to part with for a pecuniary consideration.

Aug. 22.—Arrived at the falls of Natchi. It is about three miles back from the sea-coast. It is nearly five hundred feet high. Its source is a mountain stream that comes from the range of Natchi-san. The scenery surrounding it is very wild and exceedingly grand. Within a radius of a few miles are other cascades numbering, according to native estimates, forty-eight. None of them, however, are more than half the size of this one. At its base are many shrines and tea booths for the pilgrims that flock hither every summer. On one or two occasions boats from passing steamers have landed crews to examine the falls. The people living in the vicinity are very respectful, and take very little notice of strangers. There are no regular hotels in the vicinity. The well-to-do people, living in the valley and on the steep mountain side, offer the hospitality of their roofs to visitors. When crowds are not pressing, they take turns in acting the host. We were referred well up the mountain side to a house situated on a bold crag overlooking the valley and the falls. So lovely was the place that we decided to stay here a couple of days and enjoy the scenery.

Aug. 23.—Spent in examining the falls and in visiting some of the old temples. Our host showed us some letters that had been written by some princes in the time of Yoritomo, nearly eight hundred years ago. Yanagashima had some difficulty in reading them, as the characters differed somewhat from the modern characters. One letter was from a feudal lord to his treasurer, ordering him to present a suitable gift to a certain *samurai* of another clan who had respectfully descended from his horse when his lordship came down the road. Another letter spoke about the widening of the castle moat and the securing of workmen for the task. These letters would be very interesting to any one desiring to write up a history of old times. In this vicinity are many such ancient documents. This whole promontory would be a fine field for antiquarians.

Aug. 24.—I must take it easy! I begin to find that Japanese diet is not quite so invigorating as our own. My eyes begin to be weak. The original aversion that I had for rice has disappeared. I actually relish it as the hostess dips it out of the steaming tub. Rice tastes better when eaten with chop-sticks. It should be eaten piping hot. If the Japanese were to use a little more variety in their cooking it would suit my taste more. Almost everything is boiled. They do not seem to know much about roasting and baking. Rice is used at every meal. The side dishes are varied. The landlady comes in regularly and takes our orders. Shall it be trout, or beans, or pickled radish? Or perhaps some shrimps would be preferred? When one gets accustomed to these dishes, he finds some of them very nice. But a person with a delicate taste would be a long time in getting accustomed to them. Japanese diet is certainly weak when compared with our own. You do not store up a reserve force of vitality when living on it. You can do just about so much work every day, but when you attempt to do more than your regular amount you find it very wearing. A *jinriksha* man will do splendid work for a couple of days, but if you keep him at it he breaks down. Many of these men die from heart disease every year.

Aug. 25.—Walked over the mountains some twenty miles and reached Hongu. The country is exceedingly rugged. Our course is now north-east to Coyasan and Osaca. The oldest temples in Japan are here. They antedate the shrines of Isè. They are built upon an immense rectangular platform of granite about eight feet high. They are in a dilapidated condition. They are odd structures. Innumerable crows flit over the weather-beaten roofs, and fill the somber groves with their ceaseless clamor. The legends say that in ancient times they were gifted with strange powers of speech.

Aug. 26.—We left Hongu and climbed over the Endless Mountain for about ten miles. With the exception of Fujiyama, it is the hardest climbing I have done in Japan. The amount of water that you drink is surprising. There being no springs along the roadside, your coolie has to carry a large supply along. The mountain is about five thousand feet high. The view from the summit is extremely grand. In all directions the mountains roll away in endless waves. A more rugged region can hardly be imagined. There are no large towns here, but there are great numbers of hamlets scattered all along the mountain roads. In one of the houses I found an old Tower musket with a bayonet. Inquiring whether robbers troubled the people, I was informed that wild boars gave great trouble in the potato patches, and had to be fought fiercely, as they loved potatoes and became savage on being interrupted in their meals. We traveled through this magnificent country for about twenty miles. Stopped for the night at Yagura, perched far up the mountain side.

Aug. 27.—Continued our journey twenty-eight miles along the tops of the high mountains. The scenery, to be appreciated, must be seen. A typhoon came upon us and soon made us as wet as you please. My rubber cloak came in handy. There was something so weird and grand in thus promenading nature aroused that I count this as the most enjoyable day of our excursion. Passed the night at Otake.

Aug. 28.—Walked eight miles more and made Coya-san. Determined to stop here a couple of days.

Coya monastery is at the summit of a mountain five thousand feet high. Deep groves of superb cryptomeiria that have been cultivated with the greatest care for many centuries cover the mountain to its base. For miles around the shrines betoken the vicinity of the monastery. Coya-san is the oldest Buddhist monastery in Japan. It was founded by Kobu-Daishi thirteen hundred years ago. This same man introduced Buddhism into Japan. He selected this mountain summit and built a small temple. and spent his life in propagating his creed. He lived a life of great self-denial. He rose early, prayed long and often, and fasted frequently. Instead of using a mirror, he looked into a cistern when he arranged his hair. When, after a long life of labor, his end drew near, he sent

all his companions away from the temple.   He told
them that when they no longer heard the sound of
the bell that he tapped when he prayed, they might
know that Kobu-Daishi was dead.   Faintly hummed
the bell all day long.   Fainter were its notes as
night drew on; and in the gray dawn, when the
priests slid back the *shojees*, Kobu-Daishi lay dead
upon the floor before Buddha in Nirvana, and was
devoutly clasping his rosary.

But the temple grew, and within a few years a
vast monastery covered the mountain summit.
Thousands of priests officiated at the shrines.   The
place became a city of priests.   Commerce was in-
terdicted ; trade was not allowed.   Profound peace
and quiet reigned.   Women were not allowed
within five miles of the base of the mountain.
Sacred fires were kept perpetually burning from the
original flame that Kobu-Daishi brought from
India.   Hundreds of these lights are kept in a vast
room.   They never go out.   Priests watch them
night and day.   Some of the lamps must have
been kept burning many centuries.   When a prince
dies he will donate a fund to the monastery to
keep a lamp, lit from Kobu-Daishi's flame, perpetually burning.

In front of this shrine is a huge meteoric stone
in a large cage.   The story is that when Kobu-
Daishi went to India he flung it back into Japan to
announce his arrival.

After walking through many streets and avenues
lined with shrines and temples, you strike out into

a long, somber avenue of pine trees that is over a mile and a half in length. On either hand are tombs. This is the cemetery of the monastery. Here is found the first tombstone erected in Japan. It is about five feet high. It is of stone, and is more like a pyramid in its shape than anything else I can compare it to. It is covered with Sanskrit inscriptions, like all the other graves. Many of the Daimios of Japan are buried here. Some of their tombs are very elaborate. Granite and bronze are the chief materials employed. All those buried here were first cremated. This ceremony was often attended with very imposing services.

The Buddhist literature of the monastery is very ancient and valuable. It is all in Sanskrit, and is quite unintélligible to the priests in general.

At present there are not over three hundred priests connected with Coya-san, but in its palmy days, before the Revolution, it numbered from three to five thousand.

In the house set apart for a hotel, it is curious to notice all the servants and waiters being men. They all have shaved heads. I was also much interested in seeing weasels running all over the roofs. Upon inquiry we were informed that as the priests could not take life in any form, they became rapidly overrun with rats. Weasels were then introduced, and the rats disappeared. But there was nothing to drive away the weasels. So for centuries they have become permanent fixtures. When you ask the priests why they were not responsible for causing the death of so many rats, they simply reply that the rats could have left had they found the locality too dangerous! Another feature of Coya-san is the absence of mosquitoes. So cool is the air that these tormentors are rarely seen.

Were I disposed to dream away life in profound repose and ambitionless existence, I would select Coya-san.

Aug. 30.—We are back again in Kioto, being well pleased and well tired with our tramp of six hundred miles.

I am now engaged for a year, teaching at Kioto. The Satsuma Rebellion so drained the government funds that it was found necessary to close the school in which I was teaching at Tokio. I will endeavor to give you my impressions of Kioto before long.

Yours truly,
THEOPHILUS PRATT.

THE GREAT BELL AT DAI-BUTZ TEMPLE, KIOTO.
(*Native Photograph.*)

LETTER XIV.

KIOTO, *September* 10, 1877.

DEAR JULIUS MARCELLUS:

KIOTO is the most interesting city in Japan. A thousand years of history, poetry, and romance cluster around it. It is situated in the Province of Yamashiro (Mountain Castle), in the heart of Japan. High mountains surround it on the eastern, northern, and western sides, thus protecting it from the cold winds during the winter, while, during the summer, the sea breezes cool it from the south.

Through the center of the city flows the Kamo-Gawa (River of the Wild Ducks). This noisy stream, let loose from the mountains on the north, comes tumbling along over pebbles, bowlders, and sand-bars. During heavy rains it assumes formidable proportions. Three or four long wooden bridges span it, and connect the two halves of the city. The Kamo-Gawa flows southward through Fusimè, the southern suburb of Kioto; thence it winds among foot-hills and rice-fields through a very picturesque country for about thirty miles, until it loses itself in the waters of Osaca Bay.

In 1875, before the railway was constructed,

when I visited Kioto for the first time, I had to come up this river in a long, flat-bottomed boat. In old times this river was the principal means of approach from Osaca.

In coming here from Tokio, you may choose from three routes. The quickest is by steamer to Kobè, and thence by railway for fifty miles. This journey requires about three days. The second route is by the Tokaido over Hakonè Pass, beside the base of majestic Fujisan, through the fishing villages along the coast and through Nagoya, and then around the southern end of Lake Biwa through a gap in the mountains to Kioto. This trip occupies about ten days journeying by *jinriksha*. This was the route by which I returned to Tokio in 1875. It is a magnificent highway, shaded for a great distance by cryptomeiria of centuries' growth. The third route is by the Nakasendo (Inland Road). This is the grandest of all the routes. It comes directly through the inland provinces, crossing the magnificent mountains of Shinano.

The population of Kioto numbers about five hundred thousand souls. The city is built in the usual Japanese fashion. In the center lies the now deserted Gosho, the ancient residence of the emperors. It covers but a few acres of ground, and the gardens and parks are inclosed with a high wall.

Skirting the city on all sides are groves, gardens, pagodas, temples, and monasteries. The encircling foot-hills are covered with them. These temples

and monasteries formed the pride and glory of
Kioto. At one time in the city's history there
were four thousand of them. Many of the monasteries are surrounded by deep groves and acres of
greensward and shrubbery. Immense groves of
cherry trees are scattered over all the foot-hills and
in all the gardens around the villas and temples, so
that in the spring the city seems to be fringed with
clouds of white and pink blossoms which, with a
background of majestic mountains, form a scene
of peerless beauty. Seen at such times from the
top of one of the surrounding mountains, the city
lies at your feet like a lovely garden—sweet as we
might imagine a glimpse of paradise to be.

I shall not attempt to give you a minute description of the various temples of Kioto. The task
would be indeed formidable. I send you, however,
Satow's *Guide Book to Kioto,* which will furnish you
considerable interesting information. I will only
attempt to describe three or four of the temples
that have most impressed me.

Just back of my house lies the monastery of
Chioin. It covers the entire hill side, and is one of
the largest in the empire. The central edifice is an
immense affair. Like all the native structures in
Japan, it is built entirely of wood. The huge pillars supporting the immense roof are of *kayakè.*
The roof is a wonderfully heavy affair. Taking the
tiles and rafters together, the thickness must be
about ten feet. The object of so heavy a roof is
to neutralize the effect of earthquake shocks upon

the pillars. This structure was erected two or three hundred years ago. Far up amid the tangled maze of rafters, the priest points out to you the umbrella that the architect left sticking there centuries ago. This temple is considered the finest structure of its kind in Japan. It was built regardless of expense. In the grove beside it is a belfry containing the largest bell in Japan. The height is said to be eighteen feet. I was unable to measure it for myself as it hung in the belfry, but the thickness of the bronze at its mouth measured ten inches. Like all bells in Japan, this one has no tongue, but it is struck from the outside by letting a heavy log of wood swing against its massive sides. It requires eight men to properly manipulate this huge piece of timber in order to swing it with accurate precision, so as not to deaden the sound. I had the pleasure of hearing it rung several times. The sound is a deep-toned boom—grand and magnificent beyond expression. The trembling vibrations that follow the boom last quite a while, and fill the groves with soft and deeply melancholy melody.

Leaving Chioin and skirting the suburbs in a northerly direction, we come to a singular structure known as the Kin-Kakku-Gi. In ancient times an emperor, tired of the seclusion of the Gosho, decided to abdicate. He accordingly built this residence for himself in a most lovely locality at the base of the mountains, surrounding it with extensive gardens filled with lakes, dwarfed landscape, and shrubbery. The ceilings and walls of the building were covered with sheets of pure silver. This location is specially celebrated for the superb view of the moon that can be had as it rises over the mountains. Here the emperor spent his life in meditation and in composing poetry. And the surroundings were certainly congenial to such occupations, for a lovelier locality would be difficult to find. On a clear night, the queenly moon floats above the mountain top, bathing the ravines and gardens in a soft, dreamy light; and the dwarfed pines and the shrubbery, reflected in the calm waters of the lakes, seem but unsubstantial creations of the fancy.

Upon the other side of the city is another structure of a similar character, known as the Gin-Kakku-Gi. It is upon a larger scale than the Kin-Kakku-Gi. It was built by another emperor for similar purposes. Instead of being covered with sheets of silver, however, it was covered with sheets of gold. It is embowered in gardens and groves.

I shall not attempt to give any further description of the temples of Kioto. Even at the present day, they are numbered by hundreds. Not only are the suburbs filled with these shrines and monasteries, but the surrounding mountains abound with them. Near the summit of Hiyeisan, a cone that towers to an altitude of nearly five thousand feet, about seven miles north-east of the city, is a superb monastery that I shall describe more at length hereafter.

Kioto was the religious center of Japan. The emperor was the patron of religion, and Buddhism was the preferred creed. The monasteries were famous centers of ecclesiastical learning. As the priests were learned men, their monasteries also became centers of elegant culture and refinement— famous colleges, in fact, where the gentry were educated. Emperors have received tutoring within these sacred inclosures. Kioto was built over one thousand years ago. The emperor moved to this place from Nara. Although the surroundings of Kioto are so serene and lovely, yet its history has been one of almost continued bloodshed. For centuries it was the center of intrigue and civil discord. Repeatedly has it been burned to the ground. But during the past three hundred years, under the Tokugawa *régime*, profound peace has prevailed, and the city has prospered greatly.

I found the Kioto people to be very different from the Tokio people. They regard themselves as the most cultured portion of the empire. They highly pride themselves upon their aristocratic blood. They possess much supercilious pride and a vast amount of indolence. In few parts of Japan —I will go further and say that in no part of Japan —are foreigners treated with such cool and patronizing contempt as here. Nor are the natives remarkably popular with their own countrymen. They characterize outsiders as uncultured and boorish—a criticism not very highly relished by Japanese at large, as you may naturally infer.

The people are much given up to pleasure. The theaters are numerous and well patronized. The various holidays and festivals are celebrated with processions and feastings. Religious festivals are exceedingly common. Each monastery has its fête days; the people celebrate them by turning out in immense crowds, dressed in gala costume, and thronging the streets and groves, picnicing and gossiping to their heart's content.

The most extraordinary of all the holidays is the day set apart in honor of the courtesans. In other parts of Japan the observance of this day has ceased, but it is still celebrated with much zest here. I happened to be here last July when it was being celebrated. All day long the people were busy erecting booths, platforms, and scaffoldings along the streets where the procession was going to pass in the evening. At dusk the entire city was gorgeously illuminated with paper lanterns. The courtesans slowly paraded the streets in pantomime, each group personating some domestic or social scene. One group represented a lady with her maids at work in the garden; they were sprinkling water upon the plants, dressing the shrubbery, and catching butterflies. The bushes, the flowers, the soil, and the general paraphernalia of a real garden surrounded them on all sides upon moving platforms and vehicles. The effect of the scene was capital. A lot of half-tipsy coolies helped along the ladies by pulling the vehicles through the street.

Another scene represented silk weavers. There were the looms and the shuttles. There were the revolving reels and the rapidly forming warp and woof. While to complete the domestic scene in all its details, an imitation dog lay upon the floor and wagged its tail in obedience to the skillfully manipulated string of the attendant.

In another scene the matron was in the kitchen preparing the evening meal. There were the oven and the kettle, and the mischievous child always in the way. The rice was steamed, the fish was broiled, and the salt radish was cut up, in a way fairly enough to excite the cravings of hunger.

It took several hours for the various pantomimes to pass. The courtesans were dressed with great magnificence. Some had on seven robes, each one of which would have befitted a queen. Everything was very orderly. The ceremonies were conducted with great propriety, and the crowds showed great decorum and respect, as this was considered the courtesans' yearly offering of devotion to the gods.

During the summer the people in Kioto take things very easy. The surrounding hills and mountains abound in groves, cascades, and glens. These cool resorts are thronged with jolly picnicers all day long. The amount of rice, wine, and watermelon that a Jap can annihilate on such occasions is amazing. He gives up the entire day, and frequently a succession of days, to merry-making. He calculates to arrive at the shady glen before

the heat of the day has set in. A slice of water-
melon is to be found in his hand at most any time
before lunch. He and his companions lounge
around upon matted platforms scattered all through
the glen. Between times they smoke their pipes
and gossip, occasionally stretching their limbs and
uttering stentorian yawns that fairly shake the
trees. Just before lunch they strip themselves for
a bath in the cascade. This process is conducted
with boundless *sang froid*, in view of the circumstance that the glen is swarming with people.
Having whetted their appetites sufficiently, they
take hold of a tubful of rice and a cask of *sakè* with
a zest quite impossible to describe. Raw carp and
soy are taken as relishes. After lunch, they again
fall upon their water-melons, pipes, and bathing.
Toward sundown another assault is delivered
against the rice-tub and wine-cask. And in the
cool gloaming they disperse and homeward fly,—
provided none of them have been disabled during
the assault.

Such is a brief description of the salient points of
Kioto. To go fully into the subject would require
a book—which I do not intend writing.

I am situated, as regards my house and social
surroundings, far more pleasantly than when I was
in Hirosaki.

My house is an old temple near the entrance to
the Chioin monastery. It was built about three
hundred years ago, and was originally designed as
a residence for the ladies of the Shogun's house-

hold in case they should chance to visit Kioto. But as the ladies never came, the priests utilized the house as a temple. It is very substantially built. A broad veranda surrounds it, and it has a heavy tile roof supported by massive timbers. There is but a single story, and as you may easily imagine, the ceiling is immensely high. A fine suite of six rooms constitute my apartments. The *shojees* are covered with gilt paper and are set in lacquered frames. They are beautifully ornamented. In a wing attached to my house are three rooms for the boy, and also the kitchen. This kitchen I will describe more fully in the latter part of this letter. Surrounding these premises on all sides is a lovely and extensive garden, and we are inclosed by a wall through which ingress may be obtained by a stately gateway. I could not desire a more private residence.

My neighbors are all Buddhist priests. The one on my right-hand is busily engaged every day in drilling a class of boys in the Buddhist chants. He keeps at it so regularly that I frequently find myself unconsciously humming the monotonous scores of the dreamy rhythms. The priest on my left-hand is a very religious man, judging from the amount of praying that he indulges in. He spends two or three hours daily at his matins and vespers. He begins with a slow, droning chant, tapping on a little bell betimes. His chant rapidly increases in intensity, until you hear but a prolonged whirring sound accompanied by the silvery notes of the humming bell. Then the sounds slowly subside until the prayer ends as it began in measured cadence and subdued tones. Then you know that the beads on the rosary have been counted. He goes over his rosary again and again, until I am fairly drowsy listening to him.

As you already know, it is forbidden to the Buddhists to destroy life in any shape. As a natural consequence of the following of this doctrine, the precincts of their monasteries abound in all kinds of life peculiar to the various localities. Centipedes fully six inches long are frequently seen around here in the gardens. They sometimes get into the houses, and make themselves as disagreeable as possible. Should you hang your coat upon the walls, you will probably find one of these horrid creatures in the sleeve when you attempt to put it on again. Their bites or stings are painful but not mortal. Snakes and lizards also are about as plentiful as it is possible for them to be after centuries of pampering within these sacred inclosures.

And if it were not for the friendly services of the weasels, the audacious impudence and the obtrusive familiarity of the rats and mice would speedily render the existence of man quite problematical. But it is not quite so easy to exterminate the snakes. They, however, avoid the presence of man, and keep clear of his abode. During the heavy rains last week, when I was in the bathroom, a small one fell from the rafters across my shoulder and slipped down upon my bare feet. I jumped aside with a mighty spring, and the reptile squirmed through a crack in the floor out into the garden. I can not go out into my garden without seeing half a dozen lizards basking themselves in the sunshine, and I have no doubt that in the dense shrubbery and in the extensive bamboo copses scattered all around here, snakes could be found by the score. It is very fortunate that the snakes in Japan are of a harmless nature. In the vicinity of Buddhist monasteries in the tropics you will find serpents of great size,—provided such monasteries are not in the immediate vicinity of teeming populations.

But the most surprising creatures that seek refuge within these sacred inclosures are the foxes. A family of them live under my house. They are plentiful all around here. At night-time they come out and scour the suburbs and hills for poultry and birds. They probably visit all the *Inari* shrines for miles around, feasting upon the fried wheat cakes that have been prepared for their special benefit by the fox-worshipers. During their rambles around my garden, they frequently come across my neighbors' dogs. After indulging in animated snarling and purring for about five minutes, they will part company. As the native dogs are too cowardly to come to close quarters, the foxes find their strange abodes about as safe as they can desire.

My household arrangements are upon a very

simple scale. As my contract is only for one year, it will not pay me to buy very much furniture, and if this Satsuma rebellion continues much longer to drain the government funds, I may not stay out my year. Any furniture that I might buy now would be a dead loss when I came to leave, for the natives do not use European furniture, and the few missionary families here are already well supplied.

My bedroom is adorned with severe simplicity. I sleep on the floor after the native fashion. During the day-time my bedding is stowed away in the closet. In one corner of the room stands my zinc trunk, which answers the double purpose of wardrobe and money-chest. A wash-stand and two chairs complete the furnishing of the room. All the floors throughout the house are covered with fine *tatamis*. My study has a table and two chairs, and my parlor has a table and four chairs; the walls, corners, and sides of the room being ornamented with *curios* and *bric-à-brac*. The dining-room has a table and three chairs, while the spare room is quite bare.

My kitchen is about as interesting as any part of the house. It is without any furniture whatsoever— not even a cooking range. For cooking purposes my boy uses a couple of small earthen ovens, no larger than a pair of flower-pots. It is astonishing how he manages to cook at all. Yet he certainly does marvelously well with omelets, soups, broiled chickens, and fried potatoes. His fuel is charcoal.

This produces a powerful heat, and is comparatively free from smoke. The only important utensil that he uses is a gridiron. All the other articles are of native production, and consist of an iron pot, a frying-pan, and a couple of insignificant clay bowls, in which he boils potatoes and puddings. With such primitive utensils he displays great ingenuity in preparing food. The other day I invited the two directors to dinner. The first course was tomato soup. Then came boiled fish, with egg sauce. Then came broiled venison and baked potatoes. After this came a *quasi* plum pudding, composed of currants instead of plums, and of suet and flour. The wine sauce accompanying it could not have been surpassed, although the " wine " was some brandy that he had clandestinely abstracted from my medicine chest. The dessert of this extraordinary dinner consisted of peaches, plums, and grapes.

But every rose has its thorn. My boy *will* get drunk. About once a fortnight he goes on a spree and comes staggering into the kitchen an hour or so behind time. His apologies and promises of reform are as profuse as can be desired; but his periodical sprees come in regular order nevertheless. I shall be compelled to part with him before long. But as I am in the immediate vicinity of a Treaty Port, where competent cooks are plentiful, I shall not have much trouble in replacing him. It is truly amazing how these Japs pick up our style of cooking. They all soon learn to cook fairly well; and some of them become exquisite adepts in *cuisine*.

So much for my household affairs. My school duties are similar to those in Tokio. I usually walk the three miles between my house and the school. The hours are from nine in the morning to three in the afternoon, Saturdays and Sundays being holidays. The scholars are mostly young men of the *samurai* class.

As to my social surroundings I cannot say much, as they are very limited. There are only four foreign families here, three of whom are those of American missionaries. These people are hospitable and friendly, and I spend many a profitable evening in their company.

I must now close this rambling letter. Kioto is a difficult subject to write upon if one wishes to avoid giving hackneyed information about the place.

Yours truly,

THEOPHILUS PRATT.

17

LETTER XV.

AN EXCURSION TO NARA.

KIOTO, *September* 17, 1877.

DEAR JULIUS MARCELLUS:

I TOOK a trip to Nara the other day. This city
is about thirty miles from Kioto. Having no passport, I was under the necessity of going and returning on the same day. We started off early in
the morning in our *jinrikshas*, and arrived there
about midday. This gave us fully half a day to
inspect the place; and we had the cool night in
which to return to Kioto. The trip was a thoroughly enjoyable one, although rather wearisome.
The road lay through a somewhat level country—
fairly picturesque, but rather uninteresting; and
we were glad enough to reach Nara in time for
lunch I can assure you.

Nara was the ancient capital of the emperors. It
is situated among picturesque hills near some
mountains. In its days of prosperity it was a
large and handsome city, but its present population is not over twenty thousand; and nothing remains of its ancient glory except the vast temple
and colossal image of Buddha,* or *Dai-Butz*, as

---

*The illustration on the opposite page is a reproduction
from a Japanese painting that had hung on the walls of some

THE DEATH OF BUDDHA.
(See Footnote on next page.)

the natives designate it. Otherwise the place bears no comparison with lovely Kioto.

Passing down the long, straggling street that forms the backbone of the town, you will see, on your left, an immense grove of stately pines and cedars stretching over hills and vales far away

---

monastery or temple for about fifty years prior to its sale to the author at Nagoya in 1877. It was sold because the disestablishment of Buddhism as the State religion of the Japanese Empire had produced great poverty in that sect. The illustration represents the supposed scene at the death-bed of Buddha. So great a benefactor had he been that all creation is represented as mourning at his death—personages of royal birth, celebrities of various nationalities, animals of varied species, fowls of the air, and even the fiends from hell are represented as bewailing the misfortune which the great mercifulness of Buddha's nature had rendered universal. At the top of the picture, descending upon clouds and mists, is represented the mother of Buddha, accompanied by female friends and preceded by a guide, coming from Paradise to witness the closing scene in the life of her illustrious son. Her lamentations are violent, because of the fact that the mystic medicine that she had sent to her son had been carried away from his bedside by some thieving cat, which had scampered up into a tall tree with it, thus rendering the recovery of the renowned philanthropist impossible. To the left-hand side of the picture, high up among the boughs, may be seen the unlucky bag of medicine. The contents thereof have melted, and are represented as running down the trunk of the tree. The artist, as a solemn warning to all future generations of feline depredators, and also, we may presume, as condign punishment for the immediate freebooter that had absconded with madame's physic, has failed to represent a cat in any part of his painting. The entire scene is located by the artist upon the sea-shore, where the waves may be seen through the trees. In this representation he carries out the legend which chronicles Buddha as having died upon some part of the coast of Ceylon.

into the mountains. Looming above the trees you will see the massive roof of the temple containing the monster image. The tiles are immensely heavy, and are bound together with strong iron bands. The thickness of the roof is fully ten feet. Surrounding this central figure like attendant guards, are several smaller temples, scarcely showing their gables above the trees. Coming now to a long, stately avenue, we go up for nearly half a mile through two huge gateways to the temple. The gateway, through which we first pass, merits a special description. It is a large, double-storied tower, about fifty feet high. The upper story is filled with dilapidated idols. Through the lower passes the gateway. On each side of the portal are two gigantic images about twenty feet high. Their faces are distorted in the most hideous fashion, and the weapons in their hands are poised in a threatening manner. The ancient coating of red paint has dropped from their bodies, and the heat of many centuries has warped the hard wood, so that the muscular arms and legs have split open to the center. These images are the gods of wrestlers and mighty men of valor. People desiring to excel in physical strength come here to worship. Their method of devotion is rather singular. The prayers are carefully written on small pieces of paper, which, after having been chewed up into spit-balls, are then deliberately flung at the grim deities—it being considered quite essential that the missiles should stick fast. The monsters are covered with these concise supplications.

Passing through this gateway, we enter upon a continuation of the avenue. The stately pines screen us admirably from the sun, and the greensward on all sides refreshes the eyes nearly blinded with the glare of the dusty road from Kioto. Under the trees are tea-booths furnishing refreshments to travelers and devotees. Appropriating some seats in the shade, we plunged into the depths of a water-melon, and ate vermicelli and pickled plums for the space of half an hour.

Continuing our stroll down the avenue, we came to a second gateway, through which we passed into a vast court-yard. On *fête* days, several thousand people are accommodated within this spacious inclosure. On the other side of it stands the temple. This building was originally of a bright vermilion color, but the rains of centuries have washed it bare. Across the face of the temple runs a high vestibule whose roof is supported by large wooden columns. The entire structure is of wood. The roof is supported by sixty huge wooden pillars.

From one of the pamphlets distributed by the priest within the vestibule the following information is derived :

"The original temple of Dai-Butz was built in the reign of the Emperor Shiomu, the forty-sixth Emperor of Japan, who lived about 1524 years ago. It took eleven years to cast the idol and to build the temple. Four hundred and twenty-nine years after the completion of the temple, during one of the civil feuds, Taira-Shigehira, a famous chieftain, destroyed it. Five years thereafter it was rebuilt, and the image was recast. Four hundred and eighty-four years then slipped away, and a fierce battle took place between Matsunaga-Hisahide and Miyoshi-Yasunaga, two feudal chiefs, during which the image and the temple were again destroyed. And about seven hundred years ago the present edifice was built; and the present head and shoulders, which had been melted during the previous conflagration, were recast."

Closing the pamphlet and crossing the threshold of the temple, we see Dai-Butz looming up before us to the height of seventy feet. In the middle of the temple is an immense stone platform nearly two hundred feet in circumference, and ten feet high. Upon this platform is constructed a smaller one of solid bronze, six feet high. Its surface is composed of bronze petals of the lotus flower. Seated cross-legged upon this flowery throne is Buddha in Nirvana,—a stupendous, olive-colored image. This is the largest bronze image in the world. The actual height of the idol, measuring from the bronze platform, is fifty-three feet and five inches. It is proportioned for a standing image one hundred feet high.

Turning to our pamphlet, we find that this image is seven hundred years old. Seven successive castings were made before a satisfactory piece of work could be produced.

Three thousand tons of charcoal were consumed during the operation. The total weight of the metal used is four hundred and fifty tons. The alloys are proportioned as follows:

Gold =	500	pounds avoirdupois.	
Tin =	16,827	"	"
Mercury =	1,984	"	"
Copper =	986,080	"	"
Total =	1,005,391	"	"

Taking for granted that the figures transmitted to us by antiquity are accurate, it will appear that this idol contains nearly 300,000 pounds more of metal than the Colossus of Rhodes contained. And its proportions must be almost the same. The following figures will convey to your mind some idea of the immense size of this image:

	FEET.	INCHES.
Height from throne............................	53	5
" " floor.............................	70	......
Length of face.................................	16	......
Width " "	9	5
Length of eyebrow	5	4½
" " eye.................................	3	9
Breadth of nose	2	9¾
Height " "	1	6
Length of mouth..............................	3	7
" " ear................................	8	5
Width across shoulders.........................	28	7
" " breast.............................	18	......
" " abdomen	18	......
Length of upper arm	19	......
" " forearm..............................	15	......

	FEET.	INCHES.
Length of palm	5	6
" " middle finger........................	5	......
Length from knee to foot.......................	23	8½
Diameter of knee	7	......
Circumference of *middle* finger.................	5	......
Height of each lotus petal......................	6	......
Width " " " "	30	......
Height of each curl on head....................	1	......
Diameter of each curl on head. (*There are* 966 *curls on the head.*)	......	6
Diameter of back of throne.....................	75	......
Length of each ray protruding from back of throne.	83	......
Height of temple............................	170	......
Length " "	290	......
Width " "	170	......

The image is hollow, the average thickness of the bronze being about one foot. The lower parts and the bronze pedestal, however, must be almost solid. It has been cast in separate pieces, and these have been joined together with a kind of metallic cement, leaving a barely perceptible mark. The surfaces of the lotus petals composing the pedestal are covered with minute engravings representing temples, dragons, combats between fiends, shrines perched on little knolls, various kinds of flowers, and a few other heathenish conceptions.

The left hand of the image extends along the knee, with the third and fourth fingers slightly raised. The open palm projects over the knee as if offering something to a needy individual, or showing the plausibility of some pet idea. A grand piano could easily be set upon the hand thus opened; you could comfortably lie down in the palm, and you sit upon the thumb as you would upon a log of wood. The position of the right hand is somewhat different. The wrist is slightly elevated above the right knee, the open hand being raised at right angles to the forearm as if trying to push something back,—a repelling gesture. The eyes are half shut. The face is fat and flabby. The general expression is sleepy and good natured. The image is represented as dressed in a simple priest's robe. The folds and creases have been cast with wonderful accuracy.

Behind the image is the gilt back of its throne, upon which are sixteen brackets holding sixteen bronze images, nine feet high each. In front are two colossal bronze vases, containing bronze lotus plants, twenty feet high. Perched on the rim of each vase is a large bronze butterfly, with a span across the wings of five feet; and upon each side of the image is an immense wooden statue forty feet high.

Everything, in fact, has been planned upon an immense scale. The only thing approximating to a musical instrument is a huge drum with its head battered to shreds. The floor is of hardened earth. The gigantic pillars are formed of massive, wedge-shaped slices of wood, bound together with iron bands. The ceilings and walls are quite bereft of paint; the spiders spin their webs in unbecoming proximity to His Majesty's head.

At first sight, the proportions of this image are

very deceptive. Looking up at the middle finger, you would not be apt to guess its length at more than two feet, yet, upon measurement, it will prove to be five feet long ; but, after taking a few measurements, the tremendous proportions gradually dawn upon you.

This, then, is the materialized conception of Buddha in Nirvana. The dreamy reveries of the persecuted Brahmin have thus found ponderous shape in this remote corner of the world. Under the blistering and enervating heat of India, what strange visions were evolved from the brain of that mysterious individual whose dreams of Nirvana have shaped the religious natures of millions of human beings for over two thousand years!

Leaving the drowsy atmosphere of the temple, we sauntered over the grounds of the monastery. A covered way leads to a grove on the hillside. Climbing a long flight of broad stone steps, we came to an old belfry containing a large bell. The bell, according to my pamphlet, was cast 628 A.D., having been made at the special request of *Shimo-Tenno*. Its dimensions and composition are given as follows:

Height, 13½ feet.
Diameter at mouth, 9½ feet.
Thickness of metal, 10⅜ inches.
Amount of copper, 26 tons and 600 lbs.
   "   " tin, 1 ton and 500 lbs.
Total weight, 55,100 lbs.

In the vicinity of this belfry are several booths
for the sale of trinkets, charms, and mementoes.
Old pieces of bone, horn, and ivory, have been
carved into tooth-picks, combs, hair-pins, etc., for the
devotees and visitors to purchase. You will also
see some old swords and spears, said to have been
used by the retainers of Hidèyoshi in the invasion
of Corea three hundred years ago. Returning
from their victories and conquests, they hung up
their weapons here to show their gratitude for the
successful issue of the enterprise—much in the
same way, I imagine, as the shipwrecked Roman
sailors hung up in the temples their dripping garments to testify their appreciation of Neptune's
merciful assistance. And, as the dampened tunics
have long since been taken down from the moldy
walls, so these ancient blades are rapidly disappearing before the impetuous advance of our mercenary
curio hunters.

The masses of the Japanese are very religious,
or superstitious, as some choose to term it. Buddhism gained a hold on the popular heart that
Shintoism and Confucianism failed to gain. Not
satisfied with erecting this immense image, they
constructed another one, almost as large, at Kamakura, near Yokohama. It is in a lovely glade on
the Pacific coast. It was cast about six hundred
years ago by order of the Shoguns, whose capital at
that time was Kamakura. The height of this image
is forty-four feet. The physical proportions, however, are much smaller than those of the one here

in Nara. Its head is bent forward a trifle more, and its hands are folded. In other respects it is an exact copy. The temple that formerly sheltered it was carried away by an earthquake wave. Five successive tidal billows came rolling in from the Pacific. As the last surge, black with people and the *débris* of the city, rushed down the valley, it carried the temple out to sea. So he sits there in the open air, his head looming above the pine-trees, and his face turned toward the peaceful waters of the ocean—typical of the dreamless Nirvana. The bronze is assuming a dull green color, being affected by the corrosive influence of the moist winds that come from the Pacific. There is a staircase inside of the image. A large window in the back floods the cavernous vitals with light, showing the names of scores of ambitious foreigners scrawled in all conceivable places.

Late in the afternoon we began to think of returning to Kioto. We had rambled over the grounds and had inspected every nook. The monastery showed decided marks of neglect. The leaves covered the avenues and the green-swards, and the lichens and the moss seemed to take melancholy satisfaction in creeping into all the crevices of the old shrines.

What somber reflections such scenes excite! Here in the belfry hangs the bell that sent its solemn tones through the glades and groves, calling the monks to chant their matins and vespers, while

Europe was yet in mediæval gloom. The Algon-
quins battled with the Iroquois beside the waters of
the Hudson while these mellow tones trembled
through the upland woods, summoning the votaries
to chant their monotonous rhythms before the grim
monster presiding within the sanctuary below. One
can almost fancy he sees the phantom-like procession of yellow-robed priests sweeping through yonder gateway, across the court-yard, up the steps, and
into the evening shades of the gloomy building.
They prostrate themselves before the sable god,
dimly perceptible through the dusky shadows and
the smoke of the burning incense. The huge drum
shakes the place with its bellowings, while the bell
rends the air with its throbbing notes—drowning
the murmurs of the assembled throng. The priests
now increase the volume of their chants, their
notes are pitched on a higher key, and their rapid
hummings fill the immense room with a tempest of
prayer. The immense brazen gongs strike up, the
drum shakes the place with its stupendous din, the
bell sends one continued wave of clangor rolling
up among the dusky pines and down over the town
nestled among the foot-hills—and the people then
know that the dread god is being propitiated.

As the chants increase in rapidity, the long procession marches and counter-marches, prostrates itself, kneels and rises with bewildering celerity. In
the faint twilight a weak imagination could almost
fancy the placid features of the image to relax into a
smile in contemplation, forsooth, of such pageantry.

The din now gradually dies away, the drum and the bell are silent, the torrent of supplication subsides, the tapers are extinguished, the smoking incense on the altar expends its fumes, and the procession files out in solemn order through the shadows of the portals. Unbroken silence again settles upon the place, and the people slumber peacefully, knowing that his majesty has been pacified for the night; while the belated peasant, hurrying through the somber avenues, as he sees the shadows of the gloomy pines cast upon the crimson walls of the sanctuary, hastens his steps lest his untimely intrusion arouse the latent ire of unseen powers.

When the morning mists float slowly away from the rice-fields, the long line again marches across the court-yard and through the portals; the same pageantry, din, and turmoil again rouse the echoes of the place, and the drowsy townfolk then know that the morning prayers are being offered up, and they feel safe, for how can so fine an idol turn a deaf ear to such pompous supplications?

And so, for more than twelve hundred years, this perpetual round of devotion has continued. While empires have fallen, while arts, sciences, and civilization were passing through troubled periods toward a noble maturity, the rhythm of these chants— equally unintelligible to the people and to the majority of the priests—has been supposed to propitiate the dread influences of mysterious elements. Ambitionless, spiritless, debasing, the teachings of Buddhism have given slip to the centuries, doing

but little to elevate humanity; and now the light
dawning from the east has startled the votaries at
their shrines, and has roused them from their leth-
argy. And the decayed leaves tangled amid the
unkempt grass by the gales of autumn—silent witnesses of the neglect settling upon the place—suggest the decadence of the most ingenious religion
ever invented by the human mind; and whether
our brain-proud philosophers are willing to admit
the fact or not, yet the conclusion seems clear, that
the tenets of Buddhism have been found insufficient
to raise mankind to that high plane of morality and
religious development to which the divine teachings
revealed through the Redeemer have been able to
raise the nations of Europe and America.

Riding home in the night, chasing the village
lights for hour after hour, I could not resist the
dreamy influence of the sweet tones of the monastery bells that trembled across the rice-fields at
regular intervals. Such melancholy melody! How
solemn and subdued were their suggestions! Life,
they seemed to say, is undesirable; existence is
but a curse. Let us crush all our desires, all our
passions, and all our impulses, until we have eliminated them. Then our being will be merged in
the Infinite. We shall cease to have independent
existence. We shall be Nirvana—annihilated!

Yours truly,
Theophilus Pratt.

LETTER XVI.

FUJIYAMA.

Kioto, *September* 27, 1877.

DEAR JULIUS MARCELLUS:

In looking over my journal the other day, I
came across the account of my trip up Fujiyama
two years ago. As subjects for letters are now
becoming rather scarce, I will send you a written-
up account of it. Almost everybody writing about
Japan has something to say about Fujiyama.
This naturally makes the subject somewhat stale,
nevertheless it is one that will stand much elabo-
ration.

Fujiyama is the center-piece of Japanese scenery.
It is the first point of land that the approaching
traveler sights as he comes bounding over the
waves a hundred miles away. We spied its dim
outlines at daybreak rising specter-like against the
rosy tints that suffused the horizon. All day it
loomed up before us; its flattened crest and snow-
ribbed cone towering superbly above the massive
mountain ranges around its base. How the passengers admired its magnificent proportions! One
of them, an Englishman, had climbed the stupendous cone and had slept upon the summit.
How charmed we were with his description of

sunrise as seen from that summit, and of how the water froze there in midsummer! I then resolved to climb the mountain on the first favorable occasion. We gazed on its expanding outlines and changing phases with increasing admiration. When we passed between the headlands and steamed for hours up the bay, we found much else to take our notice; yet we frequently turned our eyes Fuji-ward to admire its lovely proportions. As we lay at anchor at Yokohama, the clouds, like long banners, trailed midway from its sides, and the radiant lines of sunset formed a background of striking beauty. The lover of nature never forgets this first view of Fujiyama. Lovely Fuji! Well art thou called the matchless one! What wonder that the artists of the thirteen provinces within sight of thy stately majesty make thee their inspiration?

In August, of 1875, I made my arrangements for climbing Fujiyama. My traveling companion, whom we will designate as Jack, was also a teacher in the government schools in Tokio. Naturally we made congenial companions. Our plan was to go to Kobè by steamer, and then to return overland to Tokio by way of Kioto, and Fujiyama. We were going to climb up from the sea-shore and descend on the opposite side toward the Hakonè range.

Taking the steamer at Yokohama, we reached Kobè in a day and a half. Then we went by train to Osaca, where we tarried a couple of days "doing"

18

the place, as the "Globe Trotters" express it. Then we took a flat-bottomed river-boat and were poled and towed up the Kamogawa to Kioto, where we tarried ten days "doing" the city. Leaving Kioto, we traveled in *jinrikshas* along the Tokaido for nearly three hundred miles until we reached a village on the sea-coast near the base of Fuji-yama. Jack had already gone on ahead to meet some friends at Hakonè, intending to return and meet me at the base of the mountain by the shore, but a violent typhoon was raging along the coast, so that I was detained here a couple of days.

On the morning of the third day the storm had passed away and left the atmosphere beautifully clear. Being hidden behind a promontory, we were as yet unable to see Fuji. We now found ourselves unable to continue our journey by the Tokaido, as the torrents pouring from the mountains had swollen several brooks that ran across our road to such an extent that they were quite impassable. We therefore took a fishing-boat and determined to round the promontory and reach the base of the mountain by sea. Shipping our *jinrikshas* and luggage, we (the boy, the coolies, and myself) jumped into the boat, while a dozen fishermen put their shoulders to the prow, and we were launched with a shout into the foaming surf that came thundering in from the Pacific. The skillful scullers soon had us out into steadier water beyond the danger of capsizing.

When we had rounded the promontory, Fuji in all his majesty stood before us. The air was so clear that it seemed as if we could see the very bowlders on the summit. There was nothing to distract the gaze, as the mountain stood quite alone, many miles from any range. It swept up directly from the shore. Nature was in her loveliest mood after the hurricane. The air was as clear as crystal, and the fields of waving grain and the woods and villages upon the majestic slopes of the mountain stood out as distinctly as possible. The morning sun bathed the rugged cone with purple tints of strange beauty.

With one glance you saw the general features of the landscape; directly before us lay the beach; then came a belt of rice-fields; then came villages, orchards, and wheat-fields stretching several miles up the gentle slopes; then came a girdle of woods winding around the mountain about midway up, forming a vast band nearly ten miles wide; finally came the cone of lava and cinders, forming a massive cap fully four miles wide. The distance from shore to summit was nearly thirty miles. The altitude of the mountain is nearly thirteen thousand feet; yet so clear was the air that the summit did not seem to be further off than two or three miles.

The waves of the ocean were of a glorious blue. The bold promontories toward the north and toward the south plowed the deep half-way to the horizon, making an immense semicircular bay that bathed the base of the mountain with perpetual

foam and spray.   Lovely Fuji!   What wonder that
the fisherman along the distant coast, as he sees thy
ghostly form spread against the evening skies, ad-
mires and adores thee?   What wonder that when
thy brow is black with clouds that sink midway to
the sea,—dread harbingers of the coming storm—
he fears thee?

After sculling along the shore for some distance,
we plunged through the surf, and shot high up on
the beach.   Crossing this, we found ourselves in
rice-fields flooded with the recent rains.   The coolies were frequently half-submerged.   When we had
floundered half-way across this uninteresting section of country, we spied Jack coming from the opposite direction.   His trowsers were slung over his
shoulders, and he was wading along like a stork.
Our meeting was cordial and informal.   We spent
the greater part of the morning in wading through
this flooded district.   We finally reached a village
upon the slopes, where we changed our clothes and
lunched.

In the afternoon we journeyed several miles
around the slopes in order to reach the path that
led to the summit.   This stretch of country between
the mountain and the ocean was indescribably
beautiful.   Villages, shrines, orchards, gardens, and
wheat-fields were spread over the gently undulating
slopes in great profusion, and were wildly picturesque and charming.   The circumference of the
base of Fuji on this line around the slopes is sixty
miles.   It takes three days to make the journey,

which is one of the loveliest imaginable, as the scenery is perpetually changing with each spur that you round.

Late in the afternoon we reached the path that led to the summit. We went up the slopes for a short distance and stopped for the night at a temple that frequently was utilized for the accommodation of travelers. It would be difficult to find a more enchanting locality. Beauty was on every hand,—whether you watched the blue waves speckled with sails, or the villages nestled amid the groves and gardens, or the mists chasing the waving billows in the wheat-fields on the slopes overhead. And then the sunset bathing the landscape, and the twilight tingeing the ravines and the woods with sable hues! How shall I describe all this?

At seven o'clock next morning we packed our few articles of luggage on the back of a mountain coolie, and, with our boy, started for the summit. We walked through ten miles of wheat-fields up a gradually ascending slope. The mists lay heavily along the mountain side, obscuring the view completely; but soon after we had started the air cleared, and the day became delightfully bright and pleasant. So clear was the atmosphere that it seemed as if we could have seen almost any object on the summit twenty miles distant, yet, at that very moment the cone was thronged with white-robed pilgrims quite invisible to us.

By eleven oclock we had reached the woods.

We followed the narrow path through them for six miles until we reached the barren cone. These woods are very dense. Were you to get lost in them you would have much difficulty in getting out again. A gentleman connected with a surveying party strayed into one of the ravines here and nearly perished of hunger before he could be found. The trees are pines, beeches, and bamboos, all tangled up with vines and impenetrable underbrush.

The ascent through the woods was so steep that we made frequent halts. The foliage completely obstructed our view during this portion of the journey. At the last resting-place on the verge of the woods we stopped for dinner, which consisted of boiled rice, sardines, crackers and tea. Here was a temple in honor of the gods that preside over the mountain. Precisely what the nature of these divinities may be is a matter of doubt to myself. Great phenomena in nature seem to be always connected in the human imagination with mysterious powers. Starting with this as a basis, the Shinto priests feel themselves justified in trading on the situation by selling sacred trinkets to the pilgrims, and in setting up a huge contribution box in a conspicuous place for the offerings of the devotees. Religion and the " hat " seem to be correlatives even here. As July and August are the only months during the year in which Fuji can be safely scaled, the season for these, priests is very short ; but, as many thousands improve this opportunity to climb up, their business must declare steady and encouraging dividends.

Up to this point in the ascent, people may be carried in *kagos*, or may ride on horseback; but from this point upward everybody must walk. Arming ourselves with long, filleted staffs, purchased from the priests, we continued our journey and reached the cone at about two o'clock. The scene was immediately changed—not a bit of verdure lay before us—nothing but lava, rocks, and cinders. The temperature now became rapidly cold, and we were cautioned not to lose our breath lest we should have difficulty in regaining it in such rarefied atmosphere.

The ascent now became incredibly steep. We took a zig-zag path up the cone, for it would have been impossible to have gone straight ahead without the assistance of ropes and ladders. Even then we found our faces almost touching the rocks in front of us as we climbed. We rested every five minutes or so, and it took four hours for us to scale this last stretch to the summit. How in the name of human endurance our coolie managed to carry sixty pounds of dead weight up this mountain is a matter of marvel. I presume it is merely a question of practice, but may Providence spare me from such practice!

From the edge of the woods to the summit, at intervals of half a mile, are eight resting-places. These are huts constructed of lava rocks, and roughly floored inside. When the terrible gales are sweeping the cone, it would be impossible for anything like a house to stand here. We rested at each hut, and made and drank some tea. We were informed that all the water on the cone was brought from the base of the mountain, as there were no springs or wells in this heap of cinders, and the snow in the ravines was inaccessible. This impressed us as rather strange.. The ravines did not seem so very difficult of access after all. I presume this was merely an excuse for selling the water and netting a handsome dividend.

But what created a far more lively impression upon us was the host of fleas in all the huts. They swarmed! Pilgrims from all parts of the empire, bringing every variety of species of these insolent parasites about their clothing, had produced a cross-breed that possessed an energy and vivacity in their method of assaulting the person that were incredibly effective, and which cast quite in the shade all the efforts of their constituent ancestors.

At five o'clock we reached the last hut just beneath the summit. Here we took supper. As yet we had experienced no difficulty with our breathing. Here we had to submit to a bitter attack from our unrelenting enemies, the fleas. While we ate they did likewise, and theirs was certainly the heartier meal. Jack raved like a pirate. He scalded himself with some hot tea, which he very naturally up-

set during a frantic effort to reach the middle of
his back before the enemy had left the scene. But
we were comforted by the assurance that there were
no fleas upon the summit, and that we would consequently have a refreshing night's rest. Up to
this last hut these vile tormentors do not find the
weather too severe for them to pursue their preda-
tory habits, but upon the summit they are compelled to succumb to the cold. Upon that spot
you stand in the only place in the empire where
fleas do not exist. But fifteen minutes' climbing
lifts you from torments to serene bliss.

Leaving the eighth resting place at a quarter to
six o'clock, we proceeded to climb the last stage of
the ascent, which required about fifteen minutes of
exceedingly steep and arduous work ; and at six
o'clock we stood upon the summit. But what a
summit it was! Totally different from our expec-
tations. Seen from a distance, the top of Fujiyama
seems to be perfectly flat. We had expected to
find a sort of plateau with a kind of depression in
the center caused by the crater. But we found
the summit to be a rugged country. It was three
miles in circumference, and was covered with lava
hills, one of which was two hundred feet high at
least. The crater was encircled by these hills, and
was about two miles in circumference. It was not
over two hundred feet deep and was entirely in-
active.

We found quite a village of huts built of lava
rocks. Hundreds of pilgrims were occupying them.

The proprietors of these *quasi* hotels bring everything up from the base of the mountain, and, from
a native stand-point, keep a pretty fair larder. As
a matter of course, everything is expensive. It
costs fifty cents to pass the night on the summit.
This is very fabulous indeed for people who can be
accommodated at any of the ordinary hotels within
the empire for only twelve cents per night including
supper and breakfast.

We found a corner of one of the huts unoccupied,
and at once appropriated it to our own use. While
the boy was preparing supper, we rambled over the
hills and bowlders, viewing the matchless scenery.
We found it necessary to wrap ourselves up warmly,
as it was exceedingly cold. A scum of ice was
already forming on the water in the pails. Although the atmosphere was very rare, yet we did
not experience any difficulty with our respiratory
organs. This was probably due to the fact that
our lungs were very sound.

The view from the summit of Fujiyama is magnificent beyond description. On one hand you
have the Pacific Ocean, and on the other hand you
have thirteen provinces of Nippon. You become
dizzy as you gaze down the steep sides of the cone,
over its sable girdle of woods, and upon the slopes
at its base. It is terribly precipitous. You feel as
if you could jump down upon the empire. Thousands of feet beneath you the clouds and the evening mists are beginning to gather around the
mountain side. They mass themselves in huge

billows against the woods until it seems as if the ocean itself had risen upon the mountain; now the upward currents of air strike the clouds from below and they are tossed upward in huge columns like smoke arising from some vast battle-field,—and your view is again unobstructed. You see the grand mountain ranges of Hakonè, colossal in themselves, lying like dwarfed hills beneath you, and stretching away until merged in the obscurity that veils the horizon. In their midst lies lovely Hakonè Lake like a mirror in the hills. As far as you can see, to the east and to the south, are mountain ranges diversified with sweet valleys and lovely lakes.

The setting sun tinges this landscape with somber hues, and the deepening shades of twilight stealthily sweep the entire scene from your view. Hundreds of pilgrims are now standing around in many groups, chanting prayers, clapping their hands, and bowing their heads in reverence of the magnificent scene. Perhaps you imagine that they are worshiping the setting sun. But they do not know themselves what they are adoring. The beauty and the solemnity of the occasion would of themselves naturally call forth spontaneous expressions of superstitious admiration from simple-minded peasants. Here was the monster that, but a few years before, had sent forth a mighty stream of fire and smoke thousands of feet into the air. It covered the country with stones and ashes for nearly a hundred miles around. It roared, and thundered, and quaked. The surrounding country was terribly shaken. Yeddo was thrown to the ground, and was burnt up; while over twenty thousand of its inhabitants were destroyed in the frightful disaster. Yet here lay the crater peaceful and harmless beside us! Where had the terrible and mysterious power gone? What wonder that the untutored minds of the people were smitten with reverential awe when in the presence of such surroundings? Here reposed serenely beneath their tread the crest that had beckoned the fleets of Perry and had guided the navies of the empire.

We picked our way back to the hut and effectually demolished the supper prepared for us by the boy. Hiring several comforters from the landlord, we burrowed beneath them and slept soundly enough. In the morning we rose to see sunrise. The scene differed totally from that of sunset. The billowy clouds lay banked from the base of the cone to the horizon in every direction, just as if the ocean had risen up during the night. We were several thousand feet above them in clear air. Suddenly the clouds parted about midway toward the eastern horizon and the rays of the glorious sun shot through into our upper atmosphere, suffusing the cone with a gauzy, tremulous light, exquisitely weird and fascinating. The clouds soon rolled away to the horizon and we had the heavenly panorama of the previous evening spread around us.

In this rare atmosphere, the rays of the sun are

very powerful. While we kept within the shade,
we were blue with cold; yet when we allowed the
sun to shine directly upon us, we could almost feel
its rays blistering our skin.

Breakfasting as well as we could with chattering
teeth, we proceeded to descend the cone on the
landward side toward Shubashiri, the town whence
almost all foreigners start to climb up. We made
the descent within four hours. We ran nearly all
the way down. We rushed down the cone at a
fearful rate, taking long jumps and landing knee-
deep in cinders and ashes. Jack, in one of his flying jumps went over a huge bowlder into a group
of pilgrims climbing upward. How in the world
he avoided killing or maiming some of them is a
mystery to me. Two of them were knocked down
outright. One of them picked himself up with a
grunt and went on his way. The other one took
to his heels in great terror at the strange apparition
of a heavily bearded head, a long body, and a pair
of mammoth boots, all clattering down the rocks
without any apparent intelligence to guide their
wild career. And he was in a fair way to beat the
record down to Shubashiri when the shouts and
laughter of his companions recalled him. Poor
fellow! He was as pale as death. He had never
seen a foreigner before, and such an abrupt introduction rather unsettled his nerves. He did not
show even a scratch, yet he had been thrown upon
his back while his heels had been kicked into the
air with such force that one of his sandals had been

hurled into a neighboring ravine! He said that the only thing that frightened him was the shaggy beard of the *Ejinsan*. He did not know what to make of it ; and as he was pressed for time for reflection, he acted upon the impulse of the moment and made for home.

The ascent of Fujiyama is by no means a dangerous or very difficult one. Provided sufficient time be taken, almost any one possessing average powers of endurance can scale it. Thousands of pilgrims climb up every year. Many of these are old men. Many of them are women. We saw an old woman on the summit, who was said to be eighty years of age. I have no reason to doubt that she was.

Lunching at Shubashiri, we pushed on to Hakonè in the afternoon, arriving there in the night. We stopped at a hotel on the border of the lake. Above the mountains encircling the opposite shore of the lake, rose the cone of Fuji, continually reminding me during my stay at this delightful summer resort, of one of the pleasantest trips I have ever made. Lovely Fuji! Farewell!

Yours truly,
THEOPHILUS PRATT.

LETTER XVII.

THE SATSUMA REBELLION.

KIOTO, *November* 1, 1877.

DEAR JULIUS MARCELLUS:

THE Satsuma Rebellion, which has been raging since the beginning of the year, is now ended. As the theater of war was limited to the Island of Kiushiu, we have seen nothing of it. Nor has it been an easy matter to collect reliable information, as the reticent government officials were the principal reporters of the military operations. For eight terrible months the Imperial troops have been struggling with the rebels, shut in by the mountains and hemmed in by the sea, while we foreigners have been left to gather information as best we could. However, by means of the Yokohama newspapers, and by conversation with those returning from the scene of hostilities, I have been able to follow the course of affairs pretty well.

This war was the dying struggle of Feudalism with Imperialism. It was a contest quite as momentous to the destiny of the Japanese Empire as was, to us, our rebellion of 1861. The Imperial Government had long been expecting the outbreak, therefore they were to a certain extent prepared for it. Yet, as with us in our war, they did not anticipate so fearful a conflict.

The soul of the rebellion was the elder Saigo. The Satsuma clan, of which he was a member, were the rebels. Saigo was the ideal of feudal chivalry. He was admired and feared, not only by his own clan, but by all Japanese. All that was brave, shrewd, and magnanimous, was attributed to him. He was the ideal *samurai*,—typical of all that was noble and grand in Japanese estimation. He was considered the ablest soldier in the empire. During the war of the restoration, nine years ago, he led the Imperial forces against the Shogun, and vanquished him. As that war is but a prelude to the present conflict, I will briefly outline it here.

At the commencement of that struggle, the emperor was in the Gosho (Imperial castle in Kioto) under the surveillance of Tokugawa, who yet controlled the Imperial person. He filled the castle of Kioto with his retainers. Prestige rested on his banners. He was the authorized ruler of the empire. Those who disobeyed his orders were rebels and traitors. But his authority, while not yet openly defied, was barely tolerated by Satsuma, Tosa, and Choshiu. These mutinous and powerful clans were gathering their warriors around the Gosho ostensibly to present certain petitions to the emperor, but with the secret intention of wresting the Imperial person from the Shogun's grasp and making him the actual sovereign of the realm. Until they could accomplish this adroit diplomatic stroke their status was that of rebels and traitors; but with the Imperial person in their possession, they could obtain a revocation of the Shogun's authority to rule the empire, and could strip him of all his emoluments and power. Satsuma and his allies would then be the enforcers of the Imperial decrees; while the Shogun and his allies would be rebels and traitors if they disobeyed the Imperial mandates.

For months the hostile clans were busily occupied in collecting their forces around Kioto. Aidzu and Tokugawa gathered theirs from the north; and Tosa, Choshiu, and Satsuma hurried theirs up from the southwest. As yet there were no open hostilities, but the hostile retainers glared savagely at each other in the streets. It needed but a spark to kindle the flames of civil war. Saigo and Kirino were on hand fuming for a favorable opportunity to commence the strife, and the opportunity soon came. Kirino precipitated the conflict by expelling the Shogun's forces from the vicinity of the Gosho, and securing the "legal grip" of the emperor's person. After a series of desperate encounters, the Imperialists drove the Shogun's forces south of Fusimè toward Osaca. Here they rallied and were led back to Fusimè, with heavy reinforcements, where they were met by Saigo's forces in the rice-fields. It is said that on this occasion Saigo, by superior strategy, defeated thirty thousand troops with only seven thousand men. The larger body of soldiers found it almost impossible to deploy

19

in the slushy fields.   Saigo therefore enveloped the heads of the long columns with nimble skirmishers that speedily dissolved the huge and unwieldy masses into a routed rabble.

The Shogun fled in wild disorder to Kobè, where he embarked for Yeddo on an American steamer, and, retiring to his castle at Shidzuoka, he took no further part in the contest.   But his followers kept up the fight for a year.   They were driven slowly northward into Yesso, where they were finally vanquished.   The Province of Aidzu was terribly punished for its obstinate resistance.   Sword and flame followed that hardy clan into its mountain home in the north, and reaped a fearful harvest among the peaceful villages and hamlets of that grandly mountainous Daimiate.

At the close of hostilities, Saigo, instead of indulging in promiscuous proscription of the hostile leaders, magnanimously pardoned them.   This act endeared him greatly to the people, and made him the most popular man in the empire.

Satsuma now became the Imperial pet.   Favors without number were showered upon that warlike clan.   Saigo was made generalissimo of the Imperial forces.   The highest offices in the realm were filled by Satsuma men.   It seemed as if too much could not be done for this clan.   Its slightest frown would apparently fill the Imperial bosom with great solicitude, and the will of Saigo became law.   His family was exalted; his friends commanded the finest appointments at the emperor's disposal; the army, the navy, and the civil service were filled with Satsuma men.

At the same time it must be conceded that the Satsuma men were exceedingly brave and capable. Years of independence had developed in them executive abilities not attained by less favored clans that had been subjected to the immediate control of the hectoring Shogun. The Satsuma *samurai* were certainly clever, daring, and hospitable. At the outbreak of hostilities, Satsuma was generally conceded to be more than a match for any clan in the empire. And, by the close of the war, the ardent members of that clan began to consider themselves a match for the empire itself.

The bestowal of so much honor upon Satsuma naturally excited the jealousy of other clans by no means deficient in able men. As the government became firmer, this monopoly of Satsuma began to be abridged, and men from other clans were also favored with honors. And it soon became apparent that the power of Satsuma had ceased to be omnipotent. Although the members of that warlike clan did not exactly relish this state of affairs, yet they possessed too much good sense to take as yet any serious offense at the way the tide was turning. When the government, in 1870, abolished feudalism, and dispossessed the Daimios of their Daimiates, Satsuma obediently fell into line and supported the new *régime.* During the rebellions in Saga and in Choshiu, the allegiance of Satsuma remained unshaken.

But at last the conservative spirits of Satsuma became discontented. They stood aghast at the rapid strides civilization was making. They saw feudalism and old Japan drifting hopelessly out of sight. Truly the old days were never to return! The privileges of the *samurai* were being curtailed. Centralization had set toward the Tokio Government, and in a few years the glory of Satsuma would be merged in the empire,—its resplendent individuality would be a matter of history. Deep and ominous mutterings were heard. For two years before the actual commencement of hostilities, it was evident that a tremendous conflict was brewing between the conservative and the liberal elements in Japan. Nevertheless the government steadily pursued its policy of introducing whatever it found worth imitating in the customs of foreign countries into the political and social fabric of the new Japan.

At last the great Saigo grew sullen. He withdrew from Tokio and went to Kagoshima, the capital of Satsuma. To a great extent this province was quite independent of the government in the management of its internal affairs. Thither flocked the dissatisfied Satsuma men. The locality was eminently adapted as a place for brewing sedition, as it was perfectly free from government surveillance, and by the beginning of this year Saigo and Satsuma were in full revolt.

It was fortunate for the government that all the leading men of Satsuma did not go into revolt. It was a noticeable fact that those who had been

abroad and had obtained liberal ideas were loyal to
the emperor. The younger Saigo remained stead-
fast in his allegiance. So did Okubo, the Minister
of War. But, above all, the navy, filled with Satsuma men, and commanded by a Satsuma man, remained faithful. Had the fleet not prevented the
rebels from reaching the mainland, the issue of the
conflict would have indeed been doubtful. Had
Saigo been able to hurl twenty-five thousand men
upon Kioto or Tokio, it would have been a black
day for the government. With the navy at his disposal, the empire would have been at his mercy.

Great was the terror throughout the empire when
it became known that Satsuma and the great Saigo
had rebelled against the government. The very
name of Saigo was a tower of strength to the cause
that he advocated. His personal magnetism and
popularity were unbounded. The government
feared Satsuma less than they did that one man. I
was in Tokio at the outbreak of the war, and can
well remember the fear that pervaded all classes.
Many feared that Saigo would appear in Tokio in
a few days, leading on his fierce followers to plunder
and proscription. The emperor and his court
hastily went to Kioto, and awaited there the issue
of the conflict. The wildest stories were afloat. It
was reported that the frogs on the western shore of
some pond had been engaged in warfare with the
frogs on the eastern shore of the pond, and had
vanquished them after a long struggle. "Ah!"
said the superstitious ones, "the sword-hilt is in the

West and the chrysanthemum is in the East." Some one said that the *heimin*, or common people, composing a large part of the Imperial forces, would never be able to face the *samurai* of Satsuma,— that one *samurai* would put five *heimin* to flight; and as the troops marched through Tokio on their way south they were the recipients of pitying comments signifying that they were but so much meat for Saigo's swords.

It was now time for the men of Aidzu to have their revenge on Satsuma. They eagerly volunteered their services and flocked to the deathgrapple with their ancient enemies. Many wild young *samurai* of other clans also enlisted from mere love of fighting, and many others went in on principles of general hatred for Satsuma. These fierce warriors, trained from boyhood to the expert use of the formidable double-handed swords, were valuable auxiliaries to the government in the mountains and ravines of Kiushiu, where hand-to-hand conflicts were fierce and frequent.

Early in January Saigo took the initiative. Despairing of winning over the navy, he marched his troops northward into the Province of Higo. I presume that his precise plans will never be known. Some say that his object was to conquer the Island of Kiushiu and proclaim it an independent republic; others said that he intended to march rapidly to the Shimonosèki Straits and cross over to the mainland before the fleet could intercept him; once on the mainland, and his prospects were flat-

tering of raising the entire country in revolt and of
working his way to Kioto and Tokio with ranks
ever swelling with malcontents; while others said
that he was short in his supply of arms and ammunition and desired to equip his forces at the maga-
zines in Kumamoto Castle in the northern part of
Higo, about seventy miles north of Kagoshima.

I think the last theory is not improbable. And
it is quite likely that after overrunning Kiushiu
they would have declared an independent form of
government of some description, with Saigo at its
head. Could they but capture the castle with
a bold dash they would start with grand prestige,
and would also have a stronghold in a wild and
mountainous country from which to operate upon
any part of Kiushiu. The troops were consequently
hurried forward with great speed. Although it
was midwinter, yet the roads of that country were
entirely free from snow. The winters of southern
Japan are lovely beyond description.

Satsuma was reputed to be able to muster sixty
thousand warriors; Saigo's forces, however, did
not exceed twenty thousand men, so far as I can
ascertain. Kumamoto Castle was garrisoned by
about three thousand troops, and it was well supplied with military stores. Strategically considered, the point was of vast importance; for until
the place had been captured no army from Satsuma could get to Shimonosèki Straits, or operate
elsewhere upon the island with any degree of success. The Imperial Government was well aware

of this fact and had evidently well prepared the place for a violent attack.

Saigo's men were but partly armed with rifles. The most of them were equipped with the keen double-handed swords of feudal times, and with daggers and spears. It seemed to be their opinion that patrician *samurai* could rush into close quarters with the *heimin* and easily rout them—granting even that they were armed with rifles and bayonets. And it was reported that the astute Saigo ordered his soldiers not to kill the poor plebs in the government ranks, but rather to slash them well about the legs so as to disable them and render it necessary for each man thus wounded to be borne off the field by two able-bodied comrades—thus depriving the opposing ranks of three soldiers instead of one. This policy argued to the native mind a keen insight into the military qualities of the *heimin.*

There can be no doubt, however, that Saigo led up against Kumamoto from 15,000 to 20,000 as brave and desperate men as Japan could furnish, and, as for that matter, as formidable an array as any troops would care to face. Upon their banners was inscribed the suggestive motto, "*If we conquer, we are Imperialists ; but if we are vanquished, then are we rebels.*" In Japan, even, success constitutes the difference between patriots and traitors.

As everything depended upon celerity of action, Saigo hurled his forces fiercely upon Kumamoto.

The town and the suburbs were speedily reduced to ashes, but the troops within the castle repelled all assaults with the most unexpected bravery, pugnacity, and skill. They fought magnificently. In the first place, they were well protected by massive walls and towers from which they could use their deadly rifles with terrible effect upon the ranks beneath, and in the second place, they were officered by brave and skillful *samurai*, who filled them with courage and pugnacity by their example. Upon their stubborn resistance hung the issue of the war. In vain did Saigo clamor at the gates and hurl his legions against the walls. His slaughtered warriors filled the moats and ravines to no purpose. It must have been with boundless chagrin that he found himself compelled to settle down to a long siege of this impregnable place. His only hope was either to take the garrison by surprise, or to starve them out. On several occasions his soldiers endeavored to scale the ramparts at night, when the absence of daylight would render the rifles less deadly until close quarters had been reached, when they hoped to sweep away the hostile plebs with a few cuts with their blades. But every assault failed. The garrison was always on the *qui vive*, and it was found that swords and bayonets were not wanting skillful hands to ply them within the Imperial ranks when it came to a question of close quarters.

On one occasion, two hundred of the most desperate of Saigo's men pledged themselves to either make a lodgment within the castle or to perish in the attempt. They chose a dark and stormy night for the desperate venture. Stripping off their clothes, and taking their swords in their hands, they crept through the gloom toward the fatal moat. None of them ever came back ; and, next morning, the Imperial banners, floating defiantly above the turrets, seemed to invite other bands of fanatics to enter the slaughter pen and be butchered with rifle, revolver, bayonet, and sword.

Every day spent in besieging the castle lessened Saigo's chances of success in his enterprise. The government forces were being hurried from all parts of the empire, and were rapidly closing in around Kumamoto.

Saigo found that he would soon be environed by the Imperial troops. He decided to turn upon them and rout them before they had quite hemmed him in. Leaving a small force to watch the castle, he marched to the northward to meet the advancing forces. He came in collision with them among some mountains and rice-fields. A series of terrible conflicts ensued. The Imperial troops found great difficulty in deploying in the soft mud and narrow ravines. Before they had forced their way through this section of the country they had suffered heavy losses. They were constantly exposed to the attacks of nimble bands of *samurai* springing from every spot suitable for ambush. Hurling themselves madly against the troops, they often created sad havoc with their swords among the disordered crowds weakened by toilsome marching through a broken country. It is said that in the earlier encounters the Imperial troops were badly decimated by these sudden onslaughts, and it is not to be wondered at, for these expert swordsmen can make a bad mess in a confused crowd.

When Sir Harry Parkes visited the emperor at Kioto several years ago, his twelve dragoons, armed with lances, sabres, and revolvers, were attacked by two fanatics who suddenly sprang upon them from an alley. So quick were they in their movements that nine of the men were disabled with frightful gashes in an incredibly short space of time. The fanatics would have escaped without a scratch had they not been cut down by a couple of Japanese accompanying the body-guard.

But while the Imperialists lost heavily, the rebels also suffered severely. They found that the *heimin* possessed much obstinate pugnacity, even if they did not possess the dashing bravery of the *samurai*. In addition to all this, the Imperial forces were being constantly reinforced, while Saigo found it almost impossible to raise recruits just as soon as it became manifest that he was playing a losing game. He soon found himself facing overwhelming numbers. After several weeks of hard fighting, the rebels were forced back upon their lines at Kumamoto. They found themselves in a state of siege. For many weeks they kept up the unequal contest from behind their breastworks and trenches. The Imperialists held them there at bay while they sent troops into their rear to cut off their supplies. And, to make matters yet more hopeless, Saigo now found his supply of ammunition nearly exhausted. His hopes of success were completely blasted, yet he determined to continue the struggle.

Finding himself nearly surrounded, he raised the siege of Kumamoto Castle, and betook himself with his remaining followers to the most mountainous and inaccessible parts of Kiushiu, and there kept up an annoying guerrilla warfare for many months. At last his indomitable energy seemed to weary of the useless contest. Every hope was extinguished. He resolved to lead his followers back to Kagoshima and die in a last desperate struggle at home. Breaking away from his pursuers, who had chased him from place to place with the greatest persistency, he passed rapidly into Satsuma, in the vicinity of Kagoshima, upon which he descended like an avalanche, driving out the few soldiers that the government had left there. The astonished Imperialists, however, speedily recovered from the bewilderment produced by this sudden onset, and speedily collected thirty thousand troops around the unhappy rebels.

Then came the closing scene. A friend of mine, who was in command of one of the steamers in the harbor, gave me a full account of it. "The Imperial forces," said he, "numbered fully thirty thousand men. The rebel army had dwindled down to six hundred men. They were intrenched upon a hill-side in the immediate vicinity of the town. At daybreak I was awaked by some heavy rifle firing, and was told that Saigo was being routed out of his den on the hill-side. Climbing the mast, I could see large detachments of government troops busily at work. With my glasses, I could see bodies of men (rebels I presume) scampering over the hill in all directions. They were evidently entirely without ammunition, and were being butchered mercilessly by the troops, who could shoot them down at a distance with rare impunity. Within an hour, everything was over. When things had quieted down, I went ashore with a Japanese officer to see what we could.

"Everything seemed quiet and orderly. The soldiers were demurely standing by their arms in line of battle. There were fully thirty thousand of them, all armed with rifles. They completely surrounded the hill upon which Saigo had been intrenched. In many places they had constructed bamboo fences around the hill—so much did they fear that this terrible Saigo would again break through and escape. But he and his chiefs all lay dead upon the hill. We passed through the lines, and went to where they were all laid out in a row. They had evidently committed suicide. Saigo had performed the *hara-kiri*. A friend had then cut off his head and was running away with it when intercepted. His body was a large and fine one. Upon the breast stood the gory head of its unfortunate possessor. We stood for quite a while watching the crowds of Imperial officers that came up. This man had been their commander-in-chief for many years, and the old feeling of respect and admiration for him was yet uppermost in their minds. As each one recognized the features of Saigo in the ghastly scene before him, he instinctively saluted the corpse by touching his cap. They conversed in subdued tones, and seemed to be sincerely sorry that it had been necessary to sacrifice so fine a man."

And so ended the Satsuma Rebellion. It cost the government upward of fifteen million dollars to quell it. To us this sum seems small enough, but it is a very heavy load for Japan, I can assure you. It was a cause of grim satisfaction to the rebels that they had at least inflicted heavy losses on their enemies. The government lost upward of fifteen thousand men in battle; which, considering that they had only about forty thousand men in the field, is a tremendous percentage. But the benefits resulting from the war will be substantial and far-reaching. The government can now exercise control over the internal affairs of Satsuma, and that spirited little province will cease to be a hot-bed of sedition. The Japanese Empire is now an established fact.

Yours truly,
THEOPHILUS PRATT.

RUINS OF THE CITADEL OF AIDZU CASTLE.
(*Native Photograph.*)

LETTER XVIII.

KIOTO, *November* 10, 1877.

DEAR JULIUS MARCELLUS:

ONE of the most enjoyable excursions in the vicinity of Kioto is the trip to the summit of Hiyeisan, a mountain of almost solid granitic formation, situated about eight miles north-east of the city and overlooking Lake Biwa from an altitude of nearly five thousand feet. It was the seat of one of the finest Buddhist monasteries in Japan. Its priesthood contained over five thousand members. They owned the entire mountain and much of the territory around its base. At one time they are said to have levied tribute from some of the adjoining provinces. In those days of their power they bade defiance from their rocky eyrie to the Shoguns themselves. But about three-hundred years ago they were totally vanquished by Nobunaga, the Shogun preceding Hidèyoshi. Since that time, repeated humiliations have crushed their towering ambition. Their monastery is now almost deserted: but its surroundings and its history are nevertheless exceedingly interesting. I will, in connection with a description of the monastery, take this occasion to give you a few observations upon Buddhism, derived from several years of careful observation and eager research.

Leaving my house after breakfast, accompanied by the boy, who carried our lunch in a basket, we walked through several miles of fields and gardens until we came to the hills at the base of the mountain. The intervening country was beautiful. As we rose above the foot-hills and surrounding mountains, we obtained a view of the Yamashiro Valley, that was lovely beyond description. Kioto, embowered in groves and gardens, lay far beneath us beside the glittering shoals of the Kamogawa. There lay the religious heart of the empire, surrounded by its temples and shrines. The road up the mountain was well shaded and plentifully supplied with delightful springs of water bubbling up from numerous granite basins.

The scenery from every point was superb. The slopes were deeply wooded and formed safe retreats for wild deer and boars; and the glorious pheasants, startled by our footsteps, whirred past us ever and anon.

Just before reaching the monastery, we had a view of Lake Biwa, that was surpassingly lovely. This lake is lovelier than Lake George; and it is nearly twice as large. The scenery around its shores is far grander. The lake, with its inclosing mountains, forms a huge basin constituting Omi Province. The blue water lies beneath us, bearing

on its bosom boats and steamers. Spread around
the shores are lovely green fields and villages. I
have seen grander scenery in Japan, but there is
none more beautiful than the glimpses of Lake
Biwa as seen through the trees from the sides of
Hiyeisan.

Turning a sharp bend in the road, we come in
view of the monastery in the forests of magnificent
cryptomeria among whose topmost branches the
roofs may be seen like dovecotes in the trees.
Although the mountain was an inexhaustible quarry
of granite, yet the builders of the temples never
used a bit of stone in their buildings. Everything
was made of wood. In the old days the monastery
had scores of huge temples all through these superb
groves up here within this lovely vale, and within
half an hour's climb of the summit, and shrines
innumerable were scattered along the roadside
away down to the foot-hills.

The monastery, in the days of its prosperity,
was indeed a magnificent institution. From it, as a
center, roads branched out into all the provinces
around the base of the mountain. The abbot
claimed the entire mountain and liberal slices of
adjoining territory. His shaven emissaries made
regular circuits of his little realm, collecting the
revenues and superintending matters generally.
He was a great power in the land, not only dictating
terms to the neighboring Daimios, but frequently
waging successful war against them. The abbot
had a very elastic title. The legends report that

20

an ancient monk requested from the authorities some land upon the mountain, whereon to build a shrine in honor of Shaka (Buddha). He desired as much land as his mat would cover. This apparently modest request was readily granted. Whereupon the mat, upon which the monk was sitting, began to spread out in every direction, by means of supernatural influences, until it had covered the entire mountain, thus securing by this pious fraud an immense piece of territory. Should this abstract of title fail to convince the incredulous, the legendary archives furnish another title, to the effect that the monk was decreed as much land as he could reach with his staff while he stood still. Whereupon the stick began to lengthen until it reached the foot-hills, thus including the mountain within its scope. Should either of these claims fail to convince, I doubt not but what the incredulous will find an inexhaustible supply of titles within the monastic archives from which to choose.

Centuries ago, when the monastery was founded, the mountain was wild and rugged enough. Pine, oak, beech, *kayaki* (the finest hard wood in Japan), maple, and bamboo trees covered the slopes and cliffs, while impenetrable underbrush filled the ravines. Monkeys filled the forests, and wild boars, deer, bears, and panthers rendered the place a grand hunting-ground for valorous Daimios from the adjoining provinces. It was truly a wild and magnificent country. But in the course of years the undergrowth was cleared away from the vicinity of the monastery,

and thousands of cryptomeria were planted there,
which in a few years embowered the whole vale and
plateau in their cool embrace. Roads were laid
out through the forests on all sides. They wound
around the spurs, zig zagged down the slopes, and
hugged the edges of the ravines, until they emerged
into the green fields. The waters of the delicious
springs that had erstwhile trickled through the
rocks into the brooks gushing from the mountain
side, were zealously captured and imprisoned for
awhile within the stone fountains by the roadside,
where the weary pilgrims could drink of them and
be refreshed. Eligible localities were selected for
booths, where the travelers could with a glance
take in the Eden-like beauties of Yamashiro, or the
sparkling glories of Omi clasped with emerald fields
and sunk thousands of feet within the rugged
mountains. From these eyries you can view with
solemn feelings the majesty of the parting day as
the shadows, lingering upon the mountain sides,
stealthily creep over the fields upon the blue waves
beneath, where scudding boats are flying homeward
on bended wings. Here the moonlight and the
zephyrs, sporting with the somber hues of night,
seem to tremble at the mellow notes of the matchless bells tolling in the belfries of the monastery.
Here the tired pilgrim can drink in the beauties of
nature, while his nerves, cooled by the delicious
water and the fragrant winds, are eminently suscep-
tible to the sublime influences and the grand inspirations of the surroundings. Three times have I

climbed Hiyeisan, and yet do not find myself tired of its scenery.

The fame and popularity of the monastery spread through the entire country. Thousands of pilgrims enriched its coffers with their contributions. Princes were votaries at its shrines, being desirous of propitiating the unseen powers of this world and those of the next—whatever they might be. New temples of vast proportions and elegant design were put up. Innumerable shrines for the propitiating of every conceivable influence in the Buddhist calendar were scattered everywhere, so that the throngs could take measures to ward off all imaginable ills that might be lying in ambush against them. The simple quarters of the primitive anchorites developed into luxurious and commodious establishments. The clothing of the monks became elegant, and the food became rich. *Saké* became a common beverage. The fatted fellows too often spent their evenings in drunken stupor instead of religious meditation. The strict vegetarian diet of their sect was discarded, and flesh, fish, and fowl were abundantly partaken of to the great scandal of the orthodox brethren, who abstained from eating anything that had been animated with the breath of life. In those bacchanalian times, you doubtless would have seen the bald-headed monks sallying forth to hunt the beasts upon the mountain with spears and arrows. Ah! those were indeed roaring times, Julius Marcellus.

Nor were these fatted monks satisfied with hav-

ing the monopoly of things spiritual, but they must
needs dabble in things temporal. After centuries
of uncurbed indulgence, their soaring pride and
vaunting arrogance induced them to dictate in matters relating to the State. Now, if there is any
point upon which the Japanese temporal authorities are sensitive it is upon the question of their
prerogatives. Touch them there, and they blaze
with fury. Dare to question their authority over
the people, and you excite the fiercest and bitterest
passions in their natures. The bellicose brethren
of Hiyeisan might have gone on for ages whacking
each other's shins, and fetching the gore from each
other's shining pates, until every nerve in their
bodies jumped with anguish, while practicing the
intricacies of the fencing art with heavy bamboo
foils—nay, more, they might have exercised acts of
summary justice within their own domains to a limited extent without being interfered with. But when
they began to meddle in the general politics of the
neighboring regions and to fling their formidable
semi-spiritual and semi-military organization into
the balance, then was reached a point of audacity
that could not be tolerated by the ruling powers.
A wild and horrible contest ensued. Terrible
battles were fought. The fierce monks were forced
back from point to point. They were slowly pushed
into the ravines and up the slopes of Hiyeisan, stub-
bornly contesting every vantage ground. Finally
they were shut within the walls of their monastery,
where they were well-nigh annihilated ; and the

magnificent monastery was razed to the ground.
All the superb temples with their gorgeous paraphernalia were swept out of existence. Desolation
marked the place for years.

After the assassination of the terrible Nobunaga,
those monks that had escaped the sword timidly
came back to their mountain home and began to
build again. In a few years the ancient glories
of the place began to revive; but the monastery
never again attained its former magnificence. The
buildings, though grand, were not as magnificent
as those of yore. The monks were never as numerous as in old times; nor did they develop the military traits that characterized them before their
fearful humiliation and decimation. The place,
however, soon became a great Buddhist monastery,
and a popular resort for pilgrims.

But the monastery of to-day is almost deserted.
Since the disestablishment of the Buddhist religion
as a state religion, the funds have been cut off; and
the revenues collected from the pilgrims during the
summer are insufficient to keep up the establishment. While many pilgrims may visit the shrines,
yet, being but poor peasants, but little money is
dropped into the coffers by them. The monastery
always depended for its chief support upon dona-
tions from the wealthy classes, who now have cast
aside their ancient creeds and stand forth as arrant
atheists. But even the present temples are worth
inspecting. Although not so exquisite as those of
Nikko, nor so majestic as those of Kioto, yet they

are splendid specimens of native architecture, and the grounds of the monastery are lovely even in their unkept condition. From many parts of the place you can peep through the trees upon the blue waters of Lake Biwa,—a scene in itself sufficient to repay you for the exertions of the journey ; and if you will go beyond the monastery and climb the summit behind it, you will obtain a splendid view of the surrounding country, extending as far as Osaca Bay on the south (which may be seen on a clear day), and as far as the mountains of Echizen on the north ; while to the east and west endless mountain ranges stretch toward the horizon.

The Buddhists are the champion monastery builders of the world. In the rugged mountains of Thibet, in Ceylon, in the islands south of Asia, in the vast provinces of China, and in Japan, you will find these stately and elaborate institutions wherever an exceptionally lovely locality is to be found. Many centuries ago have these nature-loving anchorites pre-empted all the choice spots. And it must be conceded that they have rendered great service to mankind by beautifying spots and localities that otherwise would have remained wild fastnesses, and by cultivating the æsthetic part of human nature, by holding Nature herself in her loveliest moods before its gaze. Who can doubt that the thousands of peasants, who have left the slime of their native fields and the miasmas of their filthy villages, and have visited these cool retreats in clean vesture for a few days during the sultry summer, go back to their drudgery with more cheerful minds and with a few fresh ideas about the lovely world beyond the borders of their wretched hamlets?

Love for nature is one of the characteristic ideas of Buddhism. Shaka himself was powerfully influenced by it. The son of a king, brought up amid luxury and refinement, possessing a sensitive and sympathetic nature, and gifted with a keen and philosophic mind rarely found in one of his rank, he is suddenly brought in repulsive contact with human misery. The reaction upon his nature was intense. It produced melancholy meditation and a violent distaste for the garish frivolities of the sensuous court in which he had been brought up. Meditation begat a thirst for further facts relating to the affairs of human life. He flies from the court and its hateful associations. He wanders about among men, and becomes familiar with the details of human life. With his mind well stored with accurate facts, and with his heart sickened with scenes of cruelty and misery, he left the society of men and fled to the solitudes of nature, hoping there to generalize upon the facts he had collected, and to evolve some supreme principle, some great and general law that should regulate human passions and cruelty, and thus lessen the terrible misery of mankind that he saw prevailing everywhere.

After years of profound thought, he evolved the grand idea that if men would be merciful to all liv-

ing creatures, then the suffering in this world would
be greatly reduced. Carrying out this idea into
practice, he formed a law to the effect that no creat-
ure animated with life should be killed. This, he
thought, would prevent homicide and the needless
slaying of dumb creatures. Evolving yet further
from his soulful meditations, he conceived the idea
that for man to live above the miseries of this life
and to obtain an exemption from miseries hereafter,
it was necessary for him to eliminate from his mind
all thoughts and desires whatsoever, to make his
mind a void and keep it in that condition until utter
mental abstraction had been attained. Then, in the
course of years, when the body died, the mind
would merge into nothingness,—the original condition of the universe, according to his ideas,—and
the human desires and passions, which were mere ac-
cidents of matter clogging the mind, would be annihilated. And the mind would also be annihilated,
for Nirvana means nothing else.

In accordance with this theory, he enunciated
the dogma that this utter mental abstraction could
be attained before death, and whoever attained
it thus during life, would become Nirvana at death.
But that if any one neglected to attain this mental
abstraction before death, then his desires and passions would still hold his mind captive and would
force it into new forms of existence; would pass
it through ceaseless existence for cycles of time
until it had again become endowed with the human
body, when it would have another chance for Nir-

vana; which, if it again neglected to attain, it would
again be whirled through the ceaseless miseries of
mundane existence. In other words, existence is a
curse. Cease to exist, become Nirvana, and you
will be freed from everything.

The first proposition was better adapted to the
people. Hence we find them respecting animals
and treating them considerately. Although, as a
matter of course, some of them were killed for
food, yet, the effect of centuries of teaching was,
to make the people of Burmah, China, and Japan,
to a large extent, vegetarians. This accounts for
the rice diet, perhaps. It has also made them mild
in disposition.

The second part of the proposition could not, of
course, be fully comprehended or practiced by the
masses of the people. It was a theory brooded
upon by the monks alone. And even among them
it was a rare thing to see a monk endeavoring to
attain Nirvana. It was a mysterious doctrine that
but few of them tried to put into practice. But
should any of them ever feel disposed to put the
theory into practice, there was always the dark room
reserved for him in some secluded part of the
monastery where he could immure himself. The
natural result of trying to banish earthly cares
from their thoughts, led the monks to seek retired
localities among the mountains congenial to such
an existence. This led to a romantic and beautiful
system of monastery life, which was probably copied
by the Romish Church and introduced into Europe.

The monastic life in Japan, during the days when Buddhism was the state religion, must have been charming and romantic. Embowered among the grand mountains of the empire, they were secluded from the world, and yet exercised great influence upon it. The faith was introduced from Corea and China fully fourteen centuries ago, possibly earlier. It found the people to be amiable barbarians well-disposed to supplement their vague pastoral religion (Shintoism) with something more substantial. Sites for temples and monasteries were speedily selected. And in a few years, or centuries, rather, a superb system of monasteries filled the empire with unsurpassed beauty. Magnificent groves environed them. Cooling streams bubbled through their spacious grounds. The deep shade and silence of their superb forests of cryptomeria, that clothed the mountains with stately grandeur, called up the pensive moods of millions of pilgrims during many centuries. All the surroundings of these grand institutions,—the icy streams pouring from moss-covered basins, the sweet shade, the bracing air, the melancholy solitude,—all brought man into communion with nature that could not fail to benefit him.

Here lived the monks for centuries, high up in the exhilarating atmosphere with their soul-stirring surroundings. Sworn to celibacy, their ranks were replenished with recruits from the seriously inclined members of the community, usually from the middle classes. Fugitives from the vengeance of political adversaries frequently found refuge with the brotherhood. Sometimes a man of property would endow them with all his possessions, and retire within their ranks to count the beads and chant the prayers. Sometimes those saddened by reverses and disappointed in their aspirations slipped away from home and friends to dream away the balance of their lives in the routine of religious duties. But by far the larger proportion of the brotherhood was composed of those who had no special ambition or aim in life, and who could be easily induced by the proselyting monks to enter the sacred walls and be assured of a life of comparative ease and comfort.

I am not aware that any of the monks ever attained Nirvana. I do not think they were much inclined to that sort of thing. I do not think the happy, volatile, and inquisitive temperament of the Japanese could ever have endured the weary years of stupid, deadening abstraction indulged in by Chinese and Hindoo devotees. They much preferred a life of quiet contentment, with plenty to eat and drink, and with no anxiety about worldly matters. Chanting the orisons at daylight, breakfast at about seven o'clock, light household duties during the morning hours, dinner at twelve, study, meditation, and recreation in the afternoon, chanting the vespers at sunset, and a long night for sleep, —there you have the whole business in a nut-shell. What an opportunity for moral and intellectual development! What might not have been accom-

plished during a thousand years in the way of
enlightening the world!

Yet nothing was accomplished. Aside from
beautifying and developing temple architecture,
from creating magnificent forests and avenues
around their retreats, and instilling into the people
a certain amount of reverential awe and love for
Nature, the monks did nothing for the intellectual or the moral development of Japan. They
made no inventions or discoveries in any of the
departments of science. They added nothing
of any special importance to the literature of
the empire. No agricultural improvements are
attributed to them. In no way were they connected with the political advancement of the
people. Ambitionless, spiritless, deadening, their
lives were just like their creed — a hopeless
endeavor to merge existence into oblivion and
Nirvana. Their lives were perfect blanks. The
vast majority did not live by the strict rules of
their sect. They evaded almost every requirement. They followed the inclination of their volatile natures. They indulged in the entire list of
vices. They were gamblers, libertines, drunkards,
and sodomites. Rarely would you find good and
pious men ; and these were unable to stem the tide
of corruption that prevailed in the monasteries.
Although not so warlike, the monks throughout
the empire were no better than those of Hiyeisan.
A life of utter idleness and sensuous ease, without
any elevating power in their religion sufficient to

master the bent of their passions and appetites, completely neutralized any elevating effect derivable from their lovely surroundings. What literature they did produce consisted of wild and improbable legends invented by their vivid imaginations and tacked on to the life of Shaka, or on to that of some canonized monk.

* There is absolutely nothing in Buddhism to elevate mankind as the religion of Christ has done. This conclusion, I think, is sound. It is the result of long observation. The teachings of Shaka are a wild dream, a weird speculation, a fantastic theory, an ingenious hypothesis of a sincere and noble soul blindly groping for some principle that

---

* In order that you may understand why the descriptive portion of this letter should here abruptly merge into an argument, it may be well to explain that the method of reasoning herein followed was one evolved from many hours of animated discussion with my scholars during several years of teaching. Some of my pupils were keen and intelligent young men who had become versed in all the skeptical arguments of the age against Christianity. It was always understood that I, while in no sense a sectarian, was a firm believer in the doctrines of Christ; and furthermore, that I was always ready to take up the gauntlet in defense of my beliefs whenever a scholar desired to discuss such subjects; provided, however, that the discussion was in legitimate connection with the lesson of the day and did not conflict with other duties. As a matter of course, the young men, arguing in English, did not always express themselves clearly or idiomatically; but, after comprehending their full meaning, I always reduced their arguments, as a matter of courtesy, to intelligible shape, prior to combating them. The majority of their arguments were weak and easily disposed of. Some of their attacks, however, as you will probably admit in reading the balance of this letter, were by no means easy to meet.

should explain the mysteries of life and death. It is claimed by some Boston philosopher that the fundamental principles of Buddhism and those of Christianity are the same; that both are identical in underlying truths; that both are human religions, and that the religion of Christ will not elevate the Asiatics any more than the religion of Shaka has done; that each religion is specially adapted by nature to those countries where it prevails. What a wild statement! No thinking and candid man who has lived for any number of years among Buddhists would ever say this. Nobody who knows anything about the practical workings of Buddhism from personal experience could ever have the audacity to make so false a statement. Your Boston philosopher has evidently derived all his ideas of Buddhism from books. It is impossible to account for his inaccurate conclusions in any other way; unless we assume that he harbors a bitter hatred against the religion of Christ, derived, as is sometimes unfortunately the case, from bitter associations during childhood. Let us argue this matter a little.

All institutions must be judged by their effects or results. As it has been expressed, "from their fruits shall ye know them." There is no other test that can be applied. And this test is a perfectly satisfactory one. Now, I lay down the reasonable proposition that the object of religion is to elevate the spiritual and moral nature of man. If it fails to accomplish this, then what is it good for? Is it merely to breed superstition among childish men and women? If that is all it can accomplish, it had better be abolished. Now let us apply this test to the religion of Christ and to that of Shaka.

Buddhism has been in the world about twenty-five hundred years. It has prevailed for two thousand years throughout all eastern Asia. The religion of Christ has been in the world only eighteen hundred years. It has prevailed throughout western Europe for less than thirteen centuries. Twenty-five centuries ago, Buddhism commenced to operate upon people who were the most refined and civilized in existence. They had a literature fully two thousand years old. They had cities and palaces of vast size and magnificence. Eighteen centuries ago England was inhabited by a race of tattooed savages living in caves and fens. Cities were unknown. Marshes and dense forests covered a group of cheerless and uninviting islands with mists and fogs dripping from above during the greater part of the year. The condition of Denmark, Germany, and France was but little better. There were no cities, no bridges, no literature. Forests and marshes covered the face of the country. Fierce savages rendered these regions more dangerous than the wild beasts. Paganism of the grossest and stupidest description prevailed. And Spain was not much better off. While Italy was peopled by a race of warriors whose fierce natures and sensuous appetites were violently hos-

tile to such curbing as the teachings of Christ inculcated.

Now what is the moral and spiritual development of Europe to-day as compared with that of
Asia? Is it not immeasurably superior? Nay, can
you compare the moral and spiritual condition of
Europe with that of Asia at all? I think not. It
is vain and foolish to attempt to argue that the
religion of Christ has not accomplished this wonderful change. It is silly and wicked to try to
confuse the Romish Church with Christianity, and
then urge that Christianity has retarded the development of science and of man's intellectual and
spiritual nature. The religion of Christ, those
principles enunciated by Him, never were antago-
nistic to the development of human knowledge.
But, on the contrary, by purifying man's moral
nature and delivering him from the cloying appetites of his animal being, these principles, when
conscientiously practiced, have always tended to
elevate his spiritual nature and to give tone and
strength to his intellectual powers that eminently
fitted him for scientific research and profound investigation. A consistent practicing of the principles of Christianity invariably tends to develop
man's bodily, mental, and spiritual nature. A consistent practicing of Buddhism deadens and dwarfs
the bodily, the mental, and the spiritual powers of
man in a most shocking manner. In direct proportion as races consistently follow the spirit of the
teachings of Christ, in the same ratio will they be-

21

come elevated in their triple natures. This seems to me to be a sound and logical conclusion based upon accurate facts.

Therefore I say that facts show that the religion of Christ, or Christianity used in my sense, has elevated those nations consistently practicing it infinitely above those nations consistently practicing Buddhism, or the religion of Shaka. It is, therefore, the better religion, even from this stand-point alone. If the fundamental principles of Buddhism were the same as those of Christianity, they would equally have elevated the moral and spiritual nature of man, would they not? Those principles had a keen, shrewd, and intelligent race to operate upon. The races of Europe possess no faculty of mind, soul, or body that the races of Asia are not also endowed with. The vast difference between the European nature and the Asiatic nature of to-day lies in the fact that the religion of Christ has demanded the development of a higher set of faculties and qualities than Buddhism has called for. A thousand years spent in developing these nobler elements of the soul has resulted in the evolution of a race whose social, political, and moral instincts are so infinitely superior to those of Asia that you would hardly believe the people of these two continents could have sprung from the same stock. The religion of Christ has shown itself to be able to elevate mankind infinitely more than Buddhism has done. This of itself would naturally lead even a casual observer to suspect that its fundamental principles must be not only superior to those of Buddhism but also vastly different. And so they are. Let us compare them.

Buddhism teaches that existence is undesirable; that our appetites and passions should all be crushed and eliminated; that we should strive to attain Nirvana, thus merging existence into annihilation; and that if we do not attain Nirvana, we will be compelled to endure ceaseless cycles of existence. In short, it teaches that existence is a curse, and thus degrades every human faculty by endeavoring to dwarf and crush them into nothingness. If everybody put such teachings into practice, mankind would be exterminated within a generation—for it is the privilege and the duty of every Buddhist to strive to attain Nirvana. The result of such doctrines is the stultifying and deadening of all human faculties, and the production of mild, ambitionless, degraded people.

Now, on the other hand, the religion of Christ teaches that God created man for a life of happiness in this world, and for a life of greater happiness in the world to come; that He endowed us with appetites and passions that were to be curbed and enjoyed; that the proper regulation and enjoyment of them are productive of physical, mental, and spiritual development; that Christ himself, the son of God, was our example in these matters, and had set forth principles and rules for our guidance in these matters; and that if we patterned our lives after His, all would be well.

Again: The religion of Christ teaches the doctrine of the atonement, and the doctrine of the repentance and remission of sins without any earthly mediator, but by direct communion with God. Shaka never taught any such doctrine, nor have any of the prominent expounders of his faith ever breathed or hinted at so sublime a remedy for human woes. The majesty, the power, and the indefinable beauty of this doctrine alone give Christianity a hold upon the affections and sympathies of a fallen race that the stony precepts of Shaka never approximated to even.

Again: The religion of Christ teaches that we shall see our Redeemer in the next life; that we shall know and be known of him; that we shall have a conscious, happy, and glorious existence throughout all eternity upon the performance of certain easy conditions in this life. Shaka taught that we should be annihilated. Whatever his disciples in succeeding centuries may have taught, there can be no doubt that Shaka himself inculcated the doctrine of annihilation,—Nirvana.

Again: The religion of Christ recognizes the worth, the merits, and the virtues of woman in a manner absolutely unknown to Buddhism. It reaches with its fostering care that half of the human race which Buddhists not only ignore but treat with contempt.

Again: The religion of Christ is perfect. It was given to us in a perfect condition. Nothing has been added to it in eighteen centuries. Nor have the culture and refinement of nearly two thousand years been able to suggest any improvement, to make any amendment, or to find any defect therein. It is perfect,—just as we received it from the hands of God, and just as we should expect God to present a code of morality to man. It leaves no doubt as to its origin. It emphatically and distinctly declares itself to be from God, the Father. This point is dwelt upon with great clearness, and is frequently repeated. Its teachings meet all human requirements. No emergency in life is too complicated for it. If consistently and intelligently practiced, it will produce perfect happiness in this life. On the other hand, the religion of Shaka was full of imperfections. It was fearfully vague and indefinite. Its cardinal doctrines were annihilation and transmigration. It had an exceedingly meager moral code. His followers have patched up its weak points in succeeding centuries. They have built upon it an imperfect system of morality. In a word, it shows every possible trace of its human origin. It never claimed to be of divine origin. His followers may have made this claim in its behalf, but there is no satisfactory evidence that Shaka himself ever made any such claim. It is exceedingly imperfect and lamentably feeble in all its details,—just like human productions of that description.

Again: Christ is a clearly defined and distinct historical character. His birth, life, teachings, and death are pictured with great minuteness and detail. Four historians record these facts without any material contradiction, and the testimony of a vast throng of witnesses is in evidence to corroborate the substantial accuracy of those histories. He was crucified and held up to the gaze of the world so conspicuously that none of his followers have ever attempted to question that fact, no matter how humiliating and galling might be the heathen taunt about a God hung between thieves. The existence and deeds of Christ are as thoroughly established as those of Julius Cæsar.

But, on the other hand, Shaka and his deeds are almost a myth. That he was the son of some Raj in northern Hindostan,—possibly near Benares or Sarnath,—seems tolerably well established ; that he taught the doctrines of annihilation and transmigration seems pretty clear ; and that he died in exile may, perhaps, be accepted as a fact. But beyond this, everything is a mystery. The best authorities cannot make more out of his history. The mass of legends woven around his life by centuries of succeeding devotees I rule out of evidence. It is most untrustworthy hearsay. If I were to apply the rules of evidence as strictly to the historic proof of the life and deeds of Shaka as I apply them to those of Christ, he would certainly be a mythical personage.

Again : But why waste any more time? I could easily write a book showing the world-wide difference between these two great religions. But it is useless to try and make any comparison be-

tween them at all. The fundamental principles
underlying them are as divergent as the east is from
the west. The religion of Christ is divine. That
of Shaka is a superb generalization of a human
soul groping for the light. It is the device of a
sympathetic nature striving to fathom the mysteries of human life. It is the most ingenious
theory ever propounded by mortal man. That is
all it is. True, the votaries at its shrines encom-
pass one-third of the population of the globe ;
but it is fatally weak and deficient to meet the
moral requirements of mankind for all that. Nor
will another batch of legendary amendments
patched on to the mass of stupid myths already
smothering Shaka's poor generalizations ever make
it equal to Christianity. Strip off the superin-
cumbent mass of devices that the Romish Church
attempted to tack upon Christianity, and you will
have the pure doctrines of the Gospels. But when
you strip off the monastic lore from Buddhism,
what have you ? Almost nothing.

Here we have in Japan an amiable and intelligent race of people, a people whose natural endow-
ments are unsurpassed. They have lived in one of
the loveliest climates in the world, with a bracing
and exhilarating atmosphere. They have been
surrounded by scenery of matchless beauty and
magnificence. And, for nearly fifteen centuries,
they have been under the influence of Buddhism.
Surely, if there be any great elevating power in
nature and in Buddhism, it should have raised the

Japanese people beyond their present level. Surely these thousands of monks, communing with nature in their sequestered retreats for so many centuries, ought to have evolved some theory whereby their fellow-men might have been elevated. But they have not done so. This seems to me to be conclusive that men, of themselves, unaided by divine revelation, cannot rise to so exalted a condition as they can when assisted by divine revelation. They at least have never shown the disposition to do so.

But your Boston philosopher triumphantly announces that because some of the principles of Christianity are found in the teachings of modern Buddhism and in Confucianism that, therefore, Christ was merely a human reformer enunciating principles of human nature; that there was nothing supernatural about it at all; that any human being can evolve these principles from his inner consciousness by concentrating his attention thereon; that because human beings in Asia have enunciated some of the identical principles contained in the Decalogue and in the Gospels, therefore there is no reason why *all* the principles of the Decalogue and of the Gospels might not have been evolved by human beings in coming ages without any supernatural aid or Divine Revelation; that Christ was merely a reformer enunciating general principles of human nature and of human conduct, which same principles undoubtedly could have been evolved in the future by other men—because it is in evi-

dence that some men did actually evolve or enunciate some of those principles entirely by themselves.

I think I have stated the philosopher's argument
in full. Now let me state my argument in favor
of the theory that Christianity is of divine origin.

Either the universe came by chance, or it was
the creation of some intelligent being. Now,
which is more probable, that this infinite system
of revolving worlds was the work of an intelligent
creator, or that it was merely a chance? Any one
who believes that the universe came by chance is
fit to believe anything. Of course, the universe
was created by some intelligent power. Now this
Creator formed man with strong appetites and passions, and with tremendous moral powers, which,
if unrestrained and unguided, would quickly have
wrecked him. Is it not reasonable to suppose that
he would have given him a moral code whereby he
might be guided and elevated? Certainly. Of
course, it is possible to conceive that a man might
sit down and evolve these moral principles of his
nature all by himself, just as a boy might evolve in
the course of years all by himself the rules of arithmetic. But it would be the work of a lifetime in
all probability. Of course, there is nothing intellectually impossible in this conception. But the
probabilities are that it would never be accomplished by any one alone; but put an arithmetic
into the boy's hand and he will master the science
very soon. Theoretically, he might evolve every-

thing for himself, but practically it would be a pure impossibility.

Just so with the principles of Christianity. They are all simple enough when once enunciated. There is nothing intellectually impossible in conceiving men to be able to evolve them unaided by divine revelation, but has any one ever done it? The united intellects of Japan, China, and India have only worked out a few of them in several thousand years, and they might in future cycles of time evolve the balance of them; but, in the meantime, mark the moral stagnation of the people. Is it reasonable to suppose that a kind and merciful Creator, after forming man with such tremendous moral powers, would have cast him adrift to work out the problems of life with only such principles as he could himself evolve? What progress do you suppose the world would have made?

I believe Christ was divine because I do not think it would have been possible for any single man to evolve a perfect system of moral ethics. I do not believe a single man could have evolved, within thirty-three years, a code of morality so perfect that the criticism of the keenest intellects during eighteen centuries has not been able to suggest a solitary amendment thereto. None of the sciences of to-day are the work of a single individual. They are the result of the combined thought of centuries. When a man has spent a lifetime in evolving a single new principle or law we designate his intellect as colossal. We admire

and almost adore him. His praises are sung from
generation to generation. Newton spent twenty
years in evolving a theory which a school-girl
can learn and glibly rattle off with abundant explanations within a few hours—to all appearances
thoroughly comprehending it. Euclid spent twenty
years in evolving the principle of a single proposition
which a school-girl can now master in an hour ; and
can eloquently enunciate it as well as the old philosopher himself, who deemed his labors worthy of
the sacrifice of a hecatomb of oxen.

We designate Euclid and Newton as colossal intellects, and so they were. And now do you
believe that the son of a Jewish carpenter, sprung
from an ancestry of tradesmen, with no educational advantages, could have evolved a system
of moral ethics so perfect in every detail that the
civilization of the nineteenth century can not find
a single flaw therein? If you believe this, then
you can believe anything. I, for my part, believe
that Christ was God incarnate. I believe that His
teachings were divine revelations. Upon no other
hypothesis can I account for their matchless purity
and perfection. I deem them to be divine revelations because such belief is consistent with my
ideas of an intelligent and merciful Creator, giving
to the helpless being that he has endowed with
such tremendous powers, a moral code suitable for
controlling his primitive nature ; and, further, as
this being attains to higher conditions of intellectual development and social refinement, such belief

is consistent with my ideas of a kind Creator supplementing that primitive code with a system of
moral ethics suitable to the complicated conditions
of mankind in all ages and among all races.   And I
know that my belief in these doctrines has been an
anchor to my soul in the troubled waters of this
heathen community, keeping me from forms of
vice that I would have yielded to had I consulted
merely my animal instincts.

Sincerely yours,

THEOPHILUS PRATT.

LETTER XIX.

KIOTO, *November* 25, 1877.

DEAR JULIUS MARCELLUS:

AFTER generalizing upon facts derived from four years' experience among the Japanese, I have arrived at a number of conclusions that will now be submitted for your perusal.

In the first place, I regard the Japanese as the most genteel smokers in the world. The use of tobacco, as indulged in by them, so far from being a filthy habit, is, in fact, an elegant accomplishment. It is a habit in which the women can indulge with perfect propriety. It is not characterized by the disgusting expectoration so common with us. In short, tobacco smoking, as indulged in by the Japanese, is in no sense a vice. We Saxons debase ourselves by our manner of using the weed. We are not satisfied with smoking it in huge masses, but we mumble over huge quids of it, and stuff vast quantities of it up our unoffending nostrils. Such barbarism in the use of tobacco is unheard of in Japan. The natives smoke but minute quantities of it at a time. A small pellet of it is put into a delicate pipe, and only a couple of whiffs are taken thereof. That description of Japanese smoking, which characterizes it as "two whiffs and a spit," is accurate so far as the whiffing is concerned, but is entirely inaccurate as regards the spitting.

After his night's slumbers, a Jap usually gives a tremendous yawn that serves as a rising bell for the household, and brings forth his little pipe, whisking off seven or eight whiffs in rapid succession, tapping the rim of the brazier between times by way of emphasis. During the day-time he will indulge in about twenty seasons of such relaxation—supplementing the original allowance, of course, with additional puffs whenever a call is received or given. The entire amount smoked during a day would not equal, if compressed, the bulk of an ordinary cigar, or the abysmal capacity of a meerschaum bowl. Nor is the strength of the tobacco the Japanese use to be compared to the pungency of the weed that we employ. Smoking, as thus gracefully and moderately indulged in, can never injure the health.

Another advantage of the Japanese system of smoking is the utter absence of any offensive odor lingering about the clothing. I can well remember how my chum at college,—a most inveterate smoker,—would scent up, not only the clothes upon my person, but also the very bedding in the room. And, for months afterward, the carpet and the tablecloth would be impregnated with a stale and rank smell that was intensely disagreeable. But I never fully realized the vile barbarism of our method of using tobacco until I rented a Japanese house in Tokio and kept " stag hall " therein with an Englishman, who was an inveterate smoker. He always affirmed that he never expectorated while smoking. Whether he was really unconscious of any such action on his part, or was merely perpetrating a grim joke, I can not say; but the condition of the *tatamis* around the spittoons, and of the *shojees* and well-polished verandas,—silent witnesses of his inaccurate marksmanship,—must have filled the inmost soul of our landlord with horror and disgust.

On one occasion, I inspected a native house in company with the landlord. It had been occupied by a German. We went through rooms that seemed to steadily become filthier as we progressed in our tour. The previous tenant had evidently dispensed with the use of spittoons entirely. Nicotine was spattered everywhere in indelible stains. The dining room, which had evidently been the scene of the principal orgies of the fiend and his boon companions, presented a scene that fetched a groan from the depths of the landlord's innermost parts, and fastened wrinkles of disgust around the corners of his mouth that lingered there as long as we were on the premises, and I know not how long thereafter. Verily, smoking is a social problem wherein the balance of criticism is decidedly in favor of the Japanese.

But, regarding the use of *sakè*, I cannot speak quite so favorably concerning them. Drunkenness

prevails throughout the empire in a mild form. I
use the term " mild," because it certainly is mild
when compared with the gross and bestial bacchanalian displays so common with Saxons. The
tame diet of the Japanese does not tend to produce violent appetites. During the year, you do
not often see a drunken person on the streets. On
public holidays, however, and particularly around
New Year's Day, it seems to be deemed everybody's privilege to get rollicking drunk. Lord and
vassal, *samurai* and *heimin*, master and servant, indulge in *saké* until all caste distinction is forgotten,
and bacchanalian good-fellowship characterizes all
proceedings. If the master has been kind during
the year, his servants gather about him and lift
him up in the air half a dozen times or so. This
elevation is supposed to be typical of their high
esteem. Some indulge in childish tricks upon each
other ; some reel around the streets hiccoughing
forth barbaric odes that harrow up civilized tym-
panums immeasurably ; while others assume a se-
date and profound expression of serene gravity,
which ultimately culminates in a " boozy " slumber.

Saké is strongly alcoholic in its composition ; and,
when heated, it flies quickly to the head. The
Japanese, however, drink it from such small cups
that it takes them some time to get tipsy off it. The
Japanese certainly are not such swillers at drinking as Saxons are. They would gaze with amaze-
ment upon some of our Germans, who swill down
daily their ten or twenty glasses of beer ; or upon

those Englishmen who use a bottle of brandy in a day; or upon those Irishmen who drain off whisky as if it were only so much water. Yet, in the course of a year, a vast amount of *sakè* is consumed in Japan. But, on the other hand, I am not aware that *delirium tremens* is known in the empire. It is certain that drunkenness does not create the same havoc in Japan that it does in Europe and America. The reason for this may be found in the fact that *sakè* is the only liquor in the country, and it is by no means pleasant to the taste. Habitual users of it have informed me that the only reason they use it is, not because they like the taste, but because they love its exhilarating effects.

Grape wine, or wine of any other description, has never been known in Japan. Beer, ale, porter, and brandy were never made. But when these various beverages are manufactured at prices that will place them at the disposal of the people, I fear the Japanese will be afflicted with intemperance to a greater extent than they now are. They love the taste of our sparkling wines, and are fascinated with their stimulating effects. And, without any moral power to check their appetites, it may be feared that they will speedily degenerate into a nation of topers. The temperance problem is one yet to be solved by the Japanese of the future.

* But let us now compare the Japanese race a

---

* One of the most common queries of my pupils was: "Master, why is it that your skin is white, while ours is brown? And why is it that there should be different races of men?" Not being able to

little more closely with the Caucasian race. After that, we will be in a better position to review some of their social characteristics. It is my belief that all mankind sprang from Adam and Eve, and that the present vast difference in races is to be attributed to difference in climate primarily and chiefly, and to difference in diet secondarily. I do not accept the proposition that the remote progenitors of the various races were various species of anthropomorphous apes, that had been evolved from the lower forms of animal and vegetable life preceding them in those various countries. Nor do I accept the proposition that the various complexions of the various races of the present time are to be attributed to the difference of the constituent elements entering into the composition of the vegetable and animal life in these various countries. Let us reason from the logic of facts a little.

If you expose yourself in the hot sun, you become tanned. If you expose yourself to the severe winds of winter, you become chapped. In either case your complexion is darkened. But if you stay in the house all the time, your complexion becomes lighter. These are three universal and well ascer-

---

furnish them with any satisfactory answer from such scientific works as I could obtain, I was forced upon a line of investigation and generalization based upon facts derived from traveling and reading, which resulted in the conclusions herein set forth. As the subject is one that is open to much speculation, and is one yet involved in doubt, I presume that I may modestly submit my own theories as evolved from class-room discussion, without kindling the wrath of professional scientists anchored to their own pet deductions.

tained facts. Generalizing therefrom, we say that extremes of temperature darken the complexion, heat making it black and cold making it reddish. Now, as the truth of a hypothesis is established by its coincidence with existing phenomena, let us compare the above theory with existing geographical data. In the torrid zone, you will find brown and black people, and in the frigid zones you will find reddish-brown people, while in the temperate zones you will find white people, and people whose color approximates to white. But let us go a little more into details. Follow the equator around the world, and you will find the blackest people living *upon it and in its immediate vicinity.* As you leave the equator and go northward or southward toward the temperate zones, you will find that complexions become proportionately lighter. The Egyptian is lighter than the Nubian; the inhabitants of Spain, Italy, and Greece are lighter than the Moor or the Arab; while the inhabitants of 'northern Europe and of the British Islands have decidedly lighter complexions than those of southern Europe. But when you go further northward and reach the land of the Esquimaux, you find the peculiar copper complexion produced by exposure to extreme cold.

In Asia, the same law holds true. The Arab, the Afghan, the Thibetan and the Chinese are much lighter in color than the Hindoo, the Singhalese, and the Malay; and, going farther north, we find the Tartars and the Japanese to be of lighter complexion than any of those people just enumerated.

Many of the Tartars and Japanese are almost as fair as the Saxons, some, indeed, having complexions quite as fair. And, going yet further northward, we find the aborigines of Siberia along the cheerless seas of the frigid zones to have a copper complexion.

The same general law holds true in the Western Hemisphere. The aborigines on the equator in South America are darker than the Red-skins of North America. The present population of America cannot be fairly cited to uphold my theory, because they have immigrated from Europe at a comparatively recent date. But the query may arise as to whether the ultimate complexion of the people living in the United States will be reddish-brown, like that of the North American Indian. To this query a negative answer may safely be given, for the Indians throughout the North American Continent were continually exposed to climatic changes. They were more like animals living in the open air than like human beings. Whatever the darkening tendency of exposure of the skin to heat and cold might have been, it certainly had a fair opportunity to operate upon these savages. But after a few centuries, I think that the complexion of the inhabitants of the Southern States will be found to be of a tawnier hue than that of their Northern brethren.

Coming to Japan, we find our hypothesis illustrated with startling exactness. The *heimin* who labor in the fields, and whose ancestors for many centuries have been thus exposed to the sun, are darker in complexion than the higher classes. The mercantile classes who for centuries have lived in cities, dwelling within the shade, are lighter in complexion than the peasants, who for centuries have labored almost naked in the rice-fields. The fishermen along the coasts are also of a darker complexion; and the *samurai*, who from remote times have taken their ease within the shade, are quite fair in complexion, some of them, indeed, being almost as white as Saxons. Some of the court ladies, in fact, are quite as white as the fairest Saxon.

So we have here in Japan a race like ourselves; a race sprung from the same progenitors, a race with precisely the same spiritual, intellectual, and physical qualities. We have developed a higher set of faculties, and consequently possess nobler natures. Our meat diet gives us a finer physical development. Milk, butter, and meat give strength and rotundity to the flesh and muscles, and a fresh and plump appearance to the face. An exclusive rice diet gives a sallow complexion. Milk, cheese, butter, beef, and mutton have never been used by the Japanese at all. There are no goats in the empire, and but few cows. Boiled rice, with the merest nibble of meat and salt radish, has formed the diet of the masses of the people for many centuries, and they are a feeble race to-day; while the Caucasians and the Tartars, who have lived on meat and milk from time immemorial, are to-day the most vigorous portion of humanity. I have no doubt that with several generations of our diet the Japanese will become in every way our peers physically. This, however, is a social problem that must be left for time to solve.

The Japanese are a very amative race. They are not licentious like the Turks, but are strongly inclined to be sensuous. Their low diet has, to a great extent, kept down the grosser passions of their nature. We now come face to face with that strange institution of the feudal Government of Japan known as the *Yoshiwara* system. This was a system of legalized prostitution. It was not only legalized but it was under government patronage. The government support of such an institution has been whimsically accounted for by Darwin in his *Descent of Man* on the hypothesis that the government feared that the Japan Islands would become eventually too full of people, and that they therefore took this method of keeping down the population. But the *Legacy of Iyeyas* says that it was done to restrain the passions of the *samurai* within proper limits, so that there need not be endless floggings to keep the hordes of warlike retainers in order. And this is probably the true explanation. Macaulay says that an Englishman and a Frenchman will reason to opposite conclusions frequently from the same fact. And it is not an uncommon thing in the realm of science for two minds to reason to opposite conclusions from the same premises. One of these conclusions, however, must be an exceptional one. Some minds are fond of reasoning to exceptional conclusions. It seems to me that Darwin's mind was of this order. He showed it in reasoning about the descent of man from anthropomorphous apes. Given the facts that the physical structure of animals bears a striking resemblance to that of man, and that man seems to be a later production, Darwin prefers the conclusion that man was evolved from lower animal forms during countless ages instead of the conclusion that these facts argue that all creatures were made upon the same general plan by the same Creator.

The *Yoshiwara* system was undoubtedly the production of feudal licentiousness. With three millions of fierce *samurai* to control, it was no wonder that the Tokugawas should have hit upon this low method of curbing the violent natures of their retainers. What better method had they? Neither Shintoism nor Buddhism furnished any adequate moral check upon the passions of the military classes. They therefore developed the *Yoshiwara* system all over the empire. And the Daimios of the provinces heartily indorsed the system and laid out "worm-eaten spots" in all their capitals and great cities. Much money was lavished upon these foul localities and they were made attractive hells. Vice was there made to appear in its most seductive forms. Luxury and refinement were impressed into the service of this wretched avocation. The misery of the human

soul was stifled and soothed by elegant surroundings, and a tolerant and condoning social sentiment made it reputable for persons of good families to take wives from the *Yoshiwara,* and for
mothers to sell their daughters to the proprietors
of the brothels.

The history of the *Yoshiwara* system is inter-
woven with tales of the wildest debauch, of the blackest despair, and of the most romantic and hopeless
love. The brave youth from the provinces, where
valor is yet a virtue, is smitten with the subtle influence and wrecks his fortune and his health upon
some coquetting courtesan who soon bestows upon
another victim the withering spell of her hellish
charms. And now the wanton and beautiful wretch
is herself ensnared. She, upon whose smiles the
bloods of the town fondly linger, becomes touched
with the fire that burns the heart ; and, realizing
the fearful position in which she has been placed,
immolates herself upon the shrine of hopeless love,
and tinges the scandal of the town with melancholy
tales of her blighted passion. In such a social
atmosphere was the young *samurai* brought up.
What wonder that they degenerated into a class of
reckless libertines ? The only marvel to me is that
there was any virtue at all left among the people.
That wonderful provision of Providence, known as
the Natural Religion, has truly kept this people
from degenerating into a race of voluptuous
imbeciles.

Coming now to the social condition of the

Japanese, I consider it safe to say that the relative position of the sexes is about the same as it is in all countries. I am old-fashioned enough to believe that God created mankind in accordance with certain general laws that can not be changed by us. It seems manifest to me that He made man to be the unit of political power, and woman to be the unit of social power. He has made man to be the aggressive, the progressive, the governing power in the world. He has made woman to be the conservative and refining power in the world. It is man's nature to be democratic and liberal. It is woman's nature to be fond of social distinctions, to be aristocratic. It is man's nature to compete and contend not only with his fellow-man, but also with Nature herself. Following this impulse, he has developed all the political institutions of the world, and has also covered the globe with cities, railroads, navies, and productive fields. But it is woman's nature to shrink from contest and to entwine her affections around those she loves with engrossing and tender devotion. She has filled the world with homes, with sweet and tender recollections, with elevated sentiment and religious impulses. She has been the friend, the companion, and the affectionate counselior of man in all ages and in all countries. This relative position of the sexes prevails all over the world. Wherever the condition of woman is degraded, there also is the condition of man correspondingly low. And wherever the condition of woman is elevated, there is the position of man correspondingly high. But their relative positions are always about the same. Man is always the progressive, the aggressive, the governing power; woman is as generally the conservative, the refining power. Mankind cannot change this relative position of the sexes. By the force of our natures we must act out our respective parts until some greater power shall otherwise ordain.

I hate and despise the tendency in England and America to antagonize the sexes. Those female agitators, who endeavor to make their sisters dissatisfied with their lot, and who proclaim that man is but a usurper who has violently seized upon the more desirable positions in life, and has forced woman into less desirable, and inferior positions, are but insulting the dignity of their own sex. That which God has ordained, call thou not inferior. Each position is highly honorable. Neither is inferior. Neither is superior. The world cannot afford to lose the gentle qualities of women, for there is nothing in the masculine nature that can replace those qualities.

While in Japan woman has always been the friend, and the companion of man, and has been the mother of the rising generations, man, on the other hand, has always been the governing power. He did not usurp anybody's right. He was delegated by the Creator to be the controlling force. He has founded the political institutions of the empire; he has built the cities and the navies of the realm; the bridges, the highways, the temples,

AT HOME.

are all the work of his hands. All the textile manufactures, the matchless embroideries, the lovely
lacquer ware, the exquisite porcelains, the magnificent bronzes, the intricate carvings, are his productions. The carpenters, the masons, the stone-cutters,
the blacksmiths, the artisans of every description,
have always been men. All the severe labor that
has reclaimed the land of this empire from waste
and desolation, and has made it into a vast and
lovely garden, was performed by men. And the
immense annual expenditure of toil and patience
that is now required to keep these millions of acres
under a state of cultivation, is furnished by men,
and bear in mind that all this is done without any
claim of superiority on the part of the men. The
Creator has designed them for this work, and by
the force of circumstances they naturally and cheer-
fully obey the hidden power that controls them
without ever thinking of sounding their own praises
for so doing.

Generally speaking, the Japanese men make kind
and affectionate husbands ; and the women make
virtuous and exemplary wives and mothers ; and
the children are certainly the happiest little imps
in the world ; their parents fondle and spoil them
most effectually, and, at the same time, never lose
their control over them. The non-irritating nature
of the native diet has much to do with such serene
nerves and temperaments. I have never seen a
child whipped in Japan ; on three or four occasions
I have seen a reproving mother administer a mild

slap over the head, which correction invariably brings the little recalcitrants to order.

The husband has absolute control over the person of his wife ; at the same time, I have never seen a man strike a woman in Japan, yet I believe that there is considerable pinching and slapping done on occasions when those strange and ungovernable spells of exasperating ugliness, known as tantrums, settle down upon their matrimonial horizon. On these occasions there is considerable free hitting, biting, and scratching indulged in on both sides of the house ; but the greater strength of the husband invariably leaves him master of the situation, and the belligerent household speedily resumes its serene and happy course. On such occasions, unless physical force were resorted to, it would be difficult to say where matters would end ; for the women are very childish, and, in their paroxysms of fury, might speedily demolish the household, unless restrained. These family jars are not of frequent occurrence, but they make up in intensity for their rarity.

It is far more common for women to quarrel with each other than for husbands and wives to quarrel. I was once passing down a village street when I heard a tremendous commotion. Two women, upon opposite sides of a street, were railing at each other at the rate of about sixty miles an hour. The atmosphere fairly glowed with vituperation. I arrived upon the scene just as they rushed at each other, spitting, scratching, and biting like a couple of furious cats. They were clawing each other in terrible earnest when the husband of one of the combatants rushed upon them and tore them apart, hurling one of them to one side of the street and the other one to the other side, where they respectively glared at each other awhile and then cooled down. In a few minutes they were quietly discussing the misunderstanding and were, to all appearances, upon amicable terms.

When I was living in Tokio I became acquainted with an occurrence that was shocking yet unavoidable. We were keeping house in Ban-cho. Our cook lived with his wife in a distant wing of the house. His lady persisted in bathing during the summer in our front yard. We instructed our cook that this scandalous proceeding must be stopped as we did not care to have our visitors confronted with any such spectacle. He accordingly ordered her to desist from using our garden as a bath-room. But, behold! next day found her again bathing in the shrubbery. We complained to the cook at once, and he said he would see that it did not happen again. We soon heard a fearful scream. The cook quietly came into our parlor holding in his hand a hoe handle, with which he had crept up behind his unsuspecting spouse and had inflicted a terrible blow upon her bare back. He said that he did not think we would be again annoyed by his wife, but that, if we were, to report immediately and he would make her " eat stick " without limit. We felt like making him " eat stick " for the balance of the day. But, upon sober thought, we came to the conclusion that nothing could be done except to forbid any further personal chastisement upon our premises. What can you possibly do with such people? They are mere children. Yet, while all this sounds very horrible, and we feel inclined to hold up our hands and denounce such barbarism, we should modestly bear in mind that we do not need to go back very far in English history to find that women were nearly drowned in ducking stools, and were flogged upon the bare back through the streets. Truly we live in a strange world! And the incongruities of the nineteenth century are the strangest part of it.

You may easily infer that the question of Woman Suffrage has not yet agitated Japan. This question cannot arise until the question of popular enfranchisment is up for discussion. At present, no one in Japan has the right of suffrage. The emperor and his cabinet rule with absolute power. In a few years, however, there will undoubtedly be some sort of Parliament or Congress convened. Then will there be limited suffrage in some shape or other, after which it may be safely presumed that universal male suffrage will gradually be adopted. Then will the people be in the interesting position to discuss female suffrage. I apprehend, however, that by that time the general disinclination and inaptitude of women for political life will be so clearly demonstrated in Europe and

America that the Japanese will be relieved from any violent commotion on this subject. But it will be interesting, nevertheless, to briefly review some of the pet arguments advanced in favor of Woman Suffrage in Europe and America, and to see how they will fit Japan. I am constrained to stir up this hornets' nest because of the fire-brand that you inconsiderately hurled at me last month, through the medium of the United States mail, in the shape of a pamphlet written by a rabid agitator of the opposite sex, whose bitter denunciations, aimed at the sex to which I have the misfortune to belong, placed me under a cloud of humility from which I am now but timidly emerging. You will therefore kindly make allowance for my demoralized condition, and you will excuse any heresy that may chance to crop out in my very humble opinions. One favorite argument in favor of Woman Suffrage is that there should be no taxation without representation. It is urged that women hold property, and pay taxes on property, and yet do not have any voice in making the laws of the country. There is a plausible revolutionary ring about this argument that is, at first, very catching. But a close inspection will reveal its fallacy and speciousness. It is quite true that women holding property are compelled to pay taxes thereon. And this is quite just and reasonable, because this property is protected both in times of peace and in times of war by the civil and military power of the State. This power of the State is based upon masculine force. By means of this masculine force, order is maintained, enemies are kept away, and the property becomes enriched and enhanced in value by the peaceful and beneficial influence of a civilized community. Such favorable conditions would not exist in turmoil and war. Masculine force is the power that keeps the peace. This service must be paid for by property, whether owned by man or woman. This general principle holds quite as fast in Japan as in other parts of the world

It should also be borne in mind that the number of women holding property is very small when compared with the number of men holding property. Men are, and have always been, the accumulators, the originators, the makers of property. It is a rare thing for women to accumulate or make property. Other and more important duties demand their attention. Almost all the female property holders in the world have been fortunate enough to inherit their wealth from male kindred, who, perhaps, have spent years of severe toil in accumulating it ; and they must take the property with its incumbrances as well as with its benefits. They are at full liberty to revel in its princely revenues, which they have done nothing to earn. But, on the other hand, they must also pay the annual tax that the Board of Assessors placed opposite to it when it was held by father, husband, brother, or uncle. It is the property that is taxed, not the individual. If the property comes to her incumbered with mortgages, tax-arrears, or other debts of her father, she must pay off these liabilities or the property will be auctioned off by the creditors. Property is taxed irrespective of the sex of the party holding the title deeds.

Now, if the vast mass of property in this world had been accumulated by women, there would be some justice in the claim that they should have a voice in legislation affecting it. But almost all the property in this world has been accumulated by men. They are the busy workers who have developed the resources of the earth. Women rarely accumulate property, as they were not designed to compete, to struggle, to concentrate all their thoughts and efforts on such things. They have neither the time nor the inclination for severe and laborious application in pursuit of wealth. Now men have made equitable laws regulating property in general. These laws are just and impartial, and do not unjustly discriminate against property held by women. Therefore I fail to see why universal suffrage should be granted to women because a few of their more fortunate sisters have inherited from their male kindred a certain amount of property, which, in the course of time, will probably revert by inheritance to some male kinsman, or will be gradually reabsorbed by male competitors in the vicissitudes of trade. Suffrage should be based upon some general law in nature, not upon exceptions. This observation will also be found to be applicable to Japan.

23

Furthermore, legislation is powerless and absurd without the ability to enforce its mandates. The power that enforces laws should be the power to make laws. Man is the power that enforces laws in this world. Therefore I fail to see why the basing of suffrage upon man as the unit of political power is not a correct general principle. To illustrate our theory, let us suppose that universal male and female suffrage prevails in the United States. Suppose that all the women vote to have a monarchical form of government, and that all the men vote to have a republican form of government. The women, although outnumbering the men, could not enforce their wish against the men through lack of power. But, on the other hand, if all the men were to vote in favor of a monarchical form of government, and all the women were to vote in favor of a republican form of government, the men could readily enforce their wish in the matter.

Men, as a matter of courtesy, may unite and agree to give women equal right of suffrage with themselves. But this would not increase the enforcing power of the state at all. Paper money has a purchasing power when it represents gold and silver. Let the bullion cease to exist, however, and where would be the purchasing power of your paper money? If you issue twice as many bills as there is specie in the country, you reduce their purchasing power by one-half. In precisely the same manner a paper ballot represents the po-

litical unit behind it. If the voice of the ballot-box
be disobeyed, you call out your police forces and
your armies and enforce its mandate. Man is the
power, the coercive force, in the state. Without
that implied coercive force, your laws become inef-
fective and ridiculous. Women may meet in legislative halls and pass resolutions and formulate decrees at pleasure, but it is man that they call upon
to destroy the trespassing rat that is carrying consternation into their ranks and disturbing the legislative equipoise of their deliberations.

To increase the number of ballots in the box will
not necessarily increase the coercive power in the
state. Men may grant the privilege of casting
these ballots to their mothers, sisters, wives, and
daughters, under the mistaken notion that they are
merely conferring a right. But, in reality, they are
sharing their birthright as a matter of courtesy
with their families without realizing that they are
disturbing the political equipoise of the land, and
are opening the door for dangerous and humiliating complications.

Another argument that has been advanced in
favor of Woman Suffrage is that woman will purify
the ballot-box. Inasmuch as there are nearly as
many bad women in the world as there are bad
men, and as woman does not appear to have
cleansed society from its many evils in the course
of several thousand years—the realm where they
reign supreme—it is quite incomprehensible to me
how they will do any better at purifying ballot-

boxes. For you can not discriminate in this matter and give the right of suffrage to the virtuous
women alone, but you must confer this right on all
women alike. And I can assure you that I would
prefer life in a pagan country to going up to the
ballot-box in company with a gang of drunken,
cursing women on election day. Bad men are
disagreeable enough on such occasions; but may
Providence spare us from bad women !

The fact is, that if woman had been designed to
exercise the right of suffrage she would have exercised it long before our day. And, if she has not
been designed to exercise the right of suffrage, all
the legislation in the world will not create in her
any inclination or aptitude for it either in Japan or
anywhere else. I have no patience with those
women who neglect and ignore those feminine
qualities without which the world would be badly
off indeed ; who degrade their own sex by perpetually striving to be masculine in sentiment and
deed, and the burden of whose complaint seems to
be a protest against God for not having created
them as men. I do not like to see these agitators
slighting so large a portion of the human race.

Leaving, now, this great question of Woman
Suffrage to be settled by the good sense of future
Japan, we will briefly consider in conclusion the
complicated and troublesome question of Capital
and Labor in Japan.

Under the feudal system this was a very simple
question. The three great divisions of society—

the *samurai*, the tradesmen (merchants and artisans), and the peasantry, were separated by un-
yielding barriers. The *samurai* formed the aristocracy; the tradesmen dwelt in the cities and
towns; the peasantry were the country folks. In
a population of about thirty millions, it is fair to
estimate the *samurai* at about three millions, the
tradesmen at about fifteen millions, and the peasantry at about twelve millions. Centuries of culture and refinement, centuries of affluence and
power, centuries of privilege and political prerogative, had been thrown around the *samurai*,
until the laws of heredity had developed features
that were expressive of noble emotions and a deportment typical of dash and politeness. They
looked upon the tradesmen with supercilious con-
descension, and upon the peasantry with supreme
scorn. While a marriage between an impecunious
samurai and the daughter of a wealthy merchant
might be tolerated, it was impossible for a *samurai*
to marry into the family of a peasant. These two
classes have been distinct for so many centuries
that, as regards tastes, disposition, and language,
they are almost as dissimilar as different races.
The coarse *patois* of the tillers of the fields is frequently unintelligible to the *samurai;* while the
high-flown diction of the *samurai*, abundantly in-
terspersed with Chinese words and with endless
honorifics, and containing long sentences padded to
death with verbiage and circumlocutory phrases,
was utterly unintelligible to the peasantry. Com-

munication between the two classes was almost
entirely cut off. The profoundest respect was expected from the peasantry. Whenever a *samurai*
passed along the highway, the peasant must remove his head-cloth and get off from his beast of
burden.

On the other hand, what was the condition of
the peasantry? Centuries of oppression had produced a race of inoffensive and amiable boors. The
baby, tumbling around upon the *tatamis* in the
hamlet, was destined to develop into a low-browed,
plodding peasant, destitute of any ambition or
noble sentiment. How could it have been otherwise? Centuries of monotonous diet, centuries of
unvarying routine of daily occupation, have produced an uninteresting similarity of traits in all the
peasantry throughout the empire. And these circumstances have really developed a distinct class
of people, having coarse features, base natures, and
cringing dispositions. They have never enjoyed educational advantages of any description. They have
had no social advantages. Nor have they ever,
from the remotest times, been favored with any
political power or privilege. Nothing but their
animal instincts have been developed. No matter
in what part of the empire you may be traveling,
you can always single out the peasantry because of
their hereditary traits. For over a thousand years
they have been the tillers of the soil, the hewers of
wood, the bearers of burdens. Nobody has ever
encouraged them to develop the higher instincts of

their souls. None of the nobler faculties of their minds have ever been cultivated, if, indeed, they have ever been credited with possessing any such faculties at all. As a natural result of this course of treatment they are to-day ignorant, superstitious, and coarse. Yet they are industrious and frugal in their habits, amiable and docile in disposition, and exceedingly patient and submissive. But they are also very obstinate in adhering to their own ideas and customs, and, consequently, do not become ready converts to civilized innovations. Their credulity and superstition are very strong. The grossest myths to be found within the creeds of the realm have always found them to be staunch votaries. They were, in fact, but serfs cultivating the ground for their feudal lords, and their condition does not appear to have been any better than the condition of the serfs in Europe during feudal times.

Midway between these two classes come the merchants and artisans. Like the middle classes in all countries they formed the backbone of the country. They were more refined than the peasantry, having possessed for centuries better educational facilities than the poor sons of the soil. Their very occupations were a continual means of education. They did not possess the daring and the polish of the *samurai*, but they were intelligent and enterprising. They did not possess the ambitionless natures of the peasantry, yet they were thoroughly submissive, and paid cringing deference to the *samurai*. While not vacillating and cynical in their religious beliefs, yet were they not as grossly ignorant and superstitious as the peasantry. Nor were they characterized by that reckless prodigality and extravagant wastefulness that seem to accompany the leisured classes everywhere, but they were frugal, prudent, cautious, and conservative. For centuries their occupations have been hereditary, until the peculiar traits of their trades seem to have impressed themselves to a certain extent upon their natures.

Under the old feudal system, the capital of the country centered in the hands of the feudal lords, the *samurai*, and the high-grade merchants. Practically the Shogun and the Daimios controlled the capital of the entire nation. The produce of the land belonged to them. Rice was the medium of exchange. It was known how many kokus, or bushels of rice, each Daimiate was capable of producing. A certain percentage of this was claimed by the Shogun as tribute. A bare pittance was set apart for the cultivators thereof, and the balance went to the Daimios who pensioned their hordes of *samurai* with immense quantities of it, and stored the balance in their warehouses to purchase services and merchandise from the artisans and merchants. Their magnificent collections of silks, porcelains, bronzes, and lacquerware were paid for out of this reserve fund; and as they thus held the necessary of life, they were in a position to drive very one-sided bargains with the helpless trades-

men. When in special need of hard cash, they
would set their own valuation upon the rice, and
intimate irresistibly to some rich merchant their
wish that he should purchase it at that price.
These dignitaries had practically "cornered" all of
that article within the four seas of Japan. The
masses were helpless. It would be difficult to conceive of a more absolute oligarchy. Labor was
completely at their mercy; they dictated whatsoever terms they chose, and those terms were the
bare existence of the laboring classes. Labor was
looked upon by the *samurai* with absolute contempt. It was degraded and despised as only
effete aristocracies can despise it. The laboring
people were poor beyond our conception. It is no
exaggeration to say that, on an average, twenty
millions out of thirty millions of the population
lived on less than five dollars per month, and that
the average laborer lived on less than three dollars
per month. Rice and the merest nibble of vegetables and fish constituted their diet, and cotton
fabrics of coarse quality served as clothing. Only
the rich could afford silk goods, or a mixture of
silk and cotton. The average house did not cost
over five hundred dollars, and the only furniture
was a few sets of bed-quilts, cooking and household utensils, *tatamis*, and a few ornamented *shojees* and screens. Newspapers were unknown, and
books were rare. Correspondence with adjoining
provinces was phenomenal when indulged in. A
person grew up in his native hamlet, and never

went twenty miles from it in his lifetime. A person who had crossed the mountains into an adjoining province, or had, perchance, roved as far as Yeddo, acquired the reputation of a traveler, and was quoted by his neighbors as an authority on such subjects.

Nor were the wealthy people at all affluent in our sense of the term. Ten thousand dollars made a rich man. Fifty thousand dollars made an exceedingly rich man. Very few were ever worth one hundred thousand dollars. The richest merchant Japan ever had lived in Yeddo about one hundred years ago. He is reputed to have amassed by a series of bold speculations a fortune amounting to five millions of dollars. He started in life as an orange merchant; he imported them by junk from Kiushiu, a distance of over six hundred miles. On one occasion a long spell of tempestuous weather kept the various orange fleets coast-bound; he, however, boldly put to sea and reached Yeddo, where he sold his fruit on an empty market at a fine profit. On another occasion, when Yeddo was swept by one of its terrible conflagrations, he bought up all the lumber, and "cornered" the market, so that when the city was rebuilt everybody had to purchase their materials from him, and he was enabled thus to amass a fabulous fortune. But, as before observed, such fortunes were phenomenal.

The foregoing description will convey to your mind a fair idea of the condition of capital and labor during feudal times. But when the country was thrown open to foreign intercourse twenty-four years ago, the existing relations of Japanese society became changed. The tradesmen became affluent off foreign commerce; while the haughty *samurai*, scorning to defile themselves with anything savoring of labor or trade, became impoverished. This state of affairs culminated in the Revolution of 1868–1870, when the Daimios surrendered their prerogatives to the government, and the *samurai*, stripped of their hereditary privileges, were reduced to the level of common subjects. Some of the lowest grade *samurai* drifted into trade and labor; some had sufficient means to be indifferent to the change; a few actually died of starvation; but the vast proportion of them drifted into government employ and into the government schools. As matters are now shaping themselves, it is not improbable that in a few years the government will base a titled peerage upon this remnant of the old feudal aristocracy.

At present, the clashing between capital and labor is hardly known in Japan. The masses will be many years in forgetting the old distinction between themselves and the upper classes. They yet regard the *samurai* with instinctive fear and respect. They yet look upon them as beings inherently superior to themselves. But the day will surely come when the laborer will begin to question his own inferiority. He will query whether he has not more than merely the right to exist; whether he is not entitled to a few of the pleasures, and to a few of the relaxations of this life ; whether he should not have a few mental diversions and hours of leisure to devote to his spiritual development. He will rise above a condition of mere animal contentedness and be ambitious to promote the welfare of his family as well as his own. When that time comes, the Japanese will see the application of the tenth and of the eleventh commandments, which contain, in fact, the only principles that can adjust this question here or anywhere else. When men learn to do as they would be done by ; when they learn to show that consideration for the unfortunate condition of others that is demanded by the Gospels, and when those in lowly circumstances learn to curb their envy and their jealousy of those more fortunately circumstanced than themselves, then will be evolved that mutual regard and consideration between the moneyed classes and the laboring classes, that will solve this vexed problem in all countries.

Sincerely yours,
THEOPHILUS PRATT.

THE THREE ESTATES.

LETTER XX.

KIOTO, *December* 5, 1877.

DEAR JULIUS MARCELLUS:

A PERSON can not live long in Japan without coming a good deal in contact with English people. They constitute a large proportion of the foreign community in the far East, and form an important social and commercial factor in this country. Hardly had Commodore Perry concluded his famous treaty with the Shogun before England and the European Powers were loudly clamoring for similar treaty privileges, which, as a matter of course, could not well be withheld from them. They speedily filled the Treaty Ports, and, for a number of years, plied a vigorous business. The number of foreigners in Japan to-day is not over three thousand; and I do not think it an unfair estimate to place the number of English residents at fully fifty per cent. of the entire foreign community, while we Americans who opened up the country do not number over twenty per cent. of the community.

But, although our element is decidedly in the minority, yet it is a powerful and an active element, not only in the civilization of Japan, but also

in forming the social tone and the public sentiment
of the general community. Our English cousins, who
have India all to themselves, and who do pretty
much as they please in China, find in Japan an
aggressive and independent sentiment that does
not submissively yield to British ideas and dictation.
To say that the British lion chafes and growls
under this unaccustomed treatment would be putting it in exceedingly mild terms, when the English
newspapers of Yokohama, like flaming volcanoes,
are belching forth the indignation of their countrymen at some contrary action on the part of the
Japanese Government, or on the part of the refrac-
tory Americans. The continued mutterings and
rumblings of the press would keep the community
in a state of chronic disturbance were it not for the
fact that we have learned that when it is quietest,
then British interests are being conserved ; but that
when it is loudest, then our interests and those of
the country are being promoted so as to antagonize
those of our cousins aforesaid in some way that
they do not relish. We have therefore come to
look upon the press as a delicate meter indicating
the relative progress of the country and of British
interests ; and we feel cheerful when it is noisiest,
resting assured that British influence and rapacity
have been checked by some untoward event, and
we grow suspicious when the turmoil subsides for
any great length of time, fearing lest their grasping
proclivities are being unduly gratified at the expense
of the outside community.

The antagonism between British and American ideas is sharper in Japan than it is anywhere else in the Orient. Our views are perpetually coming in violent collision. Perhaps the most marked contrast between our method of dealing with the Japanese and that of the British is shown in our postal treaty with Japan, and in our theory respecting the Shimonosèki indemnity. When we made our postal treaty with the Japanese about four years ago, dealing with them as if they were intelligent equals, the new departure was met with derisive scorn by the English community. With the same verbose and acrimonious logic that they used nearly a hundred years ago in predicting the speedy failure of the "Yankee Republic,"—that, in fact, they have used at each critical juncture in our history ever since to demonstrate the worthlessness and imbecility of our democratic institutions—they said that the Japanese were unable to conduct a postal system upon foreign plans, that they were absolutely untrustworthy, and that dire confusion and endless delays would result from their inexperience and shiftlessness. Yet the Japanese have managed the matter with great ability and credit to themselves, and similar treaties will speedily be consummated with other nations.

Regarding the Shimonosèki indemnity, our theory is that it was a vast sum of money unjustly extorted from a feeble government that was rent by internal dissension, and at a time when it was vainly endeavoring to quell rebellions among semi-independent clans, and to punish those fierce clans for their aggressions upon foreigners. To extort millions of dollars from the Shogun for the acts of rebels on the borders of the empire, after he had done his best to punish them for their depredations, and after the injured parties had already exacted a sanguinary vengeance for the misdeeds, we considered unjust. We said that the indemnity thus extorted should be refunded, and we expressed our willingness to return our share of it at once. The horror and the indignation of our British cousins at being asked to return money upon which they had already tightened their grip can better be imagined than described. A tremendous controversy arose upon the subject. This strife yet continues. How it will end, I cannot tell. But I trust that our countrymen will eventually return their portion of the spoil, whether England ever does so or not.

There are three well-defined classes of Englishmen in Japan. The first class is composed of fairminded and courteous individuals who are not so bigoted in their notions about Albion's superiority as to be unwilling to concede merit to others outside of their own nation. They are willing to learn something about other countries. They do not pride themselves upon their ignorance of America and of American affairs, but they really feel gratified in being sufficiently familiar with American geography to be able to locate Yale College in Connecticut, and Harvard College in Massachusetts, and to be able to state that Philadelphia is a city,

and not a State. As far as they have any pronounced political views, they are generally liberal
and democratic in their tendencies. They are intelligent, sociable, and cosmopolitan in their natures.

The second class is composed of full-blown,
hearty specimens of humanity, who take life easy
and endeavor to avoid as far as possible all worry
and bother. They are plodding workers and honest, moderately energetic business men; but at the
same time they take all the holidays the law allows
—feeling grievously abused, should the number
be curtailed—and invariably appropriating all the
extra ones that they can legitimately obtain.
They are excellent judges of the respective merits
of porter, snipe, and pig, but have hazy and indefinite views on political theories differing from their
conservative ideas about monarchy and aristocracy.
As connoisseurs of horses, dogs, and trout, they
are *sans pareil;* but their perceptions of the beauties of republican institutions are hopelessly obtuse; and, although they are indefatigable hunters
and anglers, yet they never develop sufficient mental acumen to take exceptions to the views of the
London Times, the *Daily News*, or any other one
of the journals from which they cram their brains
with political lore. They make tough enemies,
hospitable friends, and conservative subjects; but
they invariably prefer hearty good fellowship, well
backed up with a substantial array of stuffed veal, ale,
and pudding, to exhausting political controversy.

24

And about anything relating to the history, the geography, or the institutions of America, they are mildly and complacently stupid ; nay, more, they are exasperatingly stupid. We can excuse the French poet who located alligators and palm trees upon the shores of Lake Erie, but when one of our own flesh and blood, in this age of railroads, telegraphs, and liberal ideas, does not possess a school-boy's knowledge of the United States, we must really protest against such abominable ignorance. We cannot accept the silly excuse that it can not be expected of Englishmen to be acquainted with the affairs of a country not yet a hundred years old, and whose habits and customs are not recognized among the cultured classes of Europe.

The third class of Englishmen that we come in contact with is the most disagreeable class of people imaginable. They are not only grossly ignorant about American affairs, but they glory in parading their wretched ignorance on every available occasion. They are bigoted, intolerant, and conceited. These are the individuals who rant interminably about distorted statements relating to American affairs, derived from hearsay and subsidized government periodicals. These scions of fair Albion never consider that personal experience or observation are essential to correct opinions about the practical features of republicanism. They convey the impression that an editor who has never visited the United States is specially endowed with oracular powers for expounding democratic doc-

trines, exploding democratic theories, and for predicting the speedy collapse of all institutions not
based upon "blood" and prerogative. Here be-
longs the coarse, the pedantic, the pig-headed
Cockney, who is always on the *qui vive* to hurl his
guffaws at anything American, and whose ignorance
about things American is only equaled by his
assurance in discussing them. Such are the people
who inquire with languid sympathy why Americans
always eat molasses on their pork! It will be useless for you to intimate to them that such is no
more a general custom in America than it is for
Englishmen to drink coffee and treacle together,
for they will insist that Americans themselves say
so. And when you endeavor to enlighten their
minds by informing them that the American sailors,
from whom they or their ancestors derived that
morsel of information, were only talking about marine customs, that were by no means an exponent
of general national usage, they will the more vigorously insist upon the correctness of their statement
and plunge into the subject with renewed animation. They inform you with great satisfaction that
they are able to distinguish an American before he
has spoken three words,—reposing in sublime ignorance of the fact that their own brogue and appearance render them equally conspicuous to Americans.
They express intense merriment at Americans taking only three months to "do" Europe, without
considering that their own countrymen take much
less time for "doing" America, and then seem to

consider themselves capable of discussing any feature of the country. They take it for granted that
every American is disposed to be boastful, and
therefore organize themselves into a reform committee to eradicate this idiosyncrasy ; and, while
deeming themselves entitled to assume the perfection of everything English, and considering it appropriate for John Bull to consider himself *ne plus ultra*,
they manifest unfeigned uneasiness at having other
nations assume the same premises respecting themselves, and feel highly scandalized at Brother Jona-
than's most excellent opinion respecting himself.
Being aware that no aristocracy on the Prussian
Blue system exists in America, they infer that
society must be " orridly " common, and that polite
and elegant language is not much used, and, upon
the principle of not casting pearls before swine,
they take no pains to express themselves in the
deferential phrases with which they would address
educated people of their own country, but adopt a
brusque phraseology that borders on the coarse and
impertinent. I have frequently listened in silence
to terms and forms of speech insulting to my country, because, by taking notice thereof, a noisy alter-
cation would have inevitably ensued. Should the
unkind decrees of mysterious fate ordain that you
should sit opposite to one of these people at a
dinner party, you will find your hands full for the
balance of the meal. You will find him to be as
ignorant of the principles of Lord Chesterfield's
immortal work as a horse is of rhetoric. He is not

aware of the fact that, in a promiscuous company, national peculiarities should not be offensively dwelt upon.

Those of our imperial cousins who have been endowed with thoughtful minds have collected, from history, and from a study of the social and of the political institutions of Japan, a very subtle and highly scientific series of arguments in favor of monarchical forms of governments. Generalizing from history, they argue that, before and since the days of the Jewish theocracy when the people clamored for a king to reign over them, mankind has always manifested a natural preference for monarchical forms of government. These forms of government, say they, have always been the most prevalent and the most popular in all ages and in all countries. Greece and Rome began as monarchies and ended as monarchies. All the republics that have ever existed, were eventually merged into monarchies. Society, in all countries, has always shown a natural disposition to differentiate itself. You are bound to have your high classes and your low classes at the social extremes. Ignorance, poverty, and vice will inevitably form a substratum, in any community, that will be unfit to govern itself for any length of time; and those classes wherein concentrate wealth, refinement, and intelligence, will eventually devise methods whereby to control the masses. Such evolutions of social differentiations will only be a question of time in any country, they say.

And, applying their generalizations to Japan, they fortify their theories with practical illustrations. The Ainos, the aborigines of the country, were mild tribes of pastoral people living in huts and caves, and subsisting on the spoils of the chase. In their primitive state of society, social equality prevailed. The head man of the hamlet, or of the village, was on a level with his constituents. Then came the Malays and the Mongolians with their superior bravery and intelligence. In the course of centuries, amalgamation and differentiation evolved the present triple system of Japanese society, viz.: the *samurai*, the tradesmen, and the peasantry. The descendants of each class naturally inherited the traits peculiar to that class, until each breed became so fixed in its characteristics that the features and bearing of each class could be readily distinguished. And even though feudal caste has been abolished, and all the people are merely subjects before the emperor, yet the *samurai* class still is the governing class, the tradesmen still keep on in their old avocations, and the peasants wade in the mud as of yore, hardly being aware of the vast changes around them, and being just as unfitted for governing the empire as if the laws forbade them entering the civil service.

Thus will it eventually be in the United States, they predict. In the course of centuries, the high, the middle, and the low classes will differentiate themselves into well defined types of the community. The ranks of trade will be filled with the descendants of those who manifested peculiar fitness for mercantile pursuits in by-gone years, and who have transmitted to their progeny their own peculiar mercantile aptitude and proclivities. The laboring classes will naturally be composed of the descendants of laborers. And those families that have held money and land for many generations, will develop into keen, intelligent, diplomatic classes of people who will be naturally fitted for the professions and for politics, having the inclination, the training, and the leisure to devote thereto. And, in the course of centuries, we will have three distinct classes of society transmitting to their descendants their own peculiar tastes, inclinations, characteristics and features, until we have, like the Japanese, almost three distinct races. When that time comes, then will the higher classes naturally absorb power and prerogative. Citing our immigration, they predict that in a few years there will be vast masses of Chinese in the United States, who, in connection with the millions of negroes already in the country, will form a substratum of society having but little aptitude or inclination for self-government, and expecting to be governed by the more enterprising and imperious Caucasians. This Caucasian element will be like the Malay element in Japan—fiery, intelligent, capable of governing. It will naturally form an aristocratic class. And then, as aristocrats must have a court and a monarchy, we will have, in the course of time, these institutions established in the United States. While a country is young and growing, a republican form of government is all well enough, they say; but when it has become well settled, it naturally becomes conservative and monarchical in all its tendencies. In short, the ideas of our imperial cousins, when reduced to a definite proposition, is, *that, in political matters, a cultured minority must govern the vulgar majority;* which principle, they claim, will eventually prevail in the United States. " Behold! how intensely monarchical in all their tendencies are all your Southern States. Virginia, Maryland, North Carolina, South Carolina, Georgia, and Louisiana, were all christened in honor of European monarchs; they were settled by an aristocratic element, by the sons of impecunious gentry, by the shoddy patrician classes, if you so please to express it, who emigrated, under the auspices and under the leadership of noblemen, to seek in the rich fields and favorable climate of the relaxing latitudes of the South the necessaries and the luxuries of life without being subjected to the severe toil and to the bitter climatic vicissitudes endured by the settlers of bleak New England. The salubrity and the fertility of the South having thus attracted the Bohemian element of British aristocracy, there naturally sprang up in those regions the customs and manners of patricians. A powerful slave aristocracy was rapidly developed, which perpetually collided with the republican tendencies of the plebeian North, and which would eventually have terminated in monarchy had it not

been crushed at frightful cost." Such, I ween,
would be the ideas of our thoughtful imperial
cousins, when captured and expressed in intelligible English. The shrewd and crafty aristocracy
of England had long known how matters were
drifting in the South, and, from the commencement
of the conflict, gave their unqualified and hearty
support to the mediæval confederacy of Calhoun;
and, like an evil spirit, stood ever ready to sow dissension, and to widen the gap between the North
and the South—between republicanism and monarchical tendencies, between a higher and nobler
development of democratic institutions and the
evolution of a patrician condition of society with
all its selfish and conservative theories. From afar,
they saw that this mediæval aristocracy and confederacy must either develop into feudalism or into
monarchy; in either case, republicanism, with all its
hated tendencies, would be destroyed; the white
man would forever be the imperious *samurai*, the
black man would forever be the laboring *heimin*;
and the republic of the North would be perpetually menaced by the foothold thus gained by
monarchy on the North American Continent. The
establishment of a European monarchy by force
of arms in the republic of Mexico, during the progress of our Civil War, was thoroughly in harmony
with the spirit of the British aristocracy.

But it is needless to state that untoward events
demolished the schemes of the diplomatic patricians of the old world, yet, while we have crushed

the armies of the Rebellion, we must admit that it
will take a long time for the old tendencies to fade
away. We must be ever vigilant to check the
advances of the old slave aristocracy. It will be
cheaper for us to keep the South in the Union
than to allow a vast and hostile monarchy to be
established beside our Northern republic; to be
compelled to fortify thousands of miles of frontier;
and to be compelled to keep a standing army equal
in size to the vast legions that the Southern
empire would probably keep under arms at all
times. These, however, are problems for the future to solve. I, for my part, do not think we will
fulfill the predictions or conform to the ingenious
deductions of our imperial cousins.

Undoubtedly there is considerable truth in the
foregoing enunciation. There can be no question
that monarchical forms of government have certainly been the most common in the world.
Equally evident is it that society will differentiate
itself to a certain extent in every country. We
have, and always have had, in the United States,
laboring classes, mercantile classes, and moneyed
classes decidedly aristocratic in their tendencies.
I do not think that these three general classes can
ever be done away with. There always must be social
inequality in this world until the spirit of Christ
has permeated all classes and has imbued everybody with neighborly feelings of kindness and consideration for mankind in general. We can never
make laws to compel select circles of beatified

snobs to admit the public in general to their social communings. Just fancy the utter absurdity involved in attempting to say through our legislatures to the old Knickerbocker families of New York, or to the haughty aristocracy of the Southern States, "Admit the public at large to all your social gatherings; to wit: to your balls, to your dinner parties, to your house-warmings; be perfectly impartial to every one; show no social preferences of any description whatsoever; call upon everybody, and receive calls from everybody."

Social sets and cliques, based upon likes and dislikes, similarity of tastes, and upon worldly prosperity, will invariably be organized wherever men congregate in communities, whether in monarchies or republics. And these social inequalities are perfectly consistent with our theories of political equality. But we and our descendants must be vigilant and prevent selfish and ambitious families from using their social advantages as a basis upon which to found political prerogative and privilege. Here lies the danger of the future. There can be no disgrace in candidly admitting this. Let us clearly understand it, and let us be perpetually on guard; then will our democratic institutions be safe.

I think that, as we develop the principles of the Gospels in our social and political affairs, we will find the true solution of this complicated question. Some will treat this confession of faith with contemptuous derision. But let us look into facts a little, and see if they do not support our view. Although the Constitution of the United States does not recognize any creed or religion, yet the principles upon which it is founded are eminently Christian in spirit. Equality, justice, and good-will toward all nations, breathe all through it. And, in obedience to the directions contained therein, the whole policy of our government has been to elevate and benefit the poor and weak members of the community ; and it extends these privileges to any nation whose people show any disposition to become part of the commonwealth. Has there ever been such liberality as this in the history of nations? Is it not thoroughly Christian? It has introduced into the world a description of political equality that will permit the development of such characters as Abraham Lincoln from a raw-boned peasant into a President. Who can deny that these doctrines and principles, when consist-ently practiced by every one, will develop a spirit of mutual consideration and confidence? When the poor cease to envy the fortuitous condition of the wealthy, and when those favored by fortune cease to be supercilious and selfish, then will be consummated a condition of society dimly forecast by the prophets. It is safe to say that in propor-tion as the principles of the Gospels have been faithfully and honestly applied to politics and to society, in that same proportion have they become elevated and liberalized.

In my very humble opinion, Christ's kingdom
will be nothing more nor less than a universal
republic wherein social and political equality will
be secured by mutual consideration and kindness
among all classes and nations. This state of affairs
will prevail just as soon as mankind will allow it to
do so. Christianity is the only equalizer in the
world. The poorest may practice its precepts and
secure that refinement of sentiment and action
which mere rank and riches fail to bestow. It
alone teaches that the chief end of life is the sub-
jection of the appetites and passions to the purer
and nobler impulses of the soul. Its principles,
when applied to the details of every-day life,
become a profound and wonderful science ; a complicated problem whose terms are ever varying,
whose objective point is always self-conquest,
whose arena is the human heart and brain, and
whose factors are the soul and the evil tendencies
of the flesh. All must fight the same battle. The
rich perhaps may fight under more favorable circumstances ; but, on the other hand, more is expected of them. The *samurai* acquires a polished
bearing and diction from his favorable surroundings ; but it is only a social veneer ; he carries
beneath it a cruel and lustful heart ; he is admon-
ished to combat these vile tendencies of his nature
and to subdue them ere he can enter the kingdom
of Christ. The *heimin*, on the other hand, born
into life with gross passions and ambitionless emotions, is directed to eliminate his coarse appetites

and to develop the obtuse and dwarfed faculties of his mind. The precepts of Christianity demand of one that he should crush his foul and treacherous instincts; of the other, his splenetic idiosyncrasies. Each must battle with those failings peculiar to himself; succeeding in this, their souls harmonize and are brought into congenial fellowship; herein they become equal.

I care not what may be a man's nationality; provided his soul is sincerely struggling with the base elements of his nature, he is my friend. If I see an Englishman leading a life of shame in these regions, I feel mortified and grieved. Dr. Johnson may not have had the manners of a horse, according to the standard of the patrician Chesterfield, but, beneath his boorish exterior, there dwelt the instincts of a Christian gentleman; while beneath the social veneer of the noble lord, there lurked the heart of a crafty and salacious scoundrel, who would not have hesitated to corrupt the purity of any household in Christendom, who instilled his infernal creed into the youthful mind of his son, and whose wretched precepts and example form but a miserable excuse for his fast young countrymen in the East.

When all classes and all nations practice the principles enunciated in the Gospels in all the details of their lives, I apprehend that there will be but little collision between the peoples and the nations of the earth. This peaceful condition is the one toward which mankind seems to be rapidly drifting,—a universal republic, Christ's kingdom, the millennium, whatever you choose to call it.

But whatever the future may bring forth, let our imperial cousins be mindful of the fact that, during the past century, Europe and England have developed strong democratic tendencies. Let them not be oblivious of the fact that Great Britain is far more liberal and democratic now than she was a hundred years ago ; that she has been steadily coming up to the level of the American standard of politics for many years ; that this progress on her part is rapidly lessening the difference between our two systems of government ; and that if she goes on in the same ratio of improvement, she will soon be a republic. We do not believe the doctrine that a cultivated minority can best govern the majority of the people in an intelligent and Christian community. We believe that in such communities the sentiment of the majority, upon all political questions, is apt to be safer and sounder than the sentiment of the minority ; and that the sentiment of that majority, fairly, candidly, and conscientiously expressed, should always be sovereign. Cultured minorities may reach shrewd conclusions, but they are frequently exceedingly selfish in their doctrines and policies. No, my imperial cousins, we will not discuss this matter any further. We will let the future demonstrate which is the safer and sounder theory. But I am inclined to think that the logic of facts will speedily demonstrate to the satisfaction of mankind that suffrage, based upon man as the unit of political power, is the best, the safest, and the most satisfactory of all sovereigns.

And now, Julius Marcellus, I shall probably not write any more letters from Kioto. I am not enjoying the best of health here, and it is time to be returning to my own country to resume my interrupted studies. I am seriously thinking of resigning my position and returning home by way of India and Europe. My route has been long laid out, and I have been steadily growing impatient to start off. My next letter will be definite upon this matter, and, till then, farewell!

THEOPHILUS PRATT.

LETTER XXI.

FAREWELL TO JAPAN.

YOKOHAMA, *January* 8, 1878.

DEAR JULIUS MARCELLUS:

THE time has now come for me to bid farewell to Japan. I resigned my position in Kioto last month, and have been supremely busy ever since in making preparations for my departure from these very pleasant shores. There are many strong reasons that have combined to urge me to decide to leave this country.

In the first place, I have contracted a stubborn intermittent fever, derived, I presume, from sleeping on the floor in the temple at Kioto. My contract being only for one year, I did not feel disposed to waste money on a bedstead, and therefore adopted the Japanese method of repose, which I am now prepared to characterize as not only uncomfortable, but decidedly unhealthy, as the foul air from beneath the house thus finds ready access to your lungs. I presume that I have also aggravated my malady by a series of colds which I have taken in the school-room and in my Kioto man-

25

sion. In the high rooms of the temple it was almost impossible to keep myself warm, even with a red-hot stove. In vain did I paper up all the crevices of my study, hoping thus to keep in the heat, for I discovered that the *shojees* allowed the warm air to filter through them as if they had been sieves.

In the second place, I found myself rapidly becoming a confirmed dyspeptic from the bad habit of hastily swallowing my food. Eating my meals all alone, without any enlivening conversation, was also very injurious to my digestion. My breakfast was usually disposed of in silence; my lunch was always a minus quantity, as the school was three miles from home; and my dinner was devoured with a ravenous appetite, whetted to the keenest of edges by the long walks of the day. The solitude and the silence were becoming unendurable. I had enough of that experience in Hirosaki. Life in Kioto, of course, was not nearly so lonely as that up north, but, taken in connection with the feverish condition of my system, it seemed to make it prudent for me to terminate my engagement.

In the third place, if I wish to settle down in my own country, it is high time to be returning. Nearly a quarter of a century has passed over my head, and, with my professional studies in view, time is becoming exceedingly valuable. Although Japan has a lovely climate and the most beautiful scenery, yet so different are the people from ourselves in thought, sentiment, and aspiration, that it would be impossible for me to affiliate and to grow up with them.

But it is not without much regret that I take leave of this charming land. I have spent four exceedingly happy years here, and I shall always look back to this period of my life with feelings of profound pleasure. My trips over lake, mountain, and river will forever be bright spots in my memory, that the flight of years may render dim, but can never erase.

I take this occasion to thank you for the many kind letters with which you have favored me during my exile. It is a matter of regret to me that I shall now be deprived of the pleasure of hearing the postman at my gate announcing the arrival of letters from home. You, who get your mails every day, can have but faint conception of the thrill of joyful expectancy experienced by us who receive ours but once a fortnight. I shall be amply satisfied if my own rambling correspondence shall have afforded you one-half of the pleasure that yours has afforded me.

I do not expect ever to return to Japan. Possibly in the dim future I may revisit the scenes of my youthful sojourn in these regions. But it will never be the same country to me again. It will have undergone vast changes,—all for the better, no doubt,—but it will but shadow forth the quaint reminiscences of the past. There is a lovely strain in the *Deserted Village* that floats through my

memory as I write these closing lines. Let me
conclude by quoting it :

> "Sweet Auburn ! Parent of the blissful hour !
> Thy glades forlorn confess the tyrant's power.
> Here, as I take my solitary rounds,
> Amidst thy tangling walks and ruined grounds,
> And, many a year elapsed, return to view
> Where once the cottage stood, the hawthorn grew,—
> Remembrance wakes with all her busy train,
> Swells at my breast, and turns the past to pain."

Sincerely yours,

THEOPHILUS PRATT.

INDEX.

	PAGE
Ainos	55
Assassinations—causes of	109
Avenues	86
Awomori—description of	40
" journey to	41
" meeting scholars at	41
" night scene in	41
" hotel in	42
Ban-Cho	147
Bell of Chioin Monastery	246
British Legation in Tokio	146
Browbeating the Japanese—sample of	122
Buddhist Monasteries in Japan	315
Buddhism compared with Christianity	318
Capital and Labor in Japan	356
Cascades at Nikko	186
Chapel of Iyèyas at Nikko	183
Chiusenji Lake	175
Christianity discussed by Japanese Scholars	165
Civilization and Beefsteak	224
Civilization and Religion—correlative terms	214
Complexion of Japanese	338
Compositions—samples of	168
Conjugal Relations of the Japanese	346
Court Scene in Hakodaté	105
Dai-Butz at Nara	262
Daimios —description of	65
" life of	66
" poetry of	68

	PAGE
Death of Buddha—note	258
Death of Saigo	301
Defender of the Faith	213
Desima	143
Dogs—idiosyncrasies described	178
Dutch—annual visit to Yeddo	137
Ejinsan—treatment of native house	153
Ejinsan—what	131
Empress Jingo	222
Endless Mountain	238
English Press in Yokohama	366
Execution of the Assassin	107
Family Jars	348
Farewell to Hirosaki	127
Farewell Address from Directors	128
Feudal Customs—decadence	71
Feudal Government described	76
Foreign Teachers in Japan	84
Fujiyama	272
" appearance from summit	281
" climbing	277
" cone	279
" descent	285
" general features of landscape	275
" huts on summit	282
" routes to	273
" view at base	275
" view at summit	282
Gin-Kakku-Gi—temple	247
Godown—definition of	139

PAGE

Hakodaté—description of... 38
      "   foreign popula-
            tion of........ 39
      "   battle in........ 39
      "   journey to...... 38
Hara-Kiri.......... 139; 110
Hebachi...................151
Hirosaki—my house.....49; 82
      "   meeting scholars. 49
      "   horseback ride to. 44
      "   description of.... 36
      "   "   school. 82
      "   my Boy......... 90
      "   his eccentricities.. 91
      "   musical dogs..... 96
Hotel Bill—sample of...... 221
House-keeping in Tokio 153
Inland Sea 191
Isè Temples. 230
Iwa-ki-san... ....35; 53
Iyèmitsu—shrines of........184
Iyèyas 68
Japanese Singing........... 88
      "   love of novelty in
            religious matters..203
      "   village scenery..... 45
      "   *kowtowing*........ 46
      "   soldiers.......... 57
      "   Castles—origin.... 58
      "   "   g e n e r a l
                 features. 59
      "   "   one at Hi-
                 rosaki.. 59
      "   "   a u d i e n c e
                 chamber.. 63
      "   "   present con-
                 dition 64
      "   red tape—sample of.120
Jesuit Priest in Hirosaki.....113
Jinriksha...................132
Kago......................132
Kai-Sei-Gakko.............148
Kamakura Image...........267
Kayaki Wood..............306
Kii Province. 232
Kioto—routes to...........244
      "   general characteris-
            tics............248

PAGE

Kioto—my house....... .251
      "   "   neighbors......252
      "   "   Boy...........256
      "   population..........244
      "   temples.............245
      "   Chioin temple......246
      "   religious features....248
      "   character of people..248
      "   holiday of courtesans.249
      "   picnics.............250
Kin-Kakku-Gi.............246
Kobè.............. 190
Kobu-Daishi...............239
Kumamoto Castle..........295
      "   siege......297
Lake Biwa.................304
Laws of Iyèyas..........68; 71
Life of Priests in Monasteries.317
Mikado....... ....71; 73
Mining Department.........145
Missions in Tokio.........198
      "   "   Yokohama.....199
Mitsu-Bishi Company.......189
Mitsui Bank...............216
Mission Work in Yokohama.199
      "   "   hostility to....205
Monastery of Coyasan 239
Monastery of Hiyeisan......306
      "   "   "   priests.308
      "   "   "   slaugh-
                   ter of
                   priests.309
      "   "   "   v i e w
            from.................311
Mukojima—cherry groves...158
Nagasaki..................191
Nara--temple......... ...261
      "   dimensions of image.263
      "   "   bell...266
New-Year's calling in Japan.137
Nihon-Bashi. 136
Nikko Village..............179
Nikko Temples............179
Nirvana...................313
Norimon..................86
Ono Village 225
Owari Castle...........63; 228
Pacific Railway 2

Pacific Steamers—embarking. 7
"   "   starting... 8
"   "   class of
                     passengers. 6
"   "   voyage.... 10
"   "   table scene. 11
Pappenberg 193
Pilgrimages of Natives......174
Politeness of Japanese 139
Promiscuous Bathing 187
Province of Omi — produc-
                     tions. 221
"   "   Mino   " 228
"   "   Owari   " 229
"   "   Iga   " ...230
"   "   Kii 233
"   "   Akitah—assas-
                     sin 101
Reception near Hirosaki ... 46
Rice Diet 237
Roman Catholics in Japan..111
Samurai—description.....73, 76
Satsuma Rebellion—causes..291
"   Samurai 291
"   Rebellion—Saigo ..288
"   "   outbreak.292
Sakè—use of, by Japanese...335
School-boys in Tokio......155
School-teachers' occupation..157
Schools in Tokio...........162
School Contract—sample.... 37
Sei-O-Ken—hotel 144
Shaka 312
Shimonosèki affair..........367
Shintoism 231
Shogun's Position—defined.. 72
Shojees 62
Shodo Shionin—legend con-
  cerning 180
Sir Harry Parke's Visit to
  Emperor 299
Summer Recreations in Japan 173
Takada—Prince of Iga.....224
Takashima Coal Mines......194
Tatamis—descriptive note... 42
Teaching—how conducted..163
Theatres 159

Tobacco—use of 333
Tomb of Tokugawa Iyèyas..183
Tokio—geological features..132
"   " doing " of 134
Tokio Climate 149
"   Asakusa Temple 135
"   Conflagrations 150
"   Uyèno Park 135
"   Society..............151
Tòògu—Gakko 36
Tokugawa House 68
Traveling by Jinrikisha.... 176
Truancy of Scholars.......167
Tsukidji 143
Tsuruga 223
Tycoon 71
Tsuruga Dai 148
Tsugaru Straits............ 35
Umoto Sulphur Springs.....187
Wine in Japan...........337
Woman Suffrage in Japan...350
Various Classes of English-
  men 368
Yakunin—defined.......... 77
Yamato-Yashiki............144
Yashiki 132
Yeddo—features 137
"   fires 138
"   earthquakes........139
"   merchants 140
Yesso................... 55
Yokohama—arrival......... 17
"   description..... 21
"   Curio Street ... 22
"   Bluffs 21
"   Mississippi Bay..23
"   U. S. Naval
         Hospital..... 24
"   social features.. 24
"   rifle range 23
"   recreations 25
"   Dramatic Associ-
         ation........ 27
"   public gardens.. 27
"   newspapers 28
"   trade.......... 31
Yoshiwara System....... ..342

www.ingramcontent.com/pod-product-compliance
Lightning Source LLC
Chambersburg PA
CBHW022020110726
47901CB00006B/1594